CW00828755

MUSCLES

The story of Ken Rosewall, Australia's little master of the courts

The Slattery Media Group Pty Ltd
1 Albert Street, Richmond
Victoria, Australia, 3121

First published by The Slattery Media Group Pty Ltd 2012, on behalf of Richard Naughton

Images from the Rosewall family personal collection and *Ken Rosewall: Twenty Years at the Top* by Peter Rowley with Ken Rosewall (London: Cassell, 1976). All images used with permission.

National Library of Australia Cataloguing-in-Publication entry

Author: Naughton, Richard ; Rosewall, Ken
Title: Muscles / Richard Naughton ; Rosewall, Ken ; Helen Alexander, editor.
ISBN: 9781921778568 (hbk.)
Subjects: Rosewall, Ken, 1934-. Tennis players--Australia--Biography. Tennis.
Other Authors/Contributors: Rosewall, Ken ; Alexander, Helen.
Dewey Number: 796.342092

Group Publisher: Geoff Slattery
Creative Director: Guy Shield
Authors: Richard Naughton and Ken Rosewall
Editor: Helen Alexander
Typesetting: Stephen Lording
Photo production and design: Kate Slattery

Printed and bound in Australia by Griffin Press

slatterymedia.com

MUSCLES

The story of Ken Rosewall, Australia's little master of the courts

KEN ROSEWALL
as told to RICHARD NAUGHTON
Foreword by John Barrett

Visit slatterymedia.com

CONTENTS

FOREWORD BY JOHN BARRETT

MEMORIES OF A TENNIS IMMORTAL

In every sport there are performers who, for one shining moment, flash into prominence like meteors across the night sky, and then quickly fade from view and from memory. Then there are the immortals, those legendary players who are recognised by the public, the media and their peers for the outstanding contribution they have made to the evolution of their chosen profession.

Such a man is Ken Rosewall. This ageless Australian, who won major titles 20 years apart, was at his peak during those post-war years in the 1950s and 60s when lawn tennis was evolving from an amateur game, played by talented part-timers, into the full-blown professional sport we know today.

During that period the name K. R. Rosewall was inscribed 18 times on the trophies of the four major championships, eight times in singles, nine in doubles and once in mixed. Eleven of those wins were achieved as an amateur and seven as a professional after the arrival of open tennis in 1968. Doubtless there would have been many more if open tennis had arrived sooner. By the rules of the day, during Ken's 11 years as a professional he had been ineligible to compete in 45 grand slam championships. For five of those years, from 1959-63, he had been outstandingly the best of the pros and in 1968, at 33, he beat his great rival Rod Laver in the final of the world's first open tournament in Bournemouth. Two months later he beat Rod again in the final of the first grand slam of the open era in Paris.

I met Ken during his first visit to Wimbledon in 1952 when we were drawn as first round opponents. He was 17 and had arrived in London as the winner of the boys' singles at the French Championship just two weeks earlier, a victory I had witnessed. He already possessed one of the most beautiful backhands I had ever seen. Taking the ball before it had reached the top of its bounce he would swing the racket straight through the ball with a slightly open face to impart controlling backspin. Such confidence and accuracy did he have on that shot that opponents would make errors simply trying to avoid it. With his agility and speed about the court he was already a formidable opponent, as I would discover.

Our match was scheduled for 2pm, and was among the first round of matches for the day. Well before 3pm we were back in the locker room. Ken had allowed me just four games and I had the doubtful privilege of holding the record for being the fastest loser that year!

In the years following that embarrassing first encounter we became firm friends and I am privileged to have witnessed many of his finest matches. In 1959 he played the new Wimbledon champion, Alex Olmedo, in the first round of the London Professional Indoor Championships at Wembley, an event that was the highlight of the tennis year for British fans in the days when they could see all their former heroes, men like Pancho Gonzales, Frank Sedgman, Lew Hoad and Tony Trabert. All of them came out to watch the encounter, anxious to see how the Wimbledon champion would fare in his first match as a professional. We watched in awe as Ken won the first 15 games of their best-of-five sets encounter and soon walked off the court as the winner, by 6-0 6-0 6-3. With a Slazenger colleague, Dennis Coombe, I went into Ken's dressing room afterwards to congratulate him. "What an amazing performance Ken," said Dennis. "Do you realise that in the entire match you only made four unforced errors?" "Three," replied Ken, ever the perfectionist, and then he proceeded to describe them!

Within these pages you will find many more such stories, all beautifully described by Richard Naughton whose painstaking research has produced a volume that details the remarkable rise of a grocer's son from Sydney to worldwide fame as one of the best-loved sportsmen of his generation. It is a tale that will delight readers of a certain age who remember with affection the perfection of Ken's graceful game, and for younger readers there will be the satisfaction of hearing from the master's own lips the stories behind the headlines.

This is a book you can't put down. Once you have turned the first page all thoughts of attending to the jobs you hoped to complete are forgotten. If you enjoy the journey half as much I did you will feel that your life has been enriched in the company of a great sportsman and a great human being.

John Barrett
September 2012

INTRODUCTION BY RICHARD NAUGHTON

◇◇◇◇◇◇◇

EVERYONE KNOWS 'MUSCLES'

This is a story about a little boy with remarkable sporting skills who ended up being the best professional tennis player in the world.

Since I started writing this book it's been interesting to learn that almost everyone has a view about Ken Rosewall. Maybe it's because he is small in stature, 5' 7" (170cm), and back in the 1950s and 60s everyone wanted to treat him like a younger brother or mother him somehow.

Perhaps it is because he seemed so normal—small, wiry and with a shy smile on his face. Apart from the fact that he was one of the best tennis players in the world, he looked like any average person on the street might look. As has often been explained, they called him 'Muscles' because he didn't have any.

Rosewall is also a link with the Australia of the 1950s—when he existed as an icon, alongside his fellow 'tennis twin' Lew Hoad. These two grew up a few miles apart in suburban Sydney and somehow became Davis Cup heroes. Each year, between Christmas and New Year, families tuned in their transistor radios to listen to Hoad and Rosewall take on the Americans in the Davis Cup Challenge Round.

They were different personalities of course—Hoad was something of a larrikin and a powerhouse. He had a big serve and belted the ball about the court. He was regarded as an instinctive net-rusher whose forte was the smash and brutal volley, but he also played with style and flair, swooping onto the ball and gently caressing half volleys and dropshots.

Rosewall stayed back, or maybe was an all-court player. In his early days his serve was considered a liability—a tap or a 'ploop' that merely started the point. Actually, it was probably a lot better than that as it was always deep and perfectly placed, and Rosewall had a canny tennis brain. Also, there were those perfectly played drives, most obviously a glorious backhand, so any reckless opponent approached the net at their peril.

They exhibited different focuses. Hoad was occasionally careless about important points, while Rosewall "treated all his points like match points"[1]. Tennis was a serious business for Muscles. Rex Bellamy (tennis correspondent for *The Times* during the 1960s and 70s) wrote that he played as if unforced errors were punishable by death![2]

Hoad certainly played hard off the court: "He drank enough grog to irrigate the Nullarbor Plain," was Bellamy's assessment.[3] Maybe he was too casual and easy-going to produce his best tennis consistently, and he was afflicted by back and foot injuries after turning pro in 1957. Perhaps drinking was his way of masking the pain.

I am not sure if anyone ever saw Rosewall intoxicated. Most descriptions talk of him as a man of abstemious habits who liked to be in bed early. Perhaps one glass of beer around the barbecue at night, although there was that occasion at a Barrett family barbecue during Wimbledon in 1969! Australian Davis Cup coach Harry Hopman made sure that Hoad and Rosewall didn't room together on overseas trips because their personal routines were so different.

◇◇◇◇◇◇◇

This was a time when Australia measured itself by its sporting success stories—Herb Elliot, Betty Cuthbert and Shirley Strickland on the track, Murray Rose, the Konrad kids and Dawn Fraser in the pool,

1 H Hopman, *Aces and Places*, page 123

2 R Bellamy, *The Tennis Set*, page 190

3 R Bellamy, *Three Decades of Champions*, page 14

Kel Nagle and Peter Thompson on the golf course, and Jack Brabham on the racing circuit. Peter Rowley wrote that Australia was a continent "surrounded by water and inundated with athletes"[4].

Just what are the memories that people have of Rosewall? Our parents' generation (those of them that are left) recall an intense 19-year-old winning the Davis Cup for Australia in December 1953. Alongside Hoad he managed to beat the powerful American team of Tony Trabert and Vic Seixas—but there was controversy and uncertainty associated with the tie, with odd selection decisions and rain delays. My own enduring memory is watching a 39-year-old Rosewall being trounced by a bouncy, arrogant Jimmy Connors in the 1974 Wimbledon final. He had just beaten John Newcombe and Stan Smith, but couldn't manage three in a row.

But just think about that—the 5' 7" (170cm) pocket marvel remained on top of the tennis world for 21 years. Australians considered Muscles to be the quintessential tennis champion, with one of the best backhands anyone had ever seen.

While researching this book, several people told me that Rosewall is known as a tightwad—he would stay at the cheap hotel down the road instead of the one with the other players. Then there were comments made by fellow players who admiringly observed that the Rosewall physique hadn't changed from the time he was 19 to 39: "He didn't get any heavier over the years, except in the pocket."[5] Likewise, Bud Collins joked that Rosewall has made a fortune out of tennis and "buried it beside a gum tree guarded by a wombat"[6]. I like the somewhat mean comment someone made that "Muscles wouldn't shout if a shark bit him." What else nasty could you say about Rosewall, the clean-living, all-time good guy? Back in 1965, Butch Buchholz wrote that saying Rosewall "is not a big spender is the understatement of the year, [but he] would be as generous as Lew Hoad if it came to helping a friend in need"[7].

So the man was careful with his finances, which might have something to do with his upbringing—his dad was the neighbourhood grocer with

4 P Rowley, *Ken Rosewall—Twenty Years at the Top*, page 49

5 R Bellamy, *The Tennis Set*, quoted in *The Sydney Morning Herald*, 28 January 1973

6 Quoted in P Rowley, *Ken Rosewall—Twenty Years at the Top*, page 227

7 *World Tennis*, February 1965

an eye on the till at the end of every day. Rosewall himself once said: "I come from an ordinary hard-working middle-class family. I was taught to be thrifty."[8] Tony Trabert said he was the right person to be treasurer of the players' association in the early 1960s because he was so good with money.

Peter Rowley wrote a book about Rosewall in the 1970s and spent time answering some of these comments by vouching for Rosewall's personal generosity and kindness. I can only do the same. Once Rosewall understood the type of book I wanted to write he has been 100 per cent involved in the project. We have spent many hours together discussing his career and developments in the game; he has offered hospitality and put me in contact with his friends; generously involved me in activities at the New South Wales Tennis Museum; and provided me with tickets to Wimbledon! I think that alone answers the tightwad allegation.

Another feature of Rosewall's career—perhaps another memory people might have—is that he was often overshadowed by some other personalities: most obviously by Hoad; by Gonzales; and then by Laver. Perhaps that's true. Those three players were marvellous champions with strong personalities. At different points, Peter Rowley's book reads a bit like a High Court brief making the case that Muscles was better than all his rivals. I didn't want to write a book like that. Instead, Rosewall is the perfect tool to write the story of Australian tennis for the period of his career, and to assess what was happening more broadly in the tennis world between 1950 and 1976.

◇◇◇◇◇◇◇

Why is this man relevant? This is a book about Ken Rosewall, but it is not just that. He started playing international tennis in 1952, when top 'amateur' players travelled the world under the strict disciplinarian regime imposed by Davis Cup captain, Harry Hopman. The Australian players were often engaged by sporting firms—Slazenger, Oliver, Spalding and Dunlop—and spent their off-season playing exhibitions around Australia. As amateurs they were entitled to represent their country in the Davis Cup competition and play at Wimbledon.

8 P Rowley, *Ken Rosewall—Twenty Years at the Top*, page 126

Once they became champions—by winning the Davis Cup, or a major international event—they became 'marketable' to the pro promoters, like 'Big Jake' Kramer. He immediately came sniffing around because he wanted to establish a professional tennis circuit, and make money for himself. That was fine, but as soon as amateur players signed their pro contracts they could no longer participate in the amateur Davis Cup competition or at Wimbledon.

Tennis did not become 'open' until 1968—and it was not until then that amateur and professional players could compete openly in the world's major tennis tournaments.[9] Muscles was at the forefront of all these events. He joined Kramer's professional circuit in 1957, and spent the next 11 years helping to develop a pro circuit—often playing 'one-night stands' in cycling velodromes, boxing arenas and high-school gyms. The best players in the world—Rosewall, Gonzales, Hoad and Laver—were all doing the same thing. It meant Rosewall was unable to play at Wimbledon for almost a dozen years when he was at his peak, and that is partly responsible for the sad consequence that this great player cannot claim a Wimbledon victory as part of his résumé.

While this was happening the Lawn Tennis Association of Australia (LTAA) could not quite make its mind up about where it stood regarding open tennis. One year it was in favour, another it was not. And there was a ridiculous decision made at one stage that the Kramer pros were banned from playing on LTAA or state association courts. For four years the LTAA surrendered the significant financial advantage it received from renting out courts because of its venomous dislike of Kramer.

When tennis did become open, it was not free competition between players for prize money. The International Lawn Tennis Federation (ILTF) insisted that national associations should remain in control of the game, and was alarmed by the power of professional promoters. During this period Rosewall remained a 'contract professional' with the National Tennis League (NTL) and later World Championship Tennis (WCT). Contention surrounding control of the game continued over the next

9 It was not until 1973 that professional players were able to play in the Davis Cup.

few years with WCT players being unable to play in all ILTF sanctioned tournaments (including Wimbledon) in 1972.

Another development during this period was a greater awareness on the part of the players themselves—they wanted a say in the way the international tennis circuit was managed. Rosewall was part of an early professional players' association in the 1960s, which ran the pro circuit during that time, but the Association of Tennis Professionals (ATP) was established in 1972. Its first arm-wrestle with the ILTF took place shortly after, when members of the ATP voted not to participate at Wimbledon in 1973. Again, note this—Rosewall was excluded from playing Wimbledon in 1972 and 1973.

Why is this man relevant? He is able to give a first-hand account of these events. He saw the professional game evolve from an era of playing in high-school halls, where he and his fellow pros jumped in station wagons and drove themselves to the next destination at the end of an evening, to today's multimillion dollar tennis industry.

He was also a pretty damn good tennis player.

◇◇◇◇◇◇◇

Rosewall seemed destined to become a champion tennis player. His father owned three tennis courts and his parents were good players. Newspapers talk of him having a cut-down racket in his pram, and he started playing tennis when he was three.

Robert, Rosewall's dad, read every book on the game he could get his hands on. He taught young Ken the fundamental strokes, and they remained almost unchanged throughout his career. Robert moulded young Ken's tennis skills from the age of five: "They used to practise together before Ken went to school, and would be at it again when he came home."[10] While it was important to learn the strokes, Robert also encouraged the young boy to think on the court. He was a small kid, and if he wanted to beat the bigger boys he had to outsmart them. The tennis courts were sold when Robert completed a stint with the airforce during the war,

10 O Davidson with CM Jones, *Lawn Tennis—The Great Ones*, page 127

but the family was still allowed to use them. Rosewall played there almost exclusively until he was 11.

> We lived near the courts for a while, and then moved to a small grocery shop with a living area attached in Bay Street, Rockdale. My father sold the courts to Arthur Chapman, a sports store proprietor. The shop was only half a mile or so away from those courts, and we were still able to use them. My father and I often rode our bicycles down there to play either before he went to work or I went to school.
>
> Those courts were attached to the Illawarra Tennis Club, where I played all of my junior tennis and junior competitions. I drove down there recently and most of the area now consists of housing. I think two of the courts are behind some of the units and are still attached to the tennis club, but other courts owned by Arthur are gone.
>
> After living in Rockdale our family shifted to South Hurstville when I was 10, and that's where my father joined the local backyard court group called Wianga—we played tennis in Saturday afternoon and Sunday morning men's competitions. I often practised hitting volleys between the two brick walls at the front of the shop. I caused a lot of wear and tear on the lawn outside the shop. People said they saw me hitting up against the walls as they passed by on the bus! We lived there for five years before moving to another grocery shop in Penshurst.
>
> My mother and father always played local competition tennis and because I was an only child I would go off to the tennis with them. Like any young kid, the racket was too big so my father decided he would chop part of the handle off. I liked to do things left-handed as well as right-handed, but probably was a natural left-hander. My father said: 'You should either be a left-handed player or a right-handed player. Which way do you want to pick up the racket?' So I picked it up right-handed because I think I liked making the right-handed movement on the backhand away

from my body, it felt natural, and that was probably the only reason I became a right-handed player. I did most other things on my left side. If you threw something at me I would catch it left-handed. My natural throwing motion was from my left, and so from that point of view serving left-handed would possibly have been a more natural shot. Maybe I could have changed that.

My father was really my only coach, and he was the first to admit that he could only take me so far. He learned his game from reading old tennis books. He taught me the backhand stroke. It was just a natural shot. I always knew that I was more comfortable playing a backhand than a forehand, so my forehand had some technical weaknesses. Although over the years it did improve, just like my serve did. As a kid there was really no one around to show me what I should be doing on my serve. I didn't have a natural service motion. Like I said, that might have been different if I served left-handed. In those days there wasn't the coaching available that there is now, even though I was supported by Slazenger from an early age—they started giving me rackets when I was 11 or 12.

While all this was happening there was an equally gifted young kid playing tennis in Balmain, just a few miles away. Rosewall didn't know Lew Hoad at the time but something quite extraordinary happened in January 1947. An American Davis Cup team travelled to Australia in late 1946 to challenge for the trophy in the first post-war staging of the Davis Cup. In the Challenge Round the fit and powerful Americans trounced the Australian team 5-0. Then there were a number of exhibition matches played between the Americans, and members of the Australian Davis Cup team. One of these was played at Rockdale in Sydney, and Rosewall and Hoad (aged 12 at the time) were chosen to play a preliminary singles match. Rockdale was Rosewall's home territory remember! So before the big men—Jack Kramer, Ted Schroeder, John Bromwich and Adrian Quist—strutted their stuff, the crowd was treated to these two youngsters playing against one another for the first time. Rosewall says he went about that match as if he was playing for his life, and beat Hoad 6-0, 6-0. The two boys played another exhibition contest some weeks later, and on that occasion Rosewall won 6-2, 6-3.

> We had one of those matches at Rockdale and another at Pratten Park. There were about 2000 people there and we thought it was a pretty big deal. That was the first time Lew and I had met, let alone played against one another. We had just turned 12 and although I was not all that outgoing, I can't remember being nervous. When I was playing tennis I thought the best thing was to think seriously about what I was trying to do. I had moments in my career when I went off the deep end or got upset, but generally I just got on with the game and that was how I was encouraged to play by my father. My mother was very supportive. From memory they took different turns in coming to see me play. I think overall my father saw me play more than she did.

Later that same year the boys faced one another in state age-group championship contests, and Rosewall won on both occasions. At this stage the consistent baseline strategy of Rosewall was able to doggedly unravel any questions asked by his more aggressive, hard-hitting rival. Harry Hopman wrote that there was a closeness between the pair in those early years: "They were such close friends that a growl at one brought a bark from the other."[11] Over time this closeness was replaced by a competitive rivalry. They were champions with divergent personalities.

As a young kid, Rosewall had the chance to play with two of his idols—he was 14 when he played and won a doubles match in an Easter tournament at Orange with John Bromwich, and a year later Slazenger gave him the opportunity to compete against Frank Sedgman when he and Ken McGregor entered a men's doubles event (their other opponent was George Worthington). Rosewall believed his serve and volley were pretty weak at the time. Whatever the result might have been, the 15-year-old was recognised as having enormous potential.

11 H Hopman, *Aces and Places*, page 119

Both Rosewall and Hoad left school aged 15 and went to work for sporting goods companies, although Rosewall did make some effort to keep on with his accountancy studies for at least a year or so at a business college in Sydney. Again this might have been at the insistence of his father, with his awareness of the value of pounds, shillings and pence, and the study possibly helped when Rosewall was treasurer of the international professional players' association in the mid-1960s.

◇◇◇◇◇◇◇

As we have seen, Rosewall was a remarkably good tennis player when he was 12, and he was still outstanding as a 42-year-old, when he was seeded number one in the 1976 Australian Open. He is proud of his legacy. Not only is he one of the greats of Australian tennis, he can genuinely say that by the sweat of his brow he was one of the pioneers of the professional tennis circuit. It is a legacy worth acknowledging, and who else but respected tennis commentator Rex Bellamy (who knew Rosewall well) to make a final comment in this introduction:

> *Underneath the hard remorseless professionalism is the chap next door—sensitive to the good times and the bad, appreciating the one and tolerating the other, taking everything in his stride. Rosewall smiles a lot. He is a gentle man with no fuss, no side: the modesty is genuine. Retiring rather than pushing, he has nothing to prove, no need to impress. He does that on the court. Small wonder that Rosewall has an uncommon capacity for making friends and keeping them. Long after his career has ended, we shall remember the legend with the marvellous backhand—but even more, we shall remember the man behind it.*[12]

Richard Naughton
September 2012

12 R Bellamy, *The Tennis Set*, pages 190-1

CHAPTER 1

◇◇◇◇◇◇◇

YOUNG MEN LEARNING THE GAME

In July 1949, Rosewall's name appeared in the first issue of *Australian Tennis*. Described as "the best tennis prospect for many years"[13], he had recently won the New South Wales 15-and-under schoolboys' singles championship. At 14 years old, and standing 5' 4" (162cm) tall, Rosewall went on to win the Australian junior hardcourt singles championship and by the end of the year he and Lew Hoad became the youngest players to play for New South Wales in interstate competition since Vivian McGrath in 1930. Rosewall, who turned 15 on 2 November, was the older of the pair by just three weeks.

Rosewall, with his amazing ball control, and Hoad, his blond-haired rival from Balmain, came face-to-face that same month at the semi-final of the New South Wales State junior championship. On this occasion it was Hoad's hard-hitting that won the game. The two young players travelled to Melbourne for the interstate events accompanied by Rosewall's mother, Vera. While she stayed with relatives, Rosewall and Hoad bunked out at the YMCA. It was here that Rosewall won the Victorian under-19 boys'

13 *Australian Tennis*, July 1949

singles championship, beating local player Peter Cawthorne, 6-3, 6-4. Rosewall also won the Australian junior championship in January 1950, again beating Cawthorne by 6-4, 4-6, 7-5, and together, he and Hoad won the boys' doubles competition.

> I can remember that match against Cawthorne in the Australian junior championship being delayed by rain—it took a few days to finish it. Lew and I played through the Linton Cup (an interstate competition for junior boys) and won the event for New South Wales. We ended up winning the Linton Cup on three successive occasions. We also played in New South Wales men's team matches, which was a good experience.
>
> I probably agree with the comment Harry Hopman made that Lew and I were very good friends as young kids, but things became more competitive later on. At 15, life was a bit of an adventure. We weren't exactly like brothers, but we spent a lot of time together and practised a lot. At that early stage Lew occasionally stayed at my parent's place. When we travelled overseas for the first time as 17-year-olds we were on friendly terms, but then drifted apart a bit.
>
> When we went away in teams, Harry didn't room us together because of our different personalities. While I was always happy to go to bed early, Lew liked staying up late and this resulted in a bit of a wedge between us. We got along, but there was that competitive instinct.
>
> We remained friends as we grew older, but were not as ready to do things together. He was more outgoing, and liked to have the occasional drink.

During 1950 Rosewall put in some extraordinary performances that confirmed the star quality of the young player. In one match, Rosewall beat 42-year-old Jack Crawford, a former Wimbledon champion, in Sydney's metropolitan hardcourt singles event at Naremburn. A month or so later he reached the semi-finals of another metropolitan singles event, beating Ross

Sherriff, an accomplished state-level player. *The Sydney Morning Herald* waxed lyrical about the youngster's stylish groundstrokes:

> *Rosewall favoured his flashing accurate backhand throughout and refused to be bustled by Sherriff who sought to upset his placid temperament by crowding the net at every chance. It was unusual to see a youthful tennis player stepping round his forehand to swing the ball wide off the backhand or to angle it acutely while he was attacking.*[14]

However, success was sometimes short-lived—the youngster lost in five sets to Rex Hartwig in the interstate Mars Buckley competition, prompting sports commentator Frank Tierney to claim that Hoad had greater potential than Rosewall because the latter spent too much time on the baseline. The writers of *Australian Tennis* held a different view, suggesting Rosewall had the strokes of a future world champion, but lacked a strong service, while Hoad had a devastating service and smash, but lacked the reliability or court-craft of Rosewall.

Rosewall's anticipated brilliance in senior ranks came to the fore in 1951, despite relinquishing his hold on the Australian junior championship to Hoad (6-3, 6-2). In the Queensland Championships in late October 1951, Rosewall defeated Mervyn Rose, who was five years his senior, in four sets (3-6, 7-5, 7-5, 6-4). Onlookers claimed Rosewall exhibited "typical poise and padlock control"[15]. On the same day, Hoad beat Don Candy 6-3, 7-5, 5-7, 4-6, 7-5. They were both important wins as Rose and Candy were members of Australia's Davis Cup team, and the matches signalled the beginning of a recurring pattern where Rosewall and Hoad often achieved significant victories on the same day.

Then in the New South Wales Championships, the 17-year-old Rosewall beat veteran Adrian Quist, before losing to Wimbledon champion Dick Savitt of the US in a stirring battle (6-8, 8-6, 6-3, 8-6) that lasted for more than two hours. After that match Harry Hopman, the Australian Davis

---

14 *The Sydney Morning Herald*, 11 October 1950

15 *The Sydney Morning Herald*, 1 November 1951

Cup coach, spoke of both Rosewall and Hoad as being eligible candidates to be sent overseas in order to gain international experience.

Another interested spectator was Jack Kramer, the 1947 Wimbledon champion, now involved in running the professional tennis circuit. He remarked on Rosewall's improvement having seen him play at 12 and 15 years old during his tours of Australia.

It almost came as a surprise when Rosewall lost in the semi-final of the 1951 New South Wales junior event to the American junior champion Hamilton Richardson (7-5, 1-6, 6-4), who played Hoad in the final.

> It was pretty bad weather again that week. The organisers ended up having to get a special dispensation to allow Sunday tennis to take place in order to finish the tournament.

A week or so later, Rosewall played in the 1951 Victorian Championships at Kooyong and scored an easy victory over travelling Swedish player, Lennert Bergelin, who years later earned some fame as Björn Borg's coach. On this occasion Rosewall won 6-1, 6-2, 8-6, and the Swedish gentleman was so disgusted with himself afterwards that "he brushed aside newsmen and refused even to grunt"[16]. In the quarter-finals Rosewall lost to Ken McGregor, 6-3, 9-7, 6-3.

In the semi-finals of the championships, Savitt scored a solid victory over McGregor, which appeared to guarantee himself a place playing singles for the Americans in the 1951 Challenge Round. He was the reigning Australian and Wimbledon champion. Rosewall had his moment of glory, too, beating the American player Ham Richardson in a semi-final of the junior boys' event. He then defeated Hoad in the final by 7-5, 3-6, 7-5. The performance of Rosewall and Hoad throughout the early summer tournaments meant they were signed up to the Davis Cup training squad, alongside Frank Sedgman, McGregor, Rose, Candy and Ian Ayre.

The Davis Cup Challenge Round in 1951 was played at White City in Sydney and might best be remembered for unusual selection decisions on

16 *The New York Times*, 2 December 1951

the part of both Australia and the United States. Rose was chosen as the number two player for Australia after Frank Sedgman, the holder of the US National Championship. This meant he was chosen ahead of Sedgman's doubles partner Ken McGregor, who earlier that year had reached the final of the Australian Championships and Wimbledon. It seems the chairman of selectors, Sir Norman Brookes, insisted that Rose's left-handed serve was perfectly suited to the occasionally tricky winds at White City. The decision backfired as Rose lost both his singles matches. Australia narrowly won the tie 3 rubbers to 2, with Sedgman winning both his singles matches, and Sedgman and McGregor winning the doubles.

The American captain Frank Shields chose not to play Savitt, arguably the highest-ranked US player in the tie. Instead, the American singles players were Ted Schroeder and Vic Seixas, with Schroeder and Tony Trabert playing doubles. The grumpy and fretful Savitt was furious, questioning why he had even travelled to Australia if he wasn't going to be selected for the matches.

There was talk of Sedgman and McGregor becoming professional after the Davis Cup (1930s and 40s tennis star Bobby Riggs was running the pro tour at that stage), but Sedgman reassured Australian tennis fans that he intended to play at Wimbledon in 1952, and in a further Davis Cup Challenge Round.

> My understanding of the circumstances at that time was that Bobby Riggs wanted to promote a professional tour during 1952, and he approached Frank Sedgman and Ken McGregor, but Gonzales wouldn't sign the contract. This meant the tour was cancelled in 1952, otherwise Sedgman might have become a pro the year before he eventually did. Then there was communication between Sedgman and Kramer about arrangements for a pro tour in 1953. The plan was that Kramer would play a series of head-to-head matches against Sedgman, with support matches being played between Pancho Segura, the Ecuadorian player who had been a pro for a few years, and McGregor. As we explain later, Gonzales could be a difficult customer. I'm not sure

> whether he didn't like the tour being managed by Bobby Riggs, or he wanted more money.

Another aspect of the 1951 Davis Cup matches was an incident that took place involving Jack Kramer, who was recruited as coach of the American team, and Australia's captain-coach Hopman. The Australian captain suspected Kramer was making hand signals to Schroeder during his singles match with Rose, and relayed this to referee Cliff Sproule. The discord was a sure sign of Hopman and Kramer's strained friendship, and over the next 15 years or so Hopman was continually frustrated and annoyed by Kramer attempting to sign up his best players to the pro tour.

> I have to say it was great for Lew and I to be placed in the position of being 'orange-juice boys' for that Davis Cup Challenge Round back in 1951. We were two of the youngest squad members in Davis Cup history. We were also both from Sydney and were able to watch the build up to the matches. That has now developed into a pattern that Davis Cup captains, like Neale Fraser after Hopman and those since, have always tried to blood the younger players that had potential to play Davis Cup tennis—that probably applied to Lleyton Hewitt more than anyone else. It gave younger players the chance to experience Davis Cup tennis.
>
> There was always a great deal of interest in the Challenge Round in that era. We were there to run errands or help the boys warm up. I was too young to know what was going on about that selection decision of Mervyn Rose, although he had actually played well in some of the state tournaments in the lead-up to the Challenge Round. Harry's preferred team was certainly McGregor and Sedgman, so it was all a bit of a shock when Sir Norman Brookes' knowledge about the prevailing breezes favouring left-handers was taken into account in that way. Unfortunately, Merv did not play that well on the day. But it also meant that McGregor was determined to play well when he got

a chance and he was probably the best player on the court in the Davis Cup doubles match.

◇◇◇◇◇◇◇

The 1952 Australian Championships were played at Memorial Drive in Adelaide, and in the men's singles Ken McGregor came out victorious in a finals encounter against Frank Sedgman. Perhaps this was the best way of responding to those Davis Cup selectors who overlooked him a month before. Sedgman might have been having an off day or feeling distracted (it had been a long month playing tennis and he was about to be married to Miss Jean Spence), and McGregor made the most of this opportunity.

In the semi-finals, McGregor had defeated the cranky American Savitt. There was a remarkable incident during the match when Savitt refused to play because the court surface was damp and he believed McGregor had an unfair advantage because he was wearing spikes. Savitt sulkily staged a sit-down strike, and had to be coaxed to play by senior Australian and American officials. Controversially, Schroeder and Seixas did not stay in the country for the summer tournaments, raising questions as to whether the top Australian players would be barred from playing in the US National Championships in retaliation. *The New York Times* reported top Australian administrators felt badly let down by the United States Lawn Tennis Association (USLTA).

In those Australian Championships the 17-year-old Rosewall reached his allotted place in the quarter-finals as number-six seed, and was then defeated by Rose over five sets. Hoad, the seventh seed, was beaten in the last 16 by veteran Geoff Brown, who some years earlier surprised everyone by reaching the 1946 Wimbledon final. Together, Hoad and Rosewall lost in the doubles to Americans Savitt and Ham Richardson (14-12, 1-6, 6-3, 6-1) on a day of oppressive 41°C heat. Rosewall appeared to struggle during the tournament, and was chastised for showing bad temperament in an early match. This was probably a bit harsh as Rosewall went on to register a fine result by extending Rose in their quarter-final match, after struggling back from two sets down. He went on to win the Australian junior singles title again, defeating Hoad 10-8, 6-2.

The Australian travelling team for Wimbledon and other European tournaments, and possibly America if the Lawn Tennis Association of Australasia (LTAA) selectors overcame their grievance towards the USLTA, was Sedgman (although he was travelling privately part of the time), McGregor, Rose, Rosewall and Hoad. The team captain was Hopman. The team flew directly from Australia to London, which took three days and two nights on a Super Constellation flight.

> Neither Lew or I expected to be travelling overseas at that young age. There was obviously a decision taken that the LTAA would try and develop young players.

In Paris at the French Championships the youngsters reached the semi-finals of the doubles with wins over Richardson and Trabert, Enrique Morea and Alejo Russell of Argentina, and then South Africa's Eric Sturgess and Belgium's Phillipe Washer. They finally lost to their compatriots Sedgman and McGregor by 6-4, 6-3, 3-6, 6-0.

Rosewall scored his first victory on the international circuit when he won an early singles match in the 1952 French Championships against Eugenio Saller of Brazil by 6-1, 6-4, 6-1. He explained that even though he was studying a French dictionary, he still had trouble following the scores! He subsequently lost to the lanky, 22-year-old Italian Fausto Guardini by 6-2, 6-4, 2-6, 2-6, 6-2, who humbly declared: "That boy will be a world champion in three years."[17] The French champion in 1952 was the master of clay, Jaroslav Drobny, a Czechoslovakian living in exile in Egypt, who triumphed over Frank Sedgman in the final.

There were occasional wins and some disappointing losses for the two 17-year-olds as they played and travelled the international circuit. Neither Hoad or Rosewall were seeded for the 1952 Wimbledon, while fellow Australians Sedgman, McGregor and Rose, were seeded first, fifth and eighth respectively. The Australian team played in the traditional Wimbledon lead-in tournament at Queen's Club. In that event Rosewall

---

17 *The Sydney Morning Herald*, 23 May 1952

beat experienced Sturgess in the third round, while Hoad beat Ham Richardson, the American junior. Richardson was seeded at Wimbledon, so there may have been some incentive for Hoad in this match. Both the young Australians fell in the quarter-finals.

In the first round of Wimbledon Rosewall beat Englishman John Barrett (6-2, 6-2, 6-0). Barrett later became a notable tennis journalist, broadcaster and administrator, and also married 1961 Wimbledon champion, Angela Mortimer. He became a lifelong friend of Rosewall's, who recalls meeting and losing to the Australian on four separate occasions in early rounds at Wimbledon.[18] In his second round match Rosewall faced the 10th seeded player, the veteran American Gardnar Mulloy, and was convincingly beaten. Mulloy was an extremely experienced player on the circuit, and the match was Rosewall's first experience of Wimbledon's famous centre court.

> For some reason the Wimbledon draws never did favour John Barrett. I can remember playing him a couple of times in the first round. Some years later he was British Davis Cup captain, and often travelled with junior teams. He also established the BP scholarship for junior tennis, and got Rod Laver and I involved in the BP fellowship plan in the 1960s and 70s. That was a coaching program for young British players and both of us occasionally played with the kids.
>
> That match against Mulloy was a bit of a disappointment. I was only 17, and was probably nervous. I was looking forward to playing on Wimbledon's centre court, and playing well. But then I was faced by one of the game's top players and was probably a bit overawed by the occasion, and the atmosphere of the centre court at Wimbledon.

Later in the week, Hoad and Rosewall returned to centre court to play a doubles match against the top seeded American pair of Savitt and Mulloy. It was the match that possibly established the reputation of the

18 Interview with author, 11 June 2012

two precocious Australians. Hoad and Rosewall won the first two sets 6-4, 8-6, but the Americans fought back, winning the next two sets with the loss of only four games. Hoad and Rosewall were then matched against the American duo in a do-or-die fifth set. A crowd of 17,000 packed into the stands and watched on in awe as the young men from down under played it stroke-for-stroke against their better-known rivals. Savitt and Mulloy had a match point when leading 5-4 in the final set, but the youngsters overcame that adversity. Finally they broke through Mulloy, who had been fighting a knee cramp during the final set, at 5-5. The Australians then served out the match to score a 6-4, 8-6, 1-6, 3-6, 7-5 victory and "the biggest ovation of the week"[19].

There were 25,000 people at Wimbledon that day, coping with the hottest weather London was to experience during the summer of 1952. The English patiently queued overnight, and extra police were called to handle the crowds blocking passageways. Newspapers refer to numerous cases of heat prostration during the afternoon. Allison Danzig of *The New York Times*, who became a great supporter of both Rosewall and Hoad for many years, wrote his first dispatch about the young men:

> *Hoad and Rosewall have been talked about for the past year as worthy successors to Sedgman and McGregor a few seasons hence and their performance in defeating such experienced campaigners as Savitt and Mulloy bore out the encomiums they have won. They had a bad lapse after the second set and looked like teenagers in the third and fourth, but otherwise their play was almost phenomenally good. Their shrewdness on opening the court and seizing their opportunities in rapid fire at the net had to be seen to be believed. Over and over they outmaneuvered the Americans or got the best of them in volleying exchanges. They kept their return of service low and complemented each other beautifully in setting up winning shots.*
>
> *Hoad's rifle service and his scorching forehand returns of service down the alley from the right-hand court brought explosive applause. More*

19 *The New York Times*, 29 June 1952

than once Savitt stopped in his tracks and stared unbelievingly as the sturdy blond youngster cracked back his cannonball for a winner.

But in the fifth set, Hoad and Rosewall recovered their early form and it was a battle royale all the way, with the crowd on the edge of its seats. Games followed service to 5-5 with Savitt and Mulloy hard pressed to win in the fifth and seventh and Hoad whipping through two cannonball aces to save himself, and screams of joy in the eighth in which the Americans were within a stroke of 5-3.

Then Savitt won his service, so potent most of the time, in the ninth, and in the tenth the Americans stood at match point. With the gallery holding its breath, Rosewall served and to the immense relief of the multitude Mulloy knocked the ball weakly into the net. The Floridian was tiring in the heat and his knee had been weakening from the fourth set.

Then Mulloy served in the 11th and was down 0-40. He pulled up to 30-40 and then put a backhand volley into the net. The crowd roared as the fatal break came, but its cheers were nothing compared with the outbursts in the final game.

Rosewall went back for a lob and made a marvelous return down the middle. He brought off a brilliant overhead smash angled to the sideline for 30-0. Savitt's backhand return of service found the net and the match ended as Mulloy's return of service from the backhand went out of court. A deafening roar went up to signal the victory of the teenagers.[20]

Mulloy had a reputation as a fine doubles player. Dick Savitt wasn't classified as a top doubles player but he was still effective, and as the Australian and Wimbledon champion in 1951, he was well respected. I can't remember if we got any special advice from Hop[man] about playing them. And I can't remember it being all that hot. It might have been hot by English standards! It didn't bother us too much. The match created a lot of excitement. Lew was always pretty cool, calm and collected, but deep down we were both pretty excited about winning a big match.

20 ibid

After that wonderful match, Hoad and Rosewall beat the Argentinians Morea and Russell in a quarter-final (4-6, 6-3, 6-2, 5-7, 6-4), but then fell somewhat lamely in a semi-final to the American Seixas and Sturgess of South Africa (6-4, 8-6, 6-8, 7-5).

Of course, 1952 was the year of the great Frank Sedgman at Wimbledon, where he won all three titles: beating Jaroslav Drobny in the singles; winning the doubles with McGregor; and the mixed doubles with American player, Doris Hart.

> I recall we were staying at a hotel in Kensington—nice accommodation. Even in those days the All England Club provided transportation for the players. It was usually a Bentley, with an old driver. Hopman occasionally had us out running round the Serpentine Lake in Hyde Park. A few of us might have stood behind a tree for a while! We often went to Queen's Club to train as it often rained and there were indoor courts there. That was my first experience of playing on fast indoor boards. The All England Club was very protective about its courts being used for practice games—and at that time the Wimbledon grounds were quite a small facility. It's now grown of course, but I don't think that happened until the coming of open tennis, when the club purchased more land.
>
> We all spent most of our time at the hotel, where we ate our meals, too. In spite of the restrictions on us as amateurs, we did have certain privileges. We stayed in good places and everything was laid on, and then we got pocket money of 25 shillings per day ($7 per day in America).

◇◇◇◇◇◇◇

The tennis administrators at home in Australia eventually caved in on their plan to boycott the American summer tournaments. The touring team travelled to America, where it played in lead-up tournaments to

Forest Hills.[21] At the Eastern Grass Court Championship at South Orange Tennis Club, Rosewall lost to Savitt in the fourth round by 6-4, 9-7. In spite of this loss, Rosewall's performance was praised by Al Laney of the *New York Herald Tribune*, who compared him with the Frenchman Henri Cochet due to his wonderful hand-eye coordination and astonishingly quick reflexes.

A week later Rosewall lost badly to 19-year-old American player Bob Perry (1-6, 7-5, 6-3) at the Newport Invitation event. It was Perry, along with Richardson, who the Americans now hoped might prove a counterpoint to Australia's rising stars, Rosewall and Hoad.

In the US National Championships doubles, then played as a separate tournament in Brookline, Massachusetts (just outside Boston), Hoad and Rosewall lost somewhat easily in a semi-final to Sedgman and McGregor (5-7, 6-2, 6-4, 6-2). It was reported that when the senior Australian pair "buckled down to work seriously it was really no contest"[22]. The youngsters were pinned to the baseline, and unable to force their compatriots out of attacking mode. However, what was ultimately significant about the event was that the scratch pair of Rose and Seixas scored an unexpected victory over Sedgman and McGregor in the final, by 3-6, 10-8, 10-8, 6-8, 8-6. The result was called "the biggest tennis shock of the year"[23].

In the US National Championships singles at Forest Hills, Rosewall played an early round match against Sydney Schwartz of New York, a match distinguished by the American having a temper tantrum at one point, and slamming a ball over nearby trees. Rosewall had little trouble winning the match. Conversely, poor McGregor, Australia's number-two player, led 6-3, 6-4, but was down 5-6 in the third when he approached the umpire to explain that he had to default his opening match due to a pulled stomach muscle. He was concerned the injury was serious enough to put him out of tennis altogether if he played on. However, his sporting opponent, Calvin

21 The LTAA Council insisted Hopman impress on the USLTA that American players visiting Australia for the Challenge Round should remain in Australia for the New South Wales, Victorian and Australian Championships, reported in *The Sydney Morning Herald*, 17 June 1952

22 *The New York Times*, 24 August 1952

23 *The Sydney Morning Herald*, 26 August 1952

MacCracken of Tenafly, New Jersey, joined in the discussion and pleaded with McGregor to let him default instead!

There was considerable harmony about the fact that Hoad and Rosewall scored their first major international successes in singles on the same day at the US National Championships in 1952, both reaching the quarter-finals after beating more fancied opponents. In their last 16 matches Rosewall beat Seixas, the previous year's finalist and the player ranked number four in the world in 1951, in a tight five-set battle that ended at 3-6, 6-2, 7-5, 5-7, 6-3. Hoad's victory was over Arthur 'Tappy' Larsen (6-3, 6-4, 6-4), who won the tournament in 1950. They were remarkable results on the part of the two 17-year-olds.

Those observing the tournament were particularly impressed by Rosewall's match—he played badly in the first set but managed to turn the contest around. It was the first time a knowledgeable American crowd had seen the full array of Rosewall's groundstrokes pitted against a net rusher like Seixas, and it was a dazzling spectacle. On the other hand, it was obviously a difficult loss for Seixas, normally a calm and unemotional player, and he was thoroughly despondent after the match as he pushed by photographers who wanted him to pose with Rosewall. Red Smith of the *New York Herald Tribune* described Rosewall's victory as, "a spectacle that occurs only once in a generation of big league tennis". Rosewall, he said, played "with the unruffled guile of a veteran twice his age and took a tyrannical control of tactics"[24].

> I didn't see the match between Lew and Larsen, because I was probably playing Vic Seixas on an outside court. The main tip about playing Seixas came from Ken McGregor, who told me that he liked to play a backhand passing shot down the line, so I should favour that shot if I went to the net. I wasn't really a net rusher anyway at 17 years of age. I won with a combination of passing shots, and when I went to the net I'd watch for that backhand down the line. I was very excited to have won such

24 Quoted in *Australian Tennis*, October 1952

a big match, while he obviously didn't like to lose to an unranked player. He was 11 years older than me.

Those two results were a bit of a shock to the Americans. Larsen was an exceptional player, although a bit temperamental. The story was that his nerves were a bit frayed after a period of war service. The nickname 'Tappy' came from the fact that he was constantly tapping his racket, against the net or on the ground.

I can remember him being in the old change rooms at White City in the early 1950s, and he was struggling to put on a tennis shoe for about 20 minutes. He was a strange fellow. But he was also a good player, a left-hander with a lot of touch. And on that particular day at White City he played incredibly well and beat Frank Sedgman.

That year Lew and I were staying with Mervyn Rose, Ken McGregor and Harry Hopman in an old house owned by people called Stone—'the Stone House'—which was within walking distance of the West Side Tennis Club.

The 17-year-old Rosewall was brought to earth when he played 39-year-old Gardnar Mulloy in a quarter-final of the tournament. He had already lost to Mulloy in singles at Wimbledon. The match was much closer on this occasion, a five-set battle, which the American finally won (8-6, 3-6, 4-6, 7-5, 7-5). In fact, Mulloy looked well and truly beaten when he trailed 1-4 in the fourth set, but the gritty American, playing in his national championships for the 18th time, refused to give in. Mulloy first played in the US National Championships singles before Rosewall was born. There was some delicate irony here, of course, as many years later the same was often written about Rosewall and some of his youthful rivals.

This match was also played on an outside court. Mulloy was a good player. He was 39 and I was 17. He looked after himself physically. He could sometimes get people offside because he was temperamental. I can remember watching him play at White

> City and getting upset with the crowd. He turned to the stands and said: 'Come down and say that after the match!' I was disappointed to lose that match, but it was close and a good experience for me.

In another quarter-final, Sedgman defeated Hoad 6-2, 6-1, 6-3. Then in a semi-final match the top-ranked Australian beat Rose, another member of the Australian touring team, 6-3, 6-3, 6-4. In the final it was another crushing victory to Sedgman, as he annihilated Mulloy 6-1, 6-2, 6-3 in just 47 minutes. That match was described as 'murder', with the American tired and stiff after a series of long-fought battles. What was a 39-year-old doing in the final of Forest Hills, asked some of the American papers. They suggested it meant the USLTA was a little like Old Mother Hubbard, without a bone in the cupboard![25]

On the team's trip back to Australia, Rosewall lost in the Pacific South West Championships in Los Angeles to Savitt, the number-two seed, by 6-4, 3-6, 6-3, 6-0. Hoad was defeated in the tournament by in-form junior player, Perry. In spite of these results, Hoad and Rosewall managed to beat Sedgman and McGregor in the doubles (6-4, 7-5, 6-3, 8-6), playing well enough to take control of the net away from the more highly favoured pair. The youngsters eventually lost the doubles final to the Americans, Herbie Flam and Hugh Stewart, in an agonisingly close match. The Americans won 1-6, 9-7, 1-6, 9-7, 6-2, after the youngsters held match point in the 12th game of the fourth set. For his part, Sedgman suffered one of only four losses during the year (to that point) when he was beaten by Seixas in the Pacific South West final, by 6-4, 6-4, 6-4.

Sedgman suffered from an ongoing loss of form on his return to Australia, when playing in the summer tournaments that were treated as preparation for the Davis Cup Challenge Round. He struggled to beat Rosewall in a five-set match in the semi-finals of the Queensland Championships, and then lost to Seixas in the final of the Victorian Championships by 8-6, 3-6, 6-3, 6-4. In that tournament Seixas gained some revenge over Rosewall for

25 *The New York Times*, 8 September 1952

the match at Forest Hills. He trounced the youngster 6-0, 6-2, 6-2 in the semi-finals.

Those late-season results meant there were some blemishes on Sedgman's almost perfect record in 1952. However, things were much more straightforward in the Davis Cup Challenge Round played against the Americans in Adelaide. The Australian team consisted of Sedgman, McGregor, Rose and Hoad. In that contest Sedgman scored straight-set victories against both Seixas and Trabert, and he and McGregor defeated Seixas and Trabert in the doubles. It was a crushing 4 rubbers to 1 victory to Australia.

As expected, immediately after the Challenge Round, Sedgman announced his departure to join the pro ranks, along with McGregor. Jack Kramer, the American impresario, signed on the Australians for an international pro tour—Sedgman would play Kramer in a series of matches, and McGregor was to meet Pancho Segura, the Ecuadorian who had been part of the pro circuit for five or six years. In the absence of Sedgman and McGregor, the Australians at the top of the ranking list were Rose, Rosewall and Hoad, with the last two of these having just turned 18. The question was whether the teen 'tennis twins' were ready to step up to the next level.

CHAPTER 2

◇◇◇◇◇◇◇

THE GOLDEN YEAR

What a start to the year for 18-year-old Ken! The 1953 Australian Championships singles were played at Kooyong between the 9-17 January. The holder (Ken McGregor) and Frank Sedgman had departed for pro ranks, leaving the event a little depleted, and 'open'. The relative ability of many of the new players was unknown. The top seed was Mervyn Rose, followed by Vic Seixas, Rosewall, the Italian Fausto Gardini and Lew Hoad.

It was a bad tournament for some of the higher seeds. Gardini lost in the second round to young Australian Ian Ayre; and then Hoad lost to the West Australian, Clive Wilderspin. Ayre was the surprise packet of the event as he went on to defeat Wilderspin and reach the semi-final against Rose. Things were a little more predictable in the bottom half of the draw, with Rosewall meeting Seixas in the semi-final and beating him in four sets (6-3, 2-6, 7-5, 6-4). That result confirmed the young man's standing among the best players in the world and was evidence that he continued to improve, while the American's nerves were shattered after the heavy responsibilities of the Davis Cup series. The court surface was damp by the fourth set and both players donned spikes, but this did not help Seixas. Rosewall was able to hit harder and wider, and cleanly passed Seixas on five occasions in the last two games.

> I think they tried to bring the Australian Championships forward to encourage overseas players like Seixas to stay. It was a different sort of event in those days because the best overseas players didn't really like coming out here. The field was not all that large, but I still had good matches. And you always had to beat the best Australians—like Hoad, Rose and Hartwig—and they were all among the top 10 or so in the world. I was in good shape for the match against Seixas. Lew and I had been on the Davis Cup squad and had the opportunity to practise with Sedgman and McGregor, which was good for us.

The final was a relatively easy assignment, with Rosewall beating Rose by 6-0, 6-3, 6-4. The match only lasted 75 minutes and Rosewall said he played the best tennis of his life to win. Rose was disappointed, but praised Rosewall: "The little devil would have got the ball through the eye of a needle today"[26] and conceded that he had never been passed so often. The crowd was unusually excited with the young Australian being 'mobbed' by 150 teenagers as he walked back to the clubhouse. Meanwhile, Sir Norman Brookes described Rosewall's backhand as the best of all time.

> Rose was an aggressive player and he beat me the previous year in Adelaide. I was still relying on my groundstrokes, and trying to change up my game a little, while Merv would come to the net at every opportunity. He had beaten me before, but I still thought I could win if I played decently.
>
> One good thing I remember is that Stan Nicholes, the masseur and trainer who travelled with Davis Cup teams, gave me a rub down on the Friday night, which loosened me up for the final the next day. It was not unusual for matches to take place on consecutive days, but there was no play on Sundays.
>
> I was happy and excited to win at such a young age. It was much different in those days. You had to get to the tennis by

26 G Greenwood, *The Golden Years of Australian Tennis*, page 100

> yourself on the train or the bus. It was also nice that Wilma [McIver, who Rosewall would go on to marry in 1956] was in Melbourne that year. She was playing in the Queensland Wilson Cup team. We saw a lot of one another while she was there. By that stage we had been friends for about three years. After the Wilson Cup matches finished she had to return to Brisbane to her job with Spaldings, which paid about 19s and 6d a week.

Rosewall was the youngest Australian to reach the national singles final. He received more than 100 congratulatory telegrams from all over the world after his success. It was almost expected that the youngster suffered a let-down when he lost to Rex Hartwig in a quarter-final of the South Australian Championships in a long five-set battle the following week. It was the start of a remarkable year of success for the young man[27]. Looking back, however, 1953 was also a strange year that appeared to fizzle out after Wimbledon. From then on there were constant suggestions that Rosewall was being overplayed and felt jaded. This, of course, was probably the fault of those managing his schedule. Rosewall won three of the major amateur world tennis events during 1953[28], but some argue he could have won more.

The original Australian LTAA touring team for 1953 was Rosewall, Hoad, Rose, Ayre and Wilderspin. The West Australian, Wilderspin, was considered fortunate as his selection was primarily based on him attracting public attention after beating the hard-hitting Hoad in the Australian Championships. Hartwig, hailing from Albury, was eventually included in the team after a public subscription raised the necessary funds.

The Australian team travelled to Egypt, playing exhibition matches against the Austrian Frederick Huber and Drobny, before competing in Rome. In his Rome quarter-final, Rosewall defeated the stylish American Budge Patty, before losing to Drobny (6-1, 6-4, 6-2) in the semi-final. Hoad made it all the way to the final, but the crafty Drobny was just too good on clay courts, and won in three easy sets. Hoad and Rosewall won the doubles, defeating Drobny and Patty by 6-2, 6-4, 6-2.

27 In the doubles final, Rosewall and Hoad beat the Victorians Rose and Candy 9-11, 6-4, 10-8, 6-4

28 Major amateur events at that time included: The Australian, Italian and French Championships; Wimbledon; the United States National Championships, and the Pacific South West Championships.

> That was my first match against Drobny. I knew of him by reputation, and it was a bit of a frightening experience in a way because clay was meant to be his best surface. He had already won the French Championships twice. He played with a lot of variety, and was happy to move forward and volley on faster courts. Usually he played from the back of the court on clay. As a left-hander his backhand was defensive, and a bit of a weakness. He was much more versatile on the forehand. Even so, he was able to cover up that weakness and win a lot of matches.

In Paris, Rosewall became the youngest player to reach the men's singles final of the French Championships[29] when he beat the Argentinian player Enrique Morea over five sets (2-6, 6-2, 6-4, 0-6, 6-2) in their semi-final, despite there being a stark contrast between the frail-looking 18-year-old from Australia and the 6' 3" South American. The semi-final match was described as the best in the championships to that point, with the youngster being calmer than his opponent, and displaying remarkable accuracy with his use of delicate drops and lobs. Team captain Hopman said Rosewall showed "admirable coolness and stuck to his tactics"[30] throughout.

> Morea is still around, and holds an important position with the International Tennis Federation (ITF). He was another good clay-courter. He was big and probably not all that manoeuvrable. My advantage was that I could play some short shots and use different strategy.

In the final Rosewall faced Seixas, who had defeated Drobny 6-3, 6-2, 3-6, 6-3 in their semi-final. Drobny had held the title the previous two years—beating Sedgman in 1951 and 1952—but was below form in this match, losing the first two sets in 28 minutes.

---

29 He held this record until Björn Borg won the event when he had just turned 18 in 1974. This record has since been lowered by Michael Chang, who won the championships aged 17 years and 3 months in 1989.

30 *The Sydney Morning Herald*, 30 May 1953

By beating his opponent 6-3, 6-4, 1-6, 6-2, Rosewall become the first Australian to win the French Championships since Jack Crawford in 1933. It also signalled his third win over Seixas, after earlier matches at Forest Hills in 1952 and the 1953 Australian Championships. The enthusiastic crowd cried out "*fantastique*", as the young Australian clouted his crisp and accurate groundstrokes from one side of the court to the other. At the end of the match Rosewall was greeted by the great French player Henri Cochet, who kissed him on both cheeks and said: "You played real tennis, my boy. Real tennis! And at your age, too."[31] René Lacoste, another of the 'Four Musketeers' of French tennis, spent some time comparing grips with the youngster.[32] Rosewall was immediately hailed as a great clay court player. It was an exciting prospect because in recent times the top Australians—like Sedgman—had struggled on the clay surface.

> Vic's win over Drobny in their semi-final was a surprise. He was not known as a clay court player. In that final I hit the ball well, and consistently, and was probably helped by the fact that I had already beaten him a few times before. It was exciting for me—and something to look back on. Sometimes it is difficult for young players to win major championships at that age. They may be good at 17 or 18, but then fade away. I tried to take the view that it was important to keep my feet on the ground, and there were still a lot of players who were better than me.

It was a remarkably successful tournament for the Australian travelling team as Rosewall and Hoad played off the final of the championships doubles against Mervyn Rose and Clive Wilderspin, winning 6-2, 6-1, 6-1. The two young men from Sydney did not lose a set throughout the tournament and were so dominant in the final the crowd started to barrack noisily, thinking Rose and Wilderspin were not trying!

---

31 *The Sydney Morning Herald*, 1 June 1953

32 M Brady, *The Centre Court Story*, page 211

◇◇◇◇◇◇◇

The seedings for Wimbledon in 1953 ended up showing that two 18-year-olds, Rosewall and Maureen Connolly, were favoured to win the singles crowns. After Rosewall at number one, the seeds were Seixas, Rose, Drobny, Gardnar Mulloy of America and Hoad. It was a coronation year—a big event for the colonials!

> Thinking back on it I am not sure I was ready to be seeded number one. I deserved it because I had won those two major events, but I was nervous and I ended up playing a nervous type of tournament.

Hoad raised some questions about the seedings when he defeated both Rose and then Rosewall (8-6, 10-8) in the London Grass Court Championships at Queen's Club, the week before Wimbledon. In the final, Rosewall's play was listless and inconsistent on return of serve, while for Hoad, this was his first overseas tournament win. Rosewall encountered an awkward moment when he played the Brazilian Armando Vieira in an early round at Queen's Club. At one stage the umpire referred to the Brazilian as Mr 'Veah'. In response the Brazilian stormed to the net, glared at the umpire, stomped his foot, and implored with "voice, eyes and hands: 'It is Vee-*era* if you don't mind. Please say it that way, or all these people will think I come from Korea or somewhere.'"[33]

Things were bumpy for Rosewall at Wimbledon in 1953, as he struggled to adjust to the expectations of winning. In his first match he dropped a set to the French Davis Cup player Robert Abdesselam in an unimpressive display. There was an odd match in the last 16, when Rosewall had to struggle from behind to beat a little-known Queenslander, Jack Arkinstall. Finally Rosewall "awoke as if from a bad dream"[34] to win by 4-6, 3-6, 6-1, 6-1, 6-2. It is hard to imagine what was happening through those first two sets, although the newspapers referred to Arkinstall having a magic touch on the fast surface, and Rosewall appearing unusually leaden-footed. By the end of the match, of course, Rosewall's supremacy had been reestablished.

---

33 *The Sydney Morning Herald*, 20 June 1953

34 *The Times*, 27 June 1953

That victory placed Rosewall in a quarter-final of the draw, against 22-year-old Danish player, Kurt Nielsen. The Dane, who was better-known as an indoor player, was experiencing a successful tournament and defeated fifth-seeded Mulloy in the fourth round. Nielsen was nevertheless spoken of as a rank outsider, who fluked his way into the last eight.

The Dane continued his giant-killer feats in the quarter-final to beat Rosewall in five sets with a score (7-5, 4-6, 6-8, 6-0, 6-2) that suggests Nielsen won by possessing greater stamina in the last two sets. *The Times* talks of Rosewall tiring in the fourth set, while Nielsen was as full of life as ever. It was a match played mainly from the baseline, with both players relying on effective backhand passing shots, and Nielsen was also helped by accurate serving at vital times. Clearly exhausted by the battle, it was later revealed that Rosewall's weakness on court was a result of stomach trouble that prevented him from eating anything the night before. Some months later Hopman confided to the Lawn Tennis Association of Victoria (LTAV) council at Kooyong that Rosewall had been violently ill at 2.30am on the morning of the Nielsen match, and attributed this to an attack of nerves.

> I certainly didn't have a good night's rest, although I can't remember if this was a food reaction or a nervous reaction. I ran out of puff during the match. I had my chances. Nielsen was a solid player, and grass was his best surface. I probably lost the match because I didn't win in three sets. The way I played then was mainly from the back of the court, and that was probably a disadvantage because the grass courts were quite fast. On the other hand, a good server like Nielsen had an advantage. It was also a pretty hot day! I was disappointed about losing the match and it affected me a little bit. It was a match I expected to win.

Meanwhile, Hoad lost in another tightly contested quarter-final to Seixas (5-7, 6-4, 6-3, 1-6, 9-7). Of the Australians, only Rose succeeded in reaching the semi-finals, where he lost to Seixas in another hard-fought encounter (6-4, 10-12, 9-11, 6-4, 6-3), while Nielsen added to his string of upsets by defeating Drobny (6-4, 6-3, 6-2). In the final, Seixas stamped his authority upon Nielsen, winning 9-7, 6-3, 6-4.

> Nielsen beating Drobny was interesting. That actually took place after Drobny had played an extremely long match against Budge Patty earlier in the tournament. That match lasted almost five hours and up to that point was one of Wimbledon's longest ever matches.[35] Who knows? Drobny might have been shot to pieces if I managed to win my match against Nielsen, and then played him in the semi-final. In the final Seixas played very confidently—he thought he had an edge over Nielsen.

It was another all-Australian final of the men's doubles event with Hoad and Rosewall defeating Hartwig and Rose by 6-4, 7-5, 4-6, 7-5. Rosewall's loss to Nielsen and the fact that newspapers claimed he was carried by Hoad in the doubles final raised the question of whether he was stale from too much tennis. Was Hopman driving the team too hard, asked the English tennis writers? Hopman's response was that Rosewall wasn't stale or burnt out, and if he was he'd be sent on a holiday. Speculation continued to mount when he lost badly to a Polish player in the Swiss Championships, and there was concern that the long tennis tour would leave him jaded.

> In spite of those comments it was a happy Wimbledon for the team, and it was a good win for us in the doubles event. It was good that it was an all-Australian doubles final, and that Merv won through to the semi-finals of the singles.

After Wimbledon, Hoad and Rosewall, now among the top-five players in the world, competed in the final of a junior boys' event at Rapallo in Italy, before the Australian team travelled to America for the summer grass court season. At the Eastern Grass Court Championships at South Orange, Newport, Hoad played superbly to beat Rosewall in a semi-final match

35 In their third round match Drobny beat Patty 8-6, 16-18, 3-6, 8-6, 12-10 (93 games)—the longest match played at Wimbledon up to that time.

(6-4, 6-1, 5-7 6-4) and then defeated Hartwig in the final (7-5, 6-4, 6-1). The semi-final match between the teenagers was called "the greatest display of electrifying strokes ever put on by 18-year-olds in the United States"[36]. It also showed that Hoad's play was getting better and better, while Rosewall was still slightly off his game. Even so, in an earlier quarter-final match Rosewall had beaten Trabert 6-4, 7-5. In the doubles final the Sydney youngsters beat America's top doubles team, Bill Talbert and Tony Trabert, 6-2, 6-0, 6-4.

The following week Rosewall lost to Trabert in a semi-final of the Newport Invitational event by 6-3, 6-3, 8-6. On that occasion, Allison Danzig of *The New York Times* blamed Rosewall's lack of control and constant netting for the defeat.

There was a poor result for Hoad and Rosewall when they were beaten by the American players Straight Clark and Hal Burrows in a quarter-final of the US Nationals Championships doubles at Brookline, Massachusetts, by 5-7, 14-12, 18-16, 9-7. The Americans made great use of what was termed the 'Australian formation', principally as a weapon against Rosewall's backhand service returns. Nevertheless, it was a match the Australian players should have won—their opponents were the 12th- and 17th-ranked American players respectively. Again, many commentators viewed the defeat as evidence that the youngsters were tired of tennis after such a lengthy international program. "Just why were the team members appearing in so many tournaments, exhibitions and international events during the tour?"[37] When this question was put to Hopman, he said they all needed experience.

Both Hoad and Rosewall played through to the semi-finals of the US National Championships at Forest Hills. In a quarter-final, Rosewall managed to defeat Swedish player Sven Davidson, in a match where he teetered on the brink, and survived a match point. The final score was 6-0, 8-10, 2-6, 6-0, 11-9. In the semi-finals Trabert defeated Rosewall 7-5, 6-3, 6-3, and Wimbledon champion Seixas beat Hoad 7-5, 6-4, 6-4. Rosewall's form in earlier matches at Forest Hills was disappointing. It was described

36 *The New York Times*, 9 August 1953

37 *The Sydney Morning Herald*, 1 October 1953

as "semi-sloppy" and "unimpressive and even spotty"[38]. Gayle Talbot of *American Associated Press* wrote that Rosewall was "weary", and suffered a humiliating defeat against Trabert:

> *It is not pleasant to see a nice kid thrown to the wolves, even though the spectacle proves entertaining to a stadium full of spectators and produces a welcome tennis victory for this country for a change... Our own husky Tony Trabert beat the daylights out of the weary woebegone youngster, producing a sad anticlimax to a match that had been looked forward to all week.*
>
> *Having watched the diminutive stylish play for the last two winters in his own land, we are in a position to know something of the brand of tennis he can produce when his body is fresh and his mind is not jaded by a cruel overdose of the game.*
>
> *His showing against Trabert was disillusioning to thousands who were watching him for the first time and had no way of knowing the boy was at about 20 per cent of efficiency. The other Aussies were afraid to say anything out loud as their dandy little manager-coach, Harry Hopman, was insisting to all who would listen that Ken was in perfect shape.*
>
> *It was suggested to Hopman more than a month ago by well-intentioned persons that he was overdoing the iron discipline and keeping the kids under too tight a rein for too long a period. He was urged to give his company-controlled tennis pawns at least a two-week rest from the game sometime before our nationals. He did not listen, and he drew his reward when both his 18-year-olds, Rosewall and Lewis Hoad, were knocked off in straight sets.*[39]

We had been playing a lot. As Australians we had to put up with being overseas travelling for a long time each year. It was easy to become homesick. The only contact I had with my family was through letters—telephone calls were too expensive.

38 *World Tennis*, September 1953

39 Gayle Talbot, quoted in *The Sydney Morning Herald*, 9 September 1953

In what was a minor surprise Trabert, an ex-sailor just three months out of the navy, overwhelmed Seixas in the final of the 1953 US National Championships by 6-3, 6-2, 6-3. The new US champion was described as "a young man with a crew haircut and the build of a tackle"[40]. Allison Danzig wrote that Trabert's tennis "suddenly caught fire as he never had before and attained the mastery toward which he had striven over the years"[41].

After Forest Hills the Australians played in the Pacific South West Championships with Rosewall beating Trabert in the semi-finals by 1-6, 7-5, 6-1, 6-2, where he was able take an early ball, upset Trabert's timing, and force him to hurry his shots. Rosewall went on to defeat Seixas in the final by 6-4, 1-6, 3-6, 6-1, 6-4. In a return to the best of his pre-Wimbledon form, Rosewall seemed to have regrouped and overcome some of the lackadaisicalness that marked his play at Forest Hills. Watching the final Don Budge noted that Rosewall's groundstrokes were superior to those of Seixas, and that the Australian "will always be able to take the game from him"[42].

◇◇◇◇◇◇◇

The travelling team returned to Australia in early October and it was around this time that it was announced Rosewall was unable to undertake army training because he could not wear boots! A medical examination revealed he suffered from a chronic dermatitis condition affecting his ankles, an irritating skin condition that plagued him throughout his career.

The world rankings for 1953 (issued by Lance Tingay of the *Daily Telegraph*) were: Trabert, Rosewall, Seixas, Drobny, Hoad, Rose, Nielsen, Patty, Davidson, Morea. Most of the tennis scribes placed Trabert first. The logic was that even though Rosewall and Trabert had split matches two-all during the year, Trabert won the all-important encounter at Forest Hills. It was also widely acknowledged that Rosewall's season fell apart

40 *The New York Times*, 8 September 1953. 'Tackle' is an American football (gridiron) term.

41 Allison Danzig of *The New York Times*, quoted in *The Sydney Morning Herald*, 9 September 1953.

42 *The Sydney Morning Herald*, 22 September 1953

a little after Paris. He suffered from "a succession of mediocre performances, variously attributed to being over-tennised, suffering from a stomach ailment, or being 'slave-driven' by Harry Hopman"[43].

Of course, the next major event of the year was the Davis Cup Challenge Round to be played at Melbourne's Kooyong courts between Christmas and New Year. Earlier in the year both Trabert and Mulloy stated that America would win the Challenge Round, believing Hoad and Rosewall lacked experience in Davis Cup tennis. On his arrival in Australia in early December the American captain Bill Talbert confidently stated: "We will win the Davis Cup, and I think it will be four matches to one." [44] In many ways, he had every right to be confident. He had the current Wimbledon and US champions on his team. But things weren't going to be quite so easy. Rosewall had shown an ongoing superiority over Seixas that must have worried Talbert, and since returning to Australia, Hoad had been showing his best form.

The two Australians played a high-quality final against each other in the New South Wales Championships, which Hoad won by 8-6, 4-6, 9-7, 10-8. Earlier in that event Hoad beat Trabert 6-1, 6-2, 5-7, 7-5, and Rosewall defeated Seixas 6-4, 6-2, 6-3. The two Sydney youngsters also won the doubles contest over Seixas and Trabert, even though the Rosewall serve was identified as a liability. Those in the know were saying that if America was to win the Davis Cup then Trabert had to win both his singles, and Seixas at least one. Seixas had suffered a string of injuries and setbacks since his victory at Wimbledon. He played through some of the American grass court events with supports on a knee after being injured in a fall.

Hoad also won the Queensland Championships, after Rosewall was defeated in a semi-final by Rex Hartwig, and then defeated Rosewall in the final of the Victorian Championships by 9-7, 8-6, 3-6, 6-3.

A long feature article on Hoad and Rosewall appeared in *Australian Women's Weekly* the week the Challenge Round matches were played in Melbourne. The interview had taken place during the Victorian Championships, as the two young men sat up in their beds in a Melbourne

43 *World Tennis*, November 1953

44 *World Tennis*, July 1953

hotel, eating breakfast. Hoad introduced Rosewall to the writer as Muscles, because he didn't really have any. Rosewall was described as being "small, dark, wiry", and "dead-on-the-bean". He told the writer that Hoad was jealous of him: "All his girlfriends fall for me." In answer to a question about the type of girl he found attractive, Rosewall picked up a magazine with a photograph of the film star Jean Simmonds, and gave it a cheeky kiss. He also said he thought that 21 would be about the right age to get married.

The interviewer observed that the young players were "perfect foils" for each other. Hoad was described as being "relaxed and casual", despite possessing the ability to shatter his opponent's confidence with cannonball serves. On the other hand, Rosewall was "light limbed, quick-thinking and exhibited excellent powers of concentration"[45], and confounded his opponents with beautifully anticipated backhand shots.

On the opening day of the Challenge Round, Hoad was drawn to play Seixas and Rosewall to meet Trabert. There were spectacular scenes anticipated at Kooyong, now home to the largest tennis stand in the world, with an expected crowd of 17,500 (about 10,000 people had attended the final practice matches). According to the *Washington Post*: "You could not buy a seat for love or money."[46] A world series atmosphere pervaded Melbourne and the outcome of the Challenge Round was discussed in the streets, in pubs and shops around the city. Ted Tinling, the tennis world's fashion designer, spoke of travelling to Australia with four new pairs of specially designed shorts for Australia's tennis twins.

Just as Rosewall had established an ascendancy over Seixas (having beaten him six times in a row), the Wimbledon champion from Philadelphia had consistently managed to defeat Hoad. By the time of the 1953 Challenge Round it was six straight victories in favour of Seixas, with four wins during 1953—and those matches included victories in the French Championships, at Wimbledon and at Forest Hills. On the other hand, Hoad had beaten Trabert in their only meeting, played in Sydney about a month before.

45 *Australian Women's Weekly*, 30 December 1953

46 *Washington Post*, 27 December 1953, referring to the new temporary stands erected especially for the occasion—the enormous structure swayed in the breeze as crowds cheered.

After day one of the Challenge Round, the score was level at one-all. Hoad easily beat Seixas (6-4, 6-2, 6-3), but then Trabert triumphed over Rosewall by 6-3, 6-4, 6-4. It was not a good day for Rosewall, who appeared nervous and indecisive when faced with Trabert's successful net-rushing tactics.

> I was a little on edge that day. It had always been pretty certain that Lew and I would play the singles. Harry had worked with Lew over the last few months to improve his motivation. I thought I would play better in the match against Trabert, but he was a good player with Davis Cup experience. He took the ball early and could be overpowering. In some ways I found him difficult to play. He knew my game, and had a bit of an edge for a while. I was disappointed with how I played and how it led into what happened the next day.

The following day the Australian selectors made the surprising decision to drop Rosewall from the doubles, and to play the virtually untested pair of Hoad and Hartwig. It was an unusual move to say the least, considering that Hoad and Rosewall were the reigning Australian, French and Wimbledon doubles champions. Adrian Quist wrote that it was "a wonderful Christmas present for the Americans"[47].

The Australian selectors were strongly influenced by the iron will of Sir Norman Brookes, the man who reigned as president of the LTAA for almost 30 years. Brookes was Australia's first Wimbledon champion in 1907, and more or less ruled Australian tennis as a fearless dictator. He questioned the strength of Rosewall's serve, and he and other selectors had witnessed Hoad and Hartwig defeat Sedgman and McGregor in a secret trial match at Royal South Yarra Club just before the Challenge Round. Another factor might have been that Rosewall and Hoad had lost the final of the Victorian Championships doubles to Rose and Hartwig. On that occasion it was suggested that the victors were able to exploit Rosewall's serving weakness and concentrate on him throughout the match.

---

47 *The Sydney Morning Herald*, 30 December 1953

Even so, the selectors' decision was not handled diplomatically. Rosewall and Hartwig weren't told of the arrangement until shortly before the match was about to commence. It was also made over the head of Hopman, who believed that dropping Rosewall might cause him to lose confidence for his second singles match.[48]

> I think we were told when we were in the dressing room before the match. At that time Harry spoke to me and said we were going to make a change. He talked about one of the selectors having made the decision. What could I do? I said, 'Ok. It's for the good of the team.' If they didn't want me to play the best option would probably have been to put in Rose and Hartwig, because they were a top team anyway. I think that because Lew played so well on the first day they believed he should be selected. It's all history now, but maybe the guys had a better chance of winning if they played on their usual sides of the court. Lew and I played with Hopman the following year—but the selection issue was never really raised again between Harry and me.

Critics of the decision noted that Hoad and Hartwig had never played together under tournament conditions, and were both right-court players. New South Wales tennis officials, who were no friends of Brookes, wasted little time resorting to hyperbole to describe the selectors' choice in *The Sydney Morning Herald* as: "the biggest tragedy ever to happen in Australian tennis"; a "stupid mistake"; and a "colossal blunder". The newspaper's sporting editor went on to accuse the selectors of committing sport's "biggest postwar blunder", suggesting it might have been preferable to play the tried-and-tested team of Rose and Hartwig:

> *This foolishness will now demand the breaking of the Victorian hold on tennis administration. It will give added force to the argument that tennis*

48 However, in subsequent reports, Jim Russell points to the fact that in various media interviews Hopman "defended the move as having some merit": *World Tennis*, July 1955

> *and other sports should be administered by younger men. Certainly Davis Cup selectors chosen from leading players of recent years like Quist, Hopman, Bromwich, Long and Pails could not have made a bigger blunder than that perpetuated yesterday by Sir Norman Brookes and his colleagues.*[49]

The determined combination of Trabert and Seixas had little difficulty with Australia's scratch pair, and won in straight sets. It was a 6-2, 6-4, 6-4 shellacking in front of a stunned and silent Australian crowd. The loss put the Australians well and truly on the ropes, as it was now necessary to win both remaining singles rubbers to retain the Davis Cup. Rosewall watched the doubles from the stands, taking photographs throughout the match. When speaking with friends he made no comment about being dropped: "I didn't lose any sleep last night … I'll do the job tomorrow."

> The result almost had to be expected. Seixas and Trabert were a top pair, and they were pitted against a scratch team, playing on sides of the court they weren't used to.

Writing about the match, Trabert said he could hardly believe the Australians chose Hoad and Hartwig:

> *If we'd had any doubts about winning the doubles before, we felt that there was no need to worry now, for it was asking too much from the two Australians to play their first Davis Cup match with strange partners, however good they were individually.*[50]

There was now a great deal of anxiety among Australian tennis fans and ill will towards the selectors. Australians sent telegrams to Rosewall at Kooyong encouraging him to regroup and find his form for the final match, writing: "Rats to the selectors!"[51] Hoad kept up his end of the bargain by

49 *The Sydney Morning Herald*, 30 December 1953

50 *World Tennis*, January 1954

51 A Trengove, *The Story of the Davis Cup*, page 181

scoring a thrilling five-set victory over Trabert, 13-11, 6-2, 2-6, 3-6, 7-5. It was a highly dramatic encounter:

> *The match was played on a gloomy afternoon and a thin drizzle of rain fell constantly. The players wore spikes to move safely on the rain-sodden court, but, despite the conditions, the standard of play was magnificent, especially in the climactic final set.*
>
> *An oft-repeated incident took place during the fifth set when Hoad slipped while running for a ball, falling heavily on the court. He lay motionless for some moments alarming the gallery. Then Harry Hopman ran onto the court and threw a yellow towel over Hoad's head, exclaiming, 'Get up, you clumsy oaf!' Hoad lifted the towel off his head, and grinned at the crowd. The story goes that it was a touch of Hopman inspiration as it drained the tension of the match from Hoad by making him laugh.*
>
> *When Hoad finally won after a series of thrillingly close final games, the Kooyong crowd went berserk. The crowds cheered themselves hoarse, and cushions were thrown onto the centre court. A spectator shouted out to prime minister Bob Menzies, 'Give him a knighthood, Bob, Bradman never did anything like that!'*[52]

> You have to give Lew credit. He beat Trabert under difficult conditions. He had to put on spikes that he'd never worn before. He slipped over a couple of times, but hung in there. When Trabert levelled the match at two-sets apiece it looked as if he might win, but Lew played one of the matches of his life. Hop[man] suggested that I go for a drive. I ended up stopping in a park. The worst thing was that the car didn't have a radio and I didn't know what the score was. When I got back to the courts Lew was two-sets up and I thought I was about to play. Was I nervous? At least I didn't have a prang in the car!

52 *Tennis Magazine*, December 1983

After the Hoad match, further play was abandoned due to heavy rain. It meant that Rosewall had to wait another 24 hours before he was able to finalise the proceedings. A Davis Cup ball went ahead as planned, with Rosewall as a notable absentee.

Rosewall's father had watched the first two days' play, but had to return home to mind the grocer's store in Penshurst. Gerald Patterson, another of Australia's early Wimbledon champions, persuaded the International Lawn Tennis Club of Australia to pay for Rosewall's mother Vera to fly down from Sydney to watch the match against Seixas. She said the worry of Rosewall being dropped in the doubles had left her "in a whirl... the phone has been ringing all day. Hundreds of people I don't know have said that Ken has been terribly treated ... I haven't been able to sleep properly at night. It's been a great strain." Vera's trip from Sydney was front-page news. Asked whether she had spoken to her son before the match, she said: "He wasn't worrying about tomorrow's match. He was determined to win."[53]

> I think both my mother and father were disappointed I didn't play the doubles. They thought that Lew and I were at least equal to any other combination. But the fact that I didn't perform that well on the first day had a bearing, and I recognised that even as a 19-year-old. But they obviously made a big boo-boo in having Rex and Lew play on the wrong sides of the court.

The following day, spectators saw a different Rosewall from the first rubber against Trabert. He was immediately in his stride in the first set, breaking Seixas' service with exact passing shots in the fourth game. Seixas staged a rally in the second set, but Rosewall was not prepared to take his foot off the pedal from that point. He won the match 6-2, 2-6, 6-3, 6-4. According to Trabert, Rosewall found a way to counter Seixas' tactics. He served deeper and hustled the American into errors because of his over-anxiety. *The Times* wrote that Hoad's magnificent play might have made the Davis Cup victory possible, but Rosewall suffered the greater ordeal,

53 *The Sydney Morning Herald*, 31 December 1953

being required to watch the loss of the doubles, and then suffer an extra night's agony of suspense waiting to play his final match.

> I had beaten Vic [Seixas] a couple of times before, and knew I had a good chance of winning if I played well. I guess some players like to play a certain style player, and maybe it was like that between me and Vic. That's not so much the case these days as everyone seems to play the same—with solid groundstrokes off high bouncing hard courts—but it was different in my day. Winning the Challenge Round was very exciting for us. The Americans were experienced, but it was our first go. I had my moment. I have watched the Slazenger film of the Challenge Round plenty of times. It was exciting having my mother there on the fourth day. It was one of the few times she saw me win a big match. She was sitting with my cousin, who suffered from paralysis. Them sitting together is shown on that film. They are good memories.

There were wonderful scenes after Rosewall's victory, as a brass band playing "triumphal music marched and counter-marched across the arena"[54]. Before the Victorian state governor Dallas Brooks could present the trophy to Harry Hopman it was necessary to clear away all the cushions and papers that an excited crowd had thrown onto the court. Rosewall made a remarkably sincere remark to the Kooyong crowd: "It was my first Davis Cup. And it went off *beautiful*!"

In his speech to the crowd Tony Trabert explained that he had been playing tennis since he was six, and had lost to a lot of people, but he had never been beaten by "two babes and a fox" (referring to the two 19-year-olds and their wily captain, Hopman). "I guarantee it will be my day next year,"[55] he added.

54 *The Times*, 1 January 1954
55 *The Sun-News Pictorial*, 1 January 1954

CHAPTER 3

◇◇◇◇◇◇◇

CHAMPIONS TRAVELLING THE WORLD

Winning the 1953 Davis Cup Challenge Round meant Rosewall and Hoad were national heroes and the year that followed was one of adjustment; dealing with the ups-and-downs of achieving this new status at such a young age.

After the Davis Cup matches of the previous year, Hoad was possibly considered Australia's premier player, but he was now undertaking military service and unable to compete in the Australian Championships. As a result, Rosewall was the number-one Australian seed and Trabert the number-one foreign seed for the event played at White City, Sydney, in January 1954. However, neither of these fancied players ultimately made the final. Rosewall was beaten by left-hander Mervyn Rose in a semi-final match (6-2, 6-3, 3-6, 1-6, 7-5). The youngster was completely outplayed and out-hustled by Rose's magnificent volleying in the first two sets before staging a magnificent comeback. Rosewall led 3-2 in the final set, only to miss a vital lob, and then lose three games in a row to trail 3-5. He recovered to 5-5, but then the left-handed Rose service was back at its best, and the taller man ended the match in the 12th game. Rose went on to win the championship over Rex Hartwig (6-2, 0-6, 6-4, 6-2).

> I'm not sure I want to remember that match against Merv! He was a good player. He was a hustler and played best on grass—even though he miraculously won the French Championships before turning pro in 1958.

Trabert suffered the indignity of losing to Australia's veteran player, John Bromwich, in an early round of the tournament where he was confronted by Australian crowds vigorously jeering at him and shouting: "Have a go Trabert"; "Go home you mug"; and a racecourse term, "Take a swab"[56], which is what happens when stewards decide to test a horse's saliva for dope when they believe it hasn't been trying.

Once more, Rosewall and Hoad travelled the world together in 1954 under the care of Davis Cup captain Harry Hopman, leaving Australia in early May. The team members were Rosewall, Hoad, Rose, Hartwig, Neale Fraser, Ashley Cooper and Roy Emerson. It was a larger team than in 1953 and comprised four teenagers, with Cooper and Emerson being just 17, and a decision was made to split up the team on different flights to Europe for safety reasons.

◇◇◇◇◇◇◇

Rosewall returned to Paris for the French Championships as the defending champion, and perhaps it was the heavy burden of expectation on his shoulders that caused him to lose to Sven Davidson, in the fourth round (6-3, 3-6, 6-3, 6-3). *The Times* spoke of Rosewall falling to the Swedish player's determined and skillful attack with mistakes finally being his undoing. It seemed he was not quite the brilliant champion of 12 months before. *The Sydney Morning Herald* was not so kind. It described Rosewall's performance as "a pathetic display", writing that both Rosewall and Hoad played like "tired old men"[57]. Hoad had lost a couple of days before to American veteran Gardnar Mulloy (6-2, 2-6, 7-5, 6-4).

56 *World Tennis*, March 1954
57 *The Sydney Morning Herald*, 26 May 1954

The winner of the event was Trabert, winning a straight set final over fellow American, Art Larsen, 6-4, 7-5, 6-1. The only Australian to reach the quarter-finals was Rose, who was beaten by Trabert at that stage.

> I probably wasn't too pleased about the match against Davidson. None us were. The team travelled directly to France in 1954, without playing lead-up tournaments, and before that we played exhibition matches back home in Australia. Maybe the lack of real competition didn't help when we got to play on clay in Paris.

Arriving in England, newspapers reported that the Australian players were badly in need of match practice. Confronted by a week of gloomy, wet weather the team was unable to get consistent grass court practice. In the Queen's Club event prior to Wimbledon, four Australians—Hoad, Rose, Hartwig and Rosewall—reached the semi-finals. In those matches Hoad beat Hartwig 6-3, 6-4 and Rosewall fell to Rose 7-5, 6-3.

◇◇◇◇◇◇◇

And so to Wimbledon, with the 19-year-old Rosewall being seeded third. Ahead of him in the rankings were Trabert and Hoad. In his first round match Rosewall struggled to beat the crafty South African Abe Segal in what *The Times* called "a heroic contest"[58]. Before the match Segal boasted that he might not beat Rosewall, but he'd put him through the wringer. The South African snuck into the net at every opportunity and unsettled Rosewall, and it was only at the end of the match that Rosewall was gradually able to assert himself and win by the barest of margins (7-5, 4-6, 8-6, 8-6). In the second round Rosewall appeared to be back on form as he defeated the American Herbie Flam (6-2, 8-6, 6-4) in a match for the connoisseur, with each player "full of intelligent purpose"[59]. Rosewall's third round match was against the 1948 champion, Bob Falkenburg, and he won by 6-2, 4-6, 6-1, 6-4, before defeating his teammate Cooper in the fourth round.

---

58 *The Times*, 22 June 1954

59 *The Times*, 24 June 1954

> Segal was always a bit of an intimidator. Falkenburg was probably past his prime by then. I can remember being in tears when Falkenburg beat John Bromwich in their 1948 Wimbledon final. [Bromwich led 5-2, 40-15 in the final set of the men's final.] Brom was my idol. I grew up in the same district—Illawarra—as he did and I used to play against his younger brother.

The English papers noted Rosewall had been faced with an extremely difficult draw, meeting such gifted opponents at this early stage of the tournament. In his quarter-final match Rosewall defeated Hartwig over five sets (6-3, 3-6, 3-6, 6-3, 6-1). On the other side of the draw there was a major surprise when Hoad was trounced (Drobny, by 6-4, 6-3, 6-3). At the commencement of the tournament the seeding committee only ranked Drobny at number 11, and in fact he had only been seeded because this was a year when there were 12, rather than the usual eight seeds.[60]

> I guess it was a tough draw, but you always had to take it one match at a time.

The semi-final matches saw Drobny play Budge Patty, the 1950 champion, and win by 6-2, 6-4, 4-6, 9-7, placing him in his third Wimbledon final. As an aside, when talking to the press after his own semi-final match Drobny offered some views about the Australian travelling team. He said he would always enjoy a match against Patty, win-or-lose, but it was not the same with the young Australians:

> *I have been in big tennis long enough to have learned how to take setbacks happily ... The Australians don't seem to have this approach. Rosewall never looks happy on the court, and is always stuck for something to say. Rose is bad tempered. It is bad luck that I beat Lew Hoad because he is the best of them all. But all the Australians have the same trouble. They never seem to enjoy a match. To them it is a hard day's work and they show it.*[61]

---

60 There were some critics of Drobny's seeding who felt he should have been ranked as high as number six.

61 *The Sydney Morning Herald*, 1 July 1954

In his own semi-final Rosewall beat Trabert in a match of dramatic quality by 3-6, 6-3, 4-6, 6-1, 6-1. The writer for *The Times* complained of being at a loss for words when describing the play:

> *It was almost a perfect example of the infinite variety that can spring from the highest quality of modern lawn tennis. Every stroke known to the most critical was there—and there in plenty—as well as a dozen or more that had never been played before. Indeed words must fail to describe some of Rosewall's half volleys in the forecourt exchanges, his swift and sudden volleying of smashes, and his masterly change of direction in the very middle of a stroke of beauty—all these had to be seen to be believed.*[62]

Some commentators referred to the match as the best display at Wimbledon since the war. Trabert apparently suffered from painful blisters on his hands, but refused to claim this as an excuse. It was one of the few times Rosewall managed to put Trabert away in a major amateur event.

Rosewall's parent's shared in the excitement of his journey to the final, meaning daily life at the grocery shop back in Penshurst was completely disorganised. A well-wisher from Double Bay picked up the news on shortwave radio and telephoned Rosewall's parents at 1.15am. "My wife and I haven't slept for two nights, and on top of that we've both got the flu,"[63] said Robert Rosewall. The grocer acknowledged that his customers and neighbours had been wonderful, but nevertheless complained that his business had been turned upside down.

Two days later it was 19-year-old Rosewall against 32-year-old Drobny, who immediately assumed the status of crowd favourite because he was a two-time loser at this stage of the championship and many felt this was Drobny's last chance to win the event.

Rosewall had a chance in the first set, when he had a set point at 11-10, but it came and went. It eventually boiled down to a nip-and-tuck contest in the fourth set. Drobny led 5-3, but Rosewall saved a service break, recovered to five-all, and the players then remained even at six-all and

62 *The Times*, 1 July 1954

63 *The Sydney Morning Herald*, 2 July 1954

seven-all. It was here that the crisis came. Rosewall was serving and Drobny forced a game point, and then broke the Australian's serve with a cruel net-cord winner. Drobny served for the match at 8-7, and Bud Collins picks up the tale at this point:

> *Drobny risked all—and collected—with the unexpected shot on the biggest point of his life: match point in the 1954 Wimbledon final against Rosewall. Drobny led two sets to one and 8-7 in the fourth, his serve, but Kenny was wearing him down, killing him with passing shots off that rapier backhand. They went to deuce, and Drob got the ad. One more assault. If Drob had enough left he'd put it into one last charge, wouldn't he? He went to the baseline, and Kenny set himself to return the buzzing left-handed serve beyond Drob's net-rushing reach. But there was no buzzing serve, and no assault to the net. Drob just patted a soft one to Kenny's backhand and stood there and watched. For an instant Rosewall was startled. He'd begun his swing. He tried to change it to compensate, couldn't, and he knocked the ball meekly into the net.*[64]

Drobny himself saw it this way:

> *I heard nothing, saw nothing except little Rosewall standing there waiting for my serve; a slight furrow on his forehead, his black hair tousled, his body tense and ready to spring at my service. I gave him a slice to his backhand that swung away and when it hit the ground it broke the same way. I had not given him that serve before. Rosewall mis-timed it, and mis-hit it.*[65]

The exiled Czech finally beat Rosewall by 13-11, 4-6, 6-2, 9-7. It is interesting to consider this matter with the perspective of time. Was Drobny the better player when measured over the period of the tournament, or the year, or the previous two years? Unfortunately, none of that matters in a Wimbledon final, when the question is only who is the better player

64 R Laver with B Collins, *The Education of a Tennis Player*, page 169

65 *The Sporting Globe*, 17 March 1956

during the two or three-hour contest. On the day, Drobny was the better player and fortune appeared to smile in his direction. So many of his winners merely clipped the lines, and so, if the truth be known, he was merely better by inches. Meanwhile, poor Rosewall had atrocious luck with his lobs.

What would have happened if the match stretched to a fifth set? Surely the fitter, younger man would have had a chance of spinning some magic—or else Drobny might have missed some of those startling winners. Rosewall led 40-15 in the final game, before Drobny won the next four points to take the match. Rosewall had chances, and Drobny might only have won because he was willing to change his style of play.

> The best chance I had of winning a Wimbledon final was that match against Drobny. I had won tournaments and the Davis Cup, but I still felt like an inexperienced player and needed tutoring. I think I lost to Drobny because I wasn't advised how to play. Hopman let me down. I honestly don't remember Harry telling me what I should do when playing Drobny. I wasn't smart enough to have the confidence to think about changing my game. If I had that advice it could have been different.
>
> I wasn't encouraged to go to the net, while a lot of players took advantage of Drobny's weaker backhand side.[66] Probably I should have gone to Hopman and asked for more advice. I'm not sure if other players sought advice like that. The match was reasonably close. People ask about the Wimbledon finals I played and I always think that this was my best chance. With all due respect to Harry, he got a lot of credit for things he might not have deserved. His main help in relation to tennis tactics—at least to me—was to say: "Just play your own game, and hit for the lines."
>
> I'm not sure what would have happened if I had won that fourth set against Drobny. He was still a pretty fit player. He gave the impression he wasn't fit by carrying a bit of weight, but

66 Rosewall played the match almost entirely from the back of the court. "Hopman didn't give Rosewall the right advice or make him aware of what a good volleyer he was." John Barrett, interview with author (11 June 2012)

> he was still playing a lot of tennis. He was the crowd favourite. I could understand that.

Rosewall's comments raise some interesting questions. Was Hopman the master strategist that some have claimed? The problem, to some extent, was that Hopman was in fact a master of self-promotion. He wrote his own newspaper column and often told the world that he was the creator of tennis twins Rosewall and Hoad. For a start this fails to acknowledge the role played by Robert Rosewall in developing his son's game. Most other players agree that the most advice they ever received from Hopman during an important match was to relax and go for the lines!

However, to give Hopman credit he played a notable role in the development of Australia's Davis Cup teams during the 1950s and 60s by imposing firm discipline upon team members (although one wonders whether this was necessary in the case of Rosewall), instigating new coaching methods—like two players against one in vigorous hit-up sessions—and strict fitness work. All important contributions, but one might question whether players were entitled to better advice when playing crafty veterans of the world circuit like Drobny.

Hopman ended up being firmly censured by the LTAA for criticising the Wimbledon gallery for its unfair treatment of Rosewall in his newspaper column for *The Herald* (Melbourne). He wrote that the crowd cheered Drobny because they thought he didn't have another chance of winning the title, but when Rosewall played a good shot there was only a smattering of applause. "They [the LTAA] can censure me as much as they like," was Hopman's response. "They can't possibly judge our team from 10,000 miles away."[67]

Hopman's role was always going to be a matter of controversy and in response to this outburst, Drobny wrote an open letter to Hopman:

> *It seems you are trying to defend your reputation as a world famous coach rather than trying to defend Ken Rosewall. He lost in the finals*

67 *The Sydney Morning Herald*, 19 August 1954

to me in a very sporting manner. You don't find it easy to swallow this defeat because up till now your team has not known the success it could have had. Don't blame the public. Don't criticise your team. You can blame yourself and your methods.

I have watched you closely the last two years and, although I respect you as an expert on the court, I have not the same respect for your methods on the sidelines. Between matches you treat your boys in such a way that they have forgotten what it is to smile or tell jokes. Your team would be difficult to beat if you would only treat them as individuals. The only Australian to win Wimbledon in recent years was Frank Sedgman. That was the year he was not a member of your team but was travelling on his honeymoon!

I know that you watched my final against Rosewall on television in the dressing room, from which you deduced that the crowd did not applaud Rosewall. I'll take the other side. I think that the crowds were magnificent to both of us and if they were, as you maintain, 'pro-Drobny', it is certainly the first time they have ever been against an Australian. Think back to other finals such as the one between [Bob] Falkenburg and John Bromwich or between [Frank] Sedgman and [Budge] Patty. You registered no complaints then.

I have played all over the world. I have often had the crowds against me. I have never complained about the gallery and I try to win my matches on the court and off it. You said I was not a fighter. I have only one reply. How ridiculous! How could I have reached the semi-finals four times, the finals twice and finally won the title if I were not one? You are wrong, Harry. If there is one thing I am above anything else, it's a fighter.[68]

A lot of people didn't like Harry! Obviously Drobny took exception to Hopman's comments after the final. Drobny did have the reputation of being a bit of a quitter—but I only had two or three years near him. There were stories about the Wimbledon final in 1952 against Sedgman, when Drobny was a set up and a string

68 *World Tennis*, October 1954

> broke in his favourite racket. He blamed everyone, including all the people from Dunlop, and his game went downhill after that. There were also stories about him playing in South Africa and spending a lot of time whining about other players getting paid more than he was.

In a doubles semi-final played the day before the Wimbledon final, Rosewall and Hoad lost to Seixas and Trabert in a five-set match. Rosewall also played two sets of mixed doubles that day, which Hopman did admit might have been asking too much of Rosewall. Through the tournament, Rosewall played 62 sets of tennis in singles, doubles and mixed. This contrasted with Drobny, who only played 23 sets, and did not participate in doubles.

> I didn't play mixed doubles a lot, but that year I played with Margaret Osborne Du-Pont, and we lost the final. All that play might have taken the edge off my game. I guess you have to give up something if your main goal is the singles and I didn't play in the mixed after that. In those days the play was also condensed into a shorter period of time.

◇◇◇◇◇◇◇

In the American lead-up tournaments to Forest Hills, Hoad defeated Rosewall (6-3, 6-4, 6-3) at the final of the Eastern Grass Court Championships at South Orange. (Rosewall had crushed Hartwig in a semi-final match by 6-2, 6-3, 6-1.) And there was an odd loss for Rosewall when he fell to the American, Straight Clark, in the quarter-finals of the Newport Invitation event by 6-3, 1-6, 6-0, 9-7. In the doubles event at the same tournament, Hoad and Rosewall were defeated in a shock result by teammates Hartwig and Neale Fraser, 6-3, 6-4, 9-7.

The gradual superiority of the American players—at least on home turf—was confirmed when Seixas and Trabert won the US National Championships doubles at Brookline, defeating Hoad and Rosewall by

3-6, 6-4, 8-6, 6-3. Hopman's comment was: "They were just too good for us. There was nothing much to it. Rosewall seemed a bit off for us."[69]

For the Australians at the US National Championships singles it was neither Rosewall nor Hoad who was the most successful player, but fellow team member Rex Hartwig. The defending champion was Trabert, and he was expected to provide a strong showing, but fell in the quarter-finals to Hartwig's all-court attack by 6-2, 8-6, 2-6, 6-2. Hoad was beaten by the young American Rhodes scholar, Ham Richardson, in another quarter-final, while Rosewall won against Art Larsen in a quarter-final match of fluctuating fortunes, by 9-7, 4-6, 4-6, 6-3, 6-3. It was the first time these groundstroke specialists had played each other, and the match showed that Larsen was able to play extended rallies against Rosewall, but lacked the power to put him away.

The semi-finals matched up Rosewall against Hartwig, and Richardson against the 1953 Wimbledon champion Seixas, now considered "the forgotten man of American tennis"[70] after the American team's Davis Cup loss in Melbourne.

Seixas played sparkling tennis to defeat Richardson, the national intercollegiate champion, in their semi-final, by 6-3, 12-14, 8-6, 6-2. The other semi-final match sprung a surprise as Rosewall disintegrated somewhat lamely to Hartwig, losing 6-4, 6-3, 6-4. Hartwig was six years older than Rosewall, and often forced to play second string to the two youngsters. But this result placed him in the final, and his form in the successive matches against Trabert and Rosewall was the best of his career. Rosewall did very little to break Hartwig's winning streak and had little answer to his attacking shots.

> I expected to beat Rex—his dominance was in doubles. He was a fine singles player, but maybe he didn't believe he was as good as he was. Occasionally he lost the plot in important matches.

69 *The Sydney Morning Herald*, 24 August 1954
70 *Washington Post*, 6 September 1954

In the final, the 25-year-old Hartwig played a 31-year-old Seixas, who was competing in the event for the 14th time. The American had the wholehearted support of a crowd of 11,000 in the stands at Forest Hills, and gradually pegged back Hartwig after losing the first set. Seixas won the match 3-6, 6-2, 6-4, 6-4.

> Here I think that Rex got a couple of bad calls in the final and after that he was a changed player.

As soon as the US National Championships were over most attention was placed on the relative form of the American and Australian players in the lead up to the Davis Cup Challenge Round, to be played in Sydney in December. There were some quirky issues to contend with after the Australian players reached the end of a long international tour: Hartwig was playing his best tennis; while Hoad had slipped from his great heights and was now showing a lack of interest in the game. In the Pacific South West Championships in Los Angeles the stocky blond lost a quarter-final match to the Chilean, Luis Ayala, 6-3, 8-6, 4-6, 4-6, 6-1.

Rosewall won the event the previous year, but in 1954 lost in a semi-final to Trabert (0-6, 6-3, 8-6, 5-7, 6-3), despite only allowing Trabert seven points in the first set. Trabert's success was helped by the Australian's frequent double faults.

In the final Seixas beat Trabert, 7-5, 6-3, 6-4, however Rosewall and Hoad did manage to win the doubles final over Seixas and Trabert by 9-7, 9-7, 6-4. World rankings compiled at this time by *The New York Times* read: Trabert, Drobny, Rosewall, Seixas, Hoad, Hartwig, Patty, Rose, Larsen, Richardson.

The American Davis Cup players arrived in Australia in early December, and played through some of the state championship events in the run up to the Challenge Round. Columnists began observing that things were a little awry for the Australian players during the Victorian Championships when Seixas and Trabert defeated Hoad and Rosewall (10-12, 6-2, 3-6, 6-2, 6-4) in a bitterly fought doubles semi-final match. More concerning was

Hoad's singles form. He played badly in a quarter-final match against Sven Davidson, but worse followed when his semi-final match saw him slump to a 6-4, 6-2, 7-5 defeat against Seixas. Papers reported that during the match a frustrated Hoad "slapped a ball into the wall of Kooyong stadium, and skied a ball high into the stand"[71].

Immediately the Australian press went into overdrive, blaming Hopman and his strict training methods for the number-one player's lack of form. His mother Bonnie entered the fray, saying Hoad was the victim of too much discipline. The *Melbourne Truth* published a letter chastising Hopman: "You make him think tennis, eat tennis, drink tennis and live for nothing else ... Let him blow his top to the press instead of bottling up his story for your own exclusive."[72]

James Burchard of the *New York World-Telegram and Sun* held the view that Hopman had turned his young team into robots. It wasn't necessarily his fault, this writer continued, the LTAA wanted winners and had produced them. According to Burchard, Hopman was "the most unpopular Davis Cup captain in history, and the best ... [he] wrecked his charges mentally and physically in retaining tennis supremacy"[73]. In spite of all these off-court goings-on, Hopman predicted that the Australians would win the Challenge Round. This led Bill Talbert, the American captain, to say he was either "the greatest swami in the world" or "had been reading, with deep attention, Norman Vincent Peale's *The Power of Positive Thinking*"[74]. The following year, Hopman, reflecting on Hoad's problems at this time, wrote: "He was madly in love for the first time and his previous normal life of almost complete devotion to his love of the game of tennis was badly disrupted."[75]

At the same time Rosewall was playing well, and decisively beat Hartwig in the other semi-final of the Victorian Championships. Here however, the press (who always became dedicated experts on the game at Davis Cup

71 *The Sydney Morning Herald*, 3 December 1954

72 Quoted in *World Tennis*, January 1955

73 Quoted in *World Tennis*, February 1955

74 *Sports Illustrated*, 20 December 1954

75 *Sports Illustrated*, 5 September 1955

time) criticised Hartwig for lacking interest throughout the match and his one-sided defeat.

In the final of the Victorian Championships singles Rosewall defeated Seixas by 6-1, 4-6, 6-1, 7-5, fighting back from 2-5 in the fourth set to win five successive games and the match.

Hoad's run of bad luck continued when he lost to John Bromwich in the New South Wales Championships. Rosewall played badly in this event and lost to Hartwig by 6-3, 6-2, 6-3 in the semi-finals.

◇◇◇◇◇◇◇

The Americans appeared very confident about the Davis Cup outcome. Trabert was playing at the height of his form, and they had the help of Jack Kramer, who practised with the team. Talbert arrived in Australia saying he doubted whether Rosewall would get any better, despite his age, and that Hoad was near, or at his peak. However, he couldn't deny the fact that Rosewall genuinely owned Seixas, having beaten him eight times in a row. The Americans' apparent confidence didn't make them all that popular with the Australian sporting public, with one newspaper dubbing them "Cockadoodle Yanks"[76].

It was around the time of the 1954 Davis Cup Challenge Round that it became public knowledge that 20-year-old Rosewall had more than a passing interest in Wilma McIver, now working as a Brisbane stenographer. She revealed that they wrote to one another nearly every night, but never discussed tennis. The pair met at an interschool tennis competition at Brisbane's Milton Courts some years before and Rosewall confessed that he was seriously in love.

This year the Challenge Round was played at Sydney's White City. Once again huge temporary stands (consisting of 90 miles of tubular steel) were erected to accommodate the anticipated crowds—the opening day saw 25,578 people attend the matches, significantly more than at Kooyong the year before.

76 *Sports Illustrated*, 10 January 1955

The Americans made an unexpectedly good start on that opening day. Trabert beat Hoad (6-4, 2-6, 12-10, 6-3) and Seixas managed a surprise defeat of Rosewall (8-6, 6-8, 6-4, 6-3). Rosewall seemed off colour as his impressive record against the American was broken. In so many of their previous matches Seixas had been passed blindly by Rosewall's almost perfect groundstrokes, but on this occasion Seixas was more successful in his forays to the net, and Rosewall was forced into errors. As the match progressed the errors became more frequent, and Seixas continued to successfully hammer the forehand. On this day at least, Seixas overcame the disease dubbed 'Rosewallitis' and even Hopman conceded that he could not recall a time when Seixas played better. It was a depressing day for the Australians as both Hoad and Rosewall buckled in the opening matches.

> If we played those matches a day before or a day later it might have all been different, but I think Lew and I were overawed by the occasion—playing at White City in front of a world-record crowd, and our family and friends. Lew didn't play all that well, and I was also disappointed with the way I played.

In the doubles match the next day Seixas and Trabert cleverly used 'crossover' tactics to confuse Hoad and Rosewall, and won the match by 6-2, 4-6, 6-2, 10-8. Adrian Quist wrote in *The Sydney Morning Herald* that the Americans' service returns were better than Hoad and Rosewall's, and backed up by safe volleys. They also served with greater accuracy and depth. The Americans played more solidly and cooperated as a team. American captain, Bill Talbert, confirmed that his players planned to use the 'scissors' tactics, and crossovers on big points.

> We had some wins over Seixas and Trabert, but on this occasion we didn't fire. We were motivated, but just overwhelmed again. It was disappointing for us. Maybe if the match was played somewhere else. It was such a huge crowd. When the crowd stood up for the national anthem, the stands wobbled!

Regrettably, therefore, the big silver bowl was handed back to the Americans, but the tennis twins had not gone down without a fight having saved four Davis Cup points in the fourth set of the doubles match. The American players were more consistent and better prepared on this occasion. Even after losing those points, Seixas said to Talbert at the change of ends: "Don't worry cap, they're just delaying the inevitable."[77] Gracious in victory, Trabert used the occasion to apologise for any previous comments he had made about the sportsmanship of Australian crowds, saying that feelings he might have had were erased by the way the crowd of almost 26,000 cheered the American victory.

The following day Rosewall went on to beat Trabert by 9-7, 7-5, 6-3, and Hartwig (who substituted for Hoad) defeated Seixas 4-6, 6-3, 6-2, 6-3 in the return singles. The final result showed a 3-2 win for the Americans but it was probably much more one-sided in reality, as the stars and stripes won the all-important first three rubbers. Talbert was confident that there was little chance the demoralised Australian team would win the cup back in 1955, stating: "We are not borrowing this on a short-term loan."[78]

◇◇◇◇◇◇

The 1955 Australian Championships were played in Adelaide in late January, with Rosewall seeded number one. Seixas, the US Championships winner was seeded two, then Hartwig and Trabert. Due to his current lapse, Hoad was seeded five by the match committee and now had a chance to re-establish some of his damaged reputation. In fact that is what happened, in spades. Hoad beat Seixas in the quarter-finals and then totally destroyed Hartwig in the semi-finals (6-1, 6-4, 6-4). In successive matches he had taken on, and beaten, both US Championships finalists, and showed his game was sharper than it had been for over a year. In his semi-final match on the other side of the draw Rosewall beat the sturdily built Trabert (8-6, 6-3, 6-3). It was his best match of the season, and was even better than he played against Seixas in the final of the Victorian

77 *Sports Illustrated*, 10 January 1955
78 ibid

Championships singles final. Trabert called it the best tennis of Rosewall's career: "He never made a mistake and never relaxed for a minute."[79]

> Maybe Tony was in a hurry to get back to America!

This placed the two Sydney boys in their first grand slam final. They were playing at a higher level than the Davis Cup, and there was great expectation about the match. There was a test match being played at Adelaide Oval the same weekend as the tennis finals, but many of the cricket spectators transferred across to Memorial Drive just before the final was to begin. On recent occasions, Hoad seemed to have an edge over Rosewall in important matches, but that was not the case in this final—Rosewall was consistent and employed better tactics to prevail by 9-7, 6-4, 6-4. It meant that by the tender age of 20, Rosewall was a two-time Australian champion. Adrian Quist wondered if Rosewall irritated Hoad by calmly and deliberately taking up his stance, and towelling himself off at the umpire's chair during the match. Throughout the final Hoad seemed more edgy, immediately moving to the other end to take up position.

> Perhaps Lew was spending too much time with his intended wife Jennifer at the time. She was a decent player and was in Adelaide herself that year.
>
> I can remember it being incredibly hot. I was staying at a hotel in the city and my friends John and June Mehaffey invited me to stay at their house so I could get more sleep. I may have even slept in the backyard one night because of the heat.

Losing the Davis Cup Challenge Round meant that the Australian team travelled throughout the world as 'challengers' in 1955, despite suggestions from Hopman and Brookes that the Australian team did not intend to play at Wimbledon.[80] Eventually an Australian team of Rosewall, Hoad,

79 *The Sydney Morning Herald*, 21 January 1955

80 The logic was that the team would merely participate in cup ties, but not European tournaments.

Hartwig, Fraser and Cooper (Rose decided to exclude himself from the national team) left Australia on 30 May, meaning there was no intention of participating in the French Championships. Again, following the careful policy of the LTAA, the team travelled on two separate aircraft.

> Merv was in the bad books with the LTAA at that stage, and chose to travel privately. At the start of 1955 I was at home for several months as the LTAA was not sending a team overseas until just before Wimbledon. It was our job to play exhibitions around country areas, and work for sporting companies. Tennis was always strong in the Australian country areas and this might have been partly because of these tours by the best players.

It was announced that the LTAA's main doubles pairing in 1955 would be Hoad and Hartwig, with Rosewall and Fraser making up a second string pair. As was often the case in Australia at this time, Sir Norman Brookes made this decision without consulting his fellow Davis Cup selectors. In his analysis of the matter, Jim Russell wrote that Brookes talked privately with Hopman and formed the view that the Hoad-Hartwig pairing was the answer to the ongoing dominance of Seixas and Trabert.

In the absence of the Australians the 1955 French Championships were won by Trabert, beating Sven Davidson in the final by 2-6, 6-1, 6-4, 6-2.

◇◇◇◇◇◇

Another of the many encounters between Rosewall and Hoad took place in the final of the pre-Wimbledon Queen's Club tournament, which Rosewall won 6-2, 6-3. Despite this victory, the tennis writer for *The Observer* suggested the match showed why neither player should win Wimbledon. Hoad was "limited in his range of shots, unsubtle in his tactics, and highly erratic" and even though Rosewall showed the "wonderful range and fluency of his shots" they "lacked weight and authority". Hoad had occasional moments of inspiration, and was described as "a Kirk Douglas of the courts in his forcefulness and his fallibility as well as in his looks"[81].

---

81 *The Observer*, 19 June 1955

The tennis writer might not have known it had been busy and exciting few days for Hoad. His wedding to Jenny Staley, a member of the Australian women's tennis travelling team, took place early in the morning on the same day as the final at Queen's Club. The nuptials created drama in Australia when Sir Norman Brookes sternly criticised Hopman, who gave away the bride, for not informing him of the event. Hopman's response:

> *I am becoming fed up with unwarranted and irresponsible criticism such as that reported in the statement attributed to Sir Norman Brookes. The marriage of Lew and Jennifer is a case of two young people who needed friendship, guidance and help. I spent all my energies towards helping and protecting them—what do I get from Australia?—nothing but criticism.*[82]

Hopman went on to say that he had been worried about Hoad being distracted in the lead-up to Wimbledon, and met with him and Jennifer for supper and a talk. Before he got to have his say, Hoad announced he would be getting married at 11am for next day. Hoad and his new wife were allowed a 36-hour honeymoon, but then had to move into separate hotels because Davis Cup players were not allowed to travel with their wives.

> Lew and I were supposed to be playing in the final on the last day at Queen's Club. The team had a rental car, and Neale [Fraser] and Rex were the main ones with licences who drove the car. On the Saturday morning Neale and I talked to Hop about borrowing the car to go out to Wimbledon to train. Hopman said: 'No! We're using the car.' Fraser and I then went out on the tube and walked from the Southfields station to the club. As we were walking this car goes by, with Rex driving, and it looked like Hop and Lew in the back.
>
> We got down to the club and there was no sign of them. What was happening of course was that they were at the church on the hill. Lew was getting married; Rex was best man; and Harry gave the bride away.

---

82 *Sports Illustrated*, 5 September 1955

Lew then came back to Queen's Club, and we played. I think Harry must have thought the less people who knew the better. Only Rex, Harry and maybe Adrian Quist—manager of the ladies team—knew what was going on. Neale was sharing a room with Lew, and Harry told him he had to move out, so Lew and Jenny could have their honeymoon night. Then it turned out that Jenny was already pregnant. It really made a mess of the ladies team with Adrian as captain, because he seemed so prim and proper. I don't think Jenny played in the team after that.

I spoke before about the competitive instinct that existed between Lew and I. When he got married his main focus was life with his wife. Lew and Jenny travelled independently of the team, and we didn't really see each other except at the major events.

Rosewall and Trabert were the top seeds for the 1955 Wimbledon Championships and both made light work of their preliminary matches. In the fourth round Rosewall encountered the two-handed backhand of Beppo Merlo—the Italian was apparently a nervous wreck playing on centre court for the first time and was eventually forced to abandon the match when trailing 4-6, 2-6, 1-2. Rosewall beat Sven Davidson in the quarter-final (6-4, 6-1, 6-2), playing flawlessly and producing magnificent groundstrokes. At the same stage of the tournament the newly married Hoad lost to Budge Patty (6-4, 6-4, 6-4).

The semi-final matches were played between Rosewall and Kurt Nielsen, and Patty and Trabert. Nielsen was an inspired opponent who again proved to be Rosewall's centre court nemesis—the Dane played his best ever tennis on the slick, low-bouncing courts at the All England Club and Rosewall lost the match 11-9, 6-2, 2-6, 6-4. Perhaps, as in the 1954 final, Rosewall struggled against an opponent (in that case Drobny) who reached "unexpected heights"[83]. Nielsen was almost as "nippy round the court" as Rosewall and "equally deft with short-angled volleys". Commentators remarked that they couldn't recall a match with more let cords, while on the other side of the net Rosewall's courageous shots often missed the line

83 *The Times*, 30 June 1955

by inches. "[Nielsen's] eager and persistent adventures … took Rosewall out of his rhythm when he was so often faced with early taken underspin returns, many of them down the middle that skidded through to deny him an unhurried or flowing stroke."[84]

Nielsen's victory meant that he became the first unseeded player to reach the Wimbledon final on two occasions, however Trabert had little difficulty winning the final by 6-3, 7-5, 6-1. The American's win, after triumphing in Paris and winning 16 of 18 tournaments during 1955, marked him out as the top amateur player in the world.

> I don't want to put the blame on Harry all the time. I was 20 years old and should have been more experienced. But he was the captain/manager and I would have benefitted with more advice for the Nielsen match. The kind of match I played was very poor and I wasn't aggressive enough.
>
> A lot of Nielsen's forehands floated—he didn't hit over the ball because of the grip he used—and I didn't take advantage of that. Trabert had a much better and faster service, he beat him in the final because all he did was serve and go into the net. Even so I had the agility and I think I had the game to move in and take the ball on the full against Nielsen. My volleys were improving. But that's all history now.
>
> Later in the year David Blacklock, managing director of Slazenger in Australia, said we'd better do something so Ken can win a match against Nielsen. So Nielsen was invited out to play some exhibitions and I beat him a few times. After that I didn't play him again until he joined the pro ranks.

Hoad and Hartwig won the final of the Wimbledon Championships doubles over teammates, Rosewall and Fraser, 7-5, 6-4, 6-3, after the latter two players had beaten the US Davis Cup pairing of Seixas and Trabert by 6-2, 1-6, 6-1, 4-6, 6-3.

---

84 *The Sydney Morning Herald*, 30 June 1955

◇◇◇◇◇◇◇

Being a challenger in the Davis Cup event meant playing a number of other countries in qualifying rounds in the American zone and, as a result, July 1955 was a busy month for all involved. Australia was drawn first to play Mexico, then Brazil one week later, followed by Canada, and then Japan. If successful, the Australians played the winner of the European zone (assumed to be Italy) in an inter-zone final in Philadelphia.

Australia won its qualifying matches easily. Rosewall and Hartwig played singles matches against Mexico in Chicago, while the doubles pairing was Hoad and Hartwig. (Australia won this tie 5 rubbers to 0.) Against Brazil, in Louisville, Hoad replaced Hartwig and the score was 4 rubbers to 1, with Hoad losing a singles encounter to Ronald Moreir. Hoad was replaced by Hartwig in the singles matches against Canada, where the Australians scored a 5-0 victory. They then defeated Japan by 4 rubbers to 0, with the fifth rubber cancelled because of rain.

In the inter-zone final against the Italians, Hoad and Rosewall were selected to play singles and were close to the peak of their form as they registered a 5 rubbers to 0 victory. That week saw terrible wet weather in Philadelphia—the courts were drenched and the Italians Pietrangeli and Sirola were crushed in their struggle against the Australians.

Hopman kept his players out of the US Championships doubles at Brookline, partly because of the irritating rain delays in completing the inter-zone final. The bad weather continued in Boston and there were six days of rain delays in the seven-day doubles tournament, with finals being played indoors. The Japanese players, Kosei Kamo and Atsushi Miyagi, were the eventual winners of this major event.

The Challenge Round was played at Forest Hills, and Rosewall, Hoad, Hartwig and Fraser were Australia's representatives. When the draw was announced, Rosewall was to meet Seixas in the opening match, followed by Hoad and Trabert, who were described as "the siege guns of amateur tennis"[85]. The Australian doubles pairing was Hoad and Hartwig.

The American team seemed to be on the weaker foot—following Wimbledon Trabert suffered a setback, hurting his shoulder playing in

85 *The New York Times*, 26 August 1955

a tournament in Southampton in July and not playing in a competition since. Then Seixas, compared with the previous year's form, was having a disappointing year culminating in an early loss at Wimbledon. American captain Talbert tried to give Trabert's injury a positive spin saying it might have been a blessing in disguise, giving his star player a much-needed rest. He also believed Hopman was having trouble with Hoad, who has been ill and underweight, and apparently depressed. Talbert claimed that Australia stood little chance of winning the Challenge Round unless Hoad snapped out of this malaise and reached his best form.

In spite of this, the Challenge Round proved easy meat for the Australian team. Rosewall and Hoad both won their matches on the opening day to take a 2-0 lead. Rosewall won yet again against Seixas, 6-3, 10-8, 4-6, 6-2, while Hoad defeated the Wimbledon champion, Trabert, by 4-6, 6-3, 6-3, 8-6. According to *World Tennis,* Rosewall never looked better than he did on that opening day: "His serve has shown unbelievable improvement, and his backhand passing shot was the best single shot of the Challenge Round."[86] Rosewall repeatedly passed Seixas as the American attempted to steal the net and his alleged weaknesses—service and forehand—were strong and steady. In fact, Rosewall surprised Seixas time and again by rushing to the net. When asked what had brought about the change, Rosewall mumbled: "I must have had some glucose last night."[87] Referencing Rosewall winning so many points at the net, Hopman said: "He is such a confirmed baseliner in his own mind that I had to constantly remind him not to miss an opportunity to 'go in'."[88]

During the Hoad-Trabert match Rosewall didn't take a rest—he perched on a stadium step taking films of the contest with his 8mm camera.

> Lew was happy playing Trabert. As I said, this was a case where some players suit each other's styles. Lew was motivated to do well in the Challenge Round, especially after our defeat in 1954.

---

86 *World Tennis*, October 1955

87 *Sydney Daily Mirror*, 27 August 1955

88 *Sports Illustrated*, 5 September 1955

Then on day two, Hoad and Hartwig beat Seixas and Trabert in a close battle, 12-14, 6-4, 6-3, 3-6, 7-5, to give the visitors an unassailable lead. This doubles match saw an exceptional performance by Hartwig, who Arthur Daley said "carried the burden and deserved the major share of the credit"[89]. He was voted best man on court by team captains Hopman and Talbert. The Aussies had won the cup! Although it was probably far more genteel, it seems there was a precursor to the current day 'fanatics' (Australia's travelling troupe of tennis fans) on hand to celebrate:

> *A small but very vocal section of the gallery was made up of Australians, who were sitting together just to the left of the courtside boxes. As soon as the Aussies had won, this section let out a tremendous Texas war whoop, waved their handkerchiefs and shouted gleefully to the victorious team. They even burst into song (Waltzing Matilda), and one excited spectator even threw his straw hat onto the court. Ashley Cooper and Neale Fraser pounded their smiling teammates' backs as the American gallery gave the winners a big hand.*[90]

On the final day Rosewall defeated Ham Richardson in four sets to complete an Australian victory by 5 rubbers to 0 (Hoad won his match against Seixas by 7-9, 6-1, 6-4, 6-4). In doing so, Australia became the first country in Davis Cup history to recover the cup within a year of losing it.

◇◇◇◇◇◇◇

The 1955 US Championships at Forest Hills followed. Once more the players in contention at the semi-final stage were Trabert and Seixas, and Rosewall and Hoad. In his quarter-final, Rosewall defeated Richardson, 6-4, 9-7, 2-6, 6-3, and Trabert, who was at his best, restored his reputation after the Davis Cup matches by crushing Hoad 6-4, 6-2, 6-1. *The Sydney Morning Herald* told readers that the Australian was wearing a beaming smile at the end of the match: "Why he looked so happy will be a mystery to American tennis for ever. He played like a damp squib."[91]

---

89 *The New York Times*, 28 August 1955

90 *World Tennis*, October 1955

91 *The Sydney Morning Herald*, 12 September 1955

On the other side of the draw, Rosewall scored yet another victory over Seixas, the defending champion, by 6-4, 6-4, 7-5. Seixas suffered the humiliation of losing a lead of 5-2 in the final set, only to watch "utterly baffled and bewildered" as Rosewall won the final five games. The great writer Allison Danzig of *The New York Times* was fulsome in his praise of Rosewall, who he described as an artist of the court:

> *A stylist of the classical school in the production of his groundstrokes, and a court tactician of unruffled composure and deliberation. The calm, unhurried manner in which Rosewall went about the job of defeating the energetic, fast-moving Seixas was an object lesson in conservation of energy. No one could have worked harder or expended more energy than Seixas in tearing for the net to get in his volley or smash.*[92]

The match against Seixas was a masterly performance—but it was Trabert who ultimately secured the 1955 US Championships title, winning in straight sets over Rosewall in the final by 9-7, 6-3, 6-3. Apart from the blemishes of losing to Bromwich in Australia, and to Hoad in the Challenge Round, Trabert ruled the world in 1955.

> By this time Tony had agreed to turn pro and realised this was his last amateur match. Again I didn't play as well as I wanted to, but he was playing well.

◇◇◇◇◇◇◇

As usual the Australian team stopped off in Los Angeles for the Pacific South West Championships on their way back to Australia. Here there were some odd results for both Rosewall and Hoad. Rosewall lost to an American, Gil Shea, in the fourth round by 6-3, 6-3, and was said to be playing in a listless manner, but Hoad's performance was even more disappointing. He managed to lose to Ham Richardson when holding a 6-0, 6-2, 3-1 lead following a bad call that turned the match on its head with Hoad losing the contest in five sets. Maybe the Australians were tired

92 *The New York Times*, 11 September 1955

and ready to get home after all the drama of winning back the Davis Cup. There was also plenty to distract them in Los Angeles that week. Big stars like Walter Pigeon, Ginger Rogers, Lauren Bacall and Dinah Shore were in the stands, and the team attended several social events, including visiting the Warner Brothers studios and attending the a ball at the Beverley Hills Hotel. From California, the Australian team travelled to Japan to play exhibition matches before returning home. Rosewall returned to Australia a few days ahead of other members of the team so he could attend the wedding of Wilma McIver's sister in Brisbane.

Towards the end of 1955, Jack Kramer commenced negotiations with Hoad and Rosewall about the possibility of them signing professional contracts that guaranteed them £20,000[93]. There was great concern throughout Australia about whether Rosewall and Hoad would sign with Kramer. Jim Russell, Australian correspondent for *World Tennis* magazine, wondered whether a ticker tape reception the Davis Cup team received through the crowded streets of Sydney might have been a factor in them turning down the offers. More than 150,000 people lined the streets and cheered as the players drove in open cars through to a reception at the town hall, where the Davis Cup was on show in the foyer. Rosewall's parents and Wilma were on the official platform with tennis officials.

Kramer had obtained signatures on documents from both Hoad and Rosewall, but in the end these were considered unenforceable at law because the boys remained minors, and were subject to the jurisdiction of the LTAA. The grand old man of Australian tennis, Sir Norman Brookes, congratulated Hoad and Rosewall on remaining amateurs, saying that "once they turn professional, they become outcasts"[94].

Rosewall released a statement saying that he had been made alternative offers by his then employer, a sporting goods company, as well as a milk company, for him to stay on as an amateur. But was this really amateurism asked the editor of *The Sydney Morning Herald*? Rather, the prospect of a substantial rise in salary from Slazenger and the offer of a position

93 At the time Trabert was considering a contract with a guarantee of approximately $80,000

94 *The Sydney Morning Herald*, 17 November 1955

with Carnation Milk made him see the pro offer in a less attractive light. These particular circumstances meant that "the line of demarcation between amateur and professional in Australian tennis [was] virtually indistinguishable"[95]. On the other hand, Trabert proceeded to sign a contract with Kramer guaranteeing him US$75,000.

> The ticker tape parade shows just how important winning the Davis Cup was at that time. Kramer wanted to promote further competition between Australia and America, and there were initial discussions in Los Angeles about us turning pro. However, when we considered the deal it seemed a bit lopsided, with Trabert being entitled to 30 per cent of the profits made by Kramer's company, and Lew and I only getting 15 per cent. We thought this was a bit unfair.
>
> When we ended up pulling out Rex Hartwig shifted into the pro ranks. The plan was that during the 1956 pro tour he would play Segura in a lead-in match, followed by the feature match between Gonzales and Trabert. There was controversy in this arrangement as Trabert was guaranteed the 30 per cent figure, while Gonzales earned much less. This meant Gonzales was keen to win their individual contests over 100 matches at all costs. Lew and I stayed on as amateurs.

◇◇◇◇◇◇

On returning to Australia, Rosewall played through the 1955-56 Australian summer season. In the first of the state tournaments, the Queensland Championships, he beat 19-year-old Ashley Cooper, 6-8, 6-4, 6-4, 6-4, and just a few hours after the match the president of the Queensland Lawn Tennis Association (QLTA), Cliff 'Big Bill' Edwards announced Rosewall's engagement to Wilma McIver at a dinner held in the QLTA clubrooms. Rosewall also celebrated his 21st birthday during the Brisbane tournament.

95 *The Sydney Morning Herald*, 30 October 1955

In other tournaments during that Australian summer Rosewall resumed his doubles pairing with Hoad—as a result of Hartwig's decision to turn professional, Hoad had been left without a partner. In singles tournaments, however, Hoad established an ongoing ascendancy over Rosewall and won the final of the New South Wales Championships 6-2, 6-3, 2-6, 6-1.

The 1956 Australian Championships were played in Brisbane, with Rosewall the defending champion. In the absence of a Challenge Round on Australian soil, the best Americans did not compete. There was a dramatic moment when Rosewall collapsed during an intermission in his quarter-final match against Mal Anderson. Having ducked his head under a cold shower during a break following the third set, Rosewall suffered a muscular facial spasm, preventing him from closing his mouth and causing problems with vision. Harry Hopman massaged Rosewall's face and a doctor administered a strong calcium mixture, before the Australian returned to the court looking pale and shaken. Anderson immediately ran up a 5-1 lead in the fourth set, but Rosewall managed to fight back and close the match 6-4, 6-3, 5-7, 8-6. Some people criticised the incident, citing the fact that Rosewall ended up having an intermission of 35 minutes rather than the usual 10 minutes allowed after a third set.[96]

> It was hot, so during the break after the third set I put my head under a cold shower—I started to seize up. Probably under the strictest sense of the rules I should have been forfeited, but Mal must have known what happened. He was also in the dressing room. Luckily, Harry Hopman was there and he let the referee know that I was having these problems. He also kept the press away. He requested that I get another 10 minutes, so I got back under the hot shower. It was quite a funny feeling as I recall.

In the semi-final matches Rosewall easily beat the American, Herbie Flam, a veteran player from Beverley Hills, by 6-4, 6-0, 6-2, while Hoad defeated Davis Cup teammate Neale Fraser 6-3, 6-2, 6-0. In the final match, Hoad

96 *World Tennis*, March 1956

beat Rosewall 6-4, 3-6, 6-4, 7-5, a result confirming his recent ascendancy in their rivalry. In the course of the match, Rosewall completely changed his tactics, attempting to serve-volley or else move to the net to attack Hoad's backhand. Adrian Quist noted that Rosewall played as well as he had during the last three years, but it was not enough to unsettle Hoad. That match signalled the beginning of Hoad's own 'golden' year, when he came within an ace (or at least a match) of winning the first grand slam since Don Budge in 1938.

> It was a good final, played in hot conditions. At that time Lew always thought that he had the wood on me. He had a lot of power and finesse, and things came easily to him.
>
> As an amateur his record could probably have been better, but sometimes he was a bit lackadaisical in smaller events. My game was improving. I must have been in with a chance in that match. After the national championships things pretty much went into 'recess' for all the players for a few months. I was still aligned with Slazenger and played exhibition matches around the country with other Slazenger players, like Roy Emerson and Mal Anderson, while also doing some work for Carnation Milk.

◇◇◇◇◇◇

The Australian team in 1956 comprised Rosewall, Cooper, Fraser, Anderson and Emerson; Hoad and Rose were making independent trips with their wives, while it was decided that Davis Cup coach Hopman would not accompany the team on this trip. In this absence, Cliff Sproule managed the official touring team. Later, however, a decision was taken that Hopman would travel overseas, accompanying top Australian juniors Rod Laver and Bob Mark. This trip, and Hopman's expenses, were covered by Tasmanian lotteries millionaire, Arthur Drysdale, who donated £5000 towards the venture. *The Sydney Morning Herald* questioned these circumstances, asking why the LTAA itself had not added the two youngsters players to its own squad.

The scintillating form of a thinner and trimmer Hoad was first on show in the 1956 Italian Championships, where he crushed Sven Davidson in the final. He went on to be unbeatable in Paris in the 1956 French Championships, where Rosewall was again absent. Hoad first knocked off a number of Italians, Beppo Merlo and Nicola Pietrangeli, and then, once again, Sven Davidson in the final. All those matches were straight set victories, earning the sturdy blond player the nickname 'truck driver' with writers suggesting that he hit the ball "with the frightening power of a truck barrelling down a hill"[97]. The slow clay had never been Hoad's surface, but this was his year.

> I think Lew was getting decent money 'under the table' to play in tournaments back then, and would have met up with us in Britain shortly before Wimbledon. I can't say whether I saw too much of him at the time, because he was with Jenny and I was with the team. But I am sure he would have been practising with some of our guys.
>
> After all these years it is disappointing that Australian teams didn't play in Paris a little more. With my style of play and the way tennis was played back then I was always able to perform well there. I think I could have done well in 1955 and 1956. I'm not just saying that for me, but for other Australian players who missed the chance to play in the French Championships.

In the singles final of Queen's Club, Rosewall defeated Fraser in a close match by 5-7, 6-3, 9-7, having struggled earlier to recover from match point down when playing the Indian Naresh Kumar, before eventually winning 6-4, 4-6, 9-7. Surprisingly the American pairing of Seixas and Richardson beat the star Australians, Hoad and Rosewall, by 6-8, 6-3, 6-4, in the doubles final.

> When we played doubles together in 1956 we changed sides on the court. I played on the forehand side and Lew was playing on

97 *World Tennis*, July 1956

> the backhand. I'm not sure why this happened, but maybe it was because this is the way Lew played with Rex. I was never as happy on the forehand court, but we teamed ok.

The Wimbledon seedings were limited to eight, with Hoad at number one, and Rosewall at number two. In a third round match Rosewall faced the tall Italian, Orlando Sirola who, at 6' 6", was described as "an admirable man to have on one's side in a line out". Despite his size, Sirola always showed some "surprisingly graceful shots"[98]. Rosewall was never in serious difficulty, but the Italian did stretch the match score to 7-5, 6-4, 9-7. After this, Rosewall beat the crafty American Art Larsen to reach the quarter-finals, alongside fellow Australians, Hoad, Anderson and Fraser.

The weather throughout the 1956 Wimbledon tournament was frustratingly wet and unpleasant. Ned Potter in *World Tennis* called it the wettest Wimbledon on record—which does not appear to be an unusual occurrence! In those quarter-final matches Rosewall had a relatively easy victory over Ulf Schmidt of Sweden by 6-1, 6-3, 6-2. In contrast, Hoad won a tricky four-set match over his compatriot Anderson.

The semi-finals were played between Hoad and Richardson, the sixth seed, and Rosewall and his old sparring partner Seixas. Newspapers reported that Hoad was forced through four uncomfortable sets, as a result of Richardson's shrewd play, but he eventually won 3-6, 6-4, 6-2, 6-4. On the other hand, Rosewall had won so often against Seixas it was expected he would be reasonably comfortable, but this was a naggingly close match. Rosewall finally won 6-3, 3-6, 6-8, 6-3, 7-5 in a match that suffered from annoying rain delays, with one downpour lasting over an hour, and was punctuated by outbursts from Seixas. At one point the American lost his temper over a line call decision, and slammed his racket to the ground. Peter Wilson, whose story appeared in the *Sydney Daily Mirror*, wrote that the "civilised, smart, society crowd" immediately booed him. One spectator called out, "Get on with the game!" Seixas turned to the crowd and yelled "Shut up!" All of this was unheard of at Wimbledon in those days, and Wilson, who said his hands were shaking, his heart pumping and

98 *Manchester Guardian*, 29 June 1956

his voice cracking as he wrote his story believed the American's behaviour was "disgraceful, unheard of, shocking"[99].

Again, much to Seixas' chagrin, Rosewall recovered from 2-5 down in the final set—despite looking faded and nearly dejected at one point. It was a miraculous recovery. In an effort to explain this turnaround *The Times* observed: "Genius does what it must, talent what it can."[100] This poetic analysis probably did little to assist Seixas in coming to terms with losing once more to his much younger rival. He also had to endure the criticisms of Hopman who called him "unsportsmanlike" in the French newspaper, *L'Équipe.* Apparently, Seixas blocked his ears when leaving the court so he didn't have to hear the great ovation given to Rosewall, and once more threw his racket to the ground. This led to another chorus of boos reverberating around centre court, something All England Club secretary, Colonel Duncan Macauley, said had never been heard before at Wimbledon.

> By this time my style of play had changed a little bit. I was more aggressive. It was a good semi-final and maybe a match that Seixas should have won. When he lost after leading 5-2 I think he got very dejected and upset. But his antics are insignificant considering what has taken place with players like Gonzales, Nastase and Connors.

A play-off between Hoad and Rosewall meant this was the first All-Australian final since Gerald Patterson beat Norman Brookes in the Challenge Round of the Wimbledon singles back in 1919. This 1956 final saw Rosewall seek to blunt the brute power of Hoad with clever tactics and skill. However, as was the case with many of their recent encounters, Hoad won 6-2, 4-6, 6-2, 6-4. On 7 July, the *Manchester Guardian* wrote: "Hoad won through greater strength and more consistent power in service, but Rosewall provided most of the decorations and luxuries of the match. Hoad took most of his points quickly and swiftly by single blows. Rosewall

---

99 *Sydney Daily Mirror*, 5 July 1956

100 *The Times*, 5 July 1956

won the prizes for most of the long rallies." Despite being a contest between two of the world's best amateurs, the pair had played one another so often that there was a lack of emotion, and the match lacked an international rivalry to excite the crowd who perceived it as a national championship rather than a world-title bout. In spite of these reservations, it was described by *The Times* as a glorious final and watched by keen spectators, including Princess Margaret, Princess Marina, the Duchess of Kent—who was also president of the All England Club—and the prime ministers of Great Britain, Australia and New Zealand.

> I think that generally English people liked Australians playing against each other—and I often seemed to get a lot of support. Probably on reflection the Drobny final was more a clash of opposites—youth versus experience—and the involvement of a sentimental favourite. This was probably less the case between Lew and myself, and maybe no one really cared who won. It was like one of our regular matches, but at this stage Lew had the slight edge in our rivalry. There was genuine excitement when I led 4-1 in the fourth set. I think I got ahead of myself. I thought we were heading for a fifth set, but he won five games in a row and then all of a sudden the match was over.

The handsome blond hulk from down under was on top of the world, with a Wimbledon title to add to his 1956 Australian and French crowns. It was a good week all round for Australian sportsmen. The previous day Melbourne's Peter Thompson won the British Open golf championship for the third successive time, prompting the *The Sydney Morning Herald* to call it the "greatest ever day in Australian sport", before detailing the efforts of various Australian cricketers playing in county cricket fixtures.[101] Hoad and Rosewall enjoyed further success, beating Italians Pietrangeli and Sirola to win the men's doubles event by 7-5, 6-2, 6-1.

---

101 *The Sydney Morning Herald*, 8 July 1956

Bill Talbert claimed the Australians now straddled men's amateur tennis like "two colossi":

> *They are no longer timid little boys tied to Harry Hopman's apron strings. They don't easily panic any more. They are now on their fifth trip around the world. They have gained independence and with it a poise and confidence that turns stroke-making excellence, which they have always had, into an instrument of destruction. It isn't a comforting picture for us Yankees who took one of the largest squads in history to Wimbledon, hoping to produce a single spark of hope for our coming Davis Cup battles. The spark never materialised.*[102]

◇◇◇◇◇◇◇

At this stage in 1956 Hoad and Rosewall were the best doubles pairing in amateur tennis, and the best two singles players in the world. The highly successful doubles pairing continued their form when they played in the US National doubles tournament at Brookline, beating their Davis Cup teammates Cooper and Fraser (10-8, 6-4, 10-8) in the semi-final and taking on Seixas and Richardson in the final—the American pair had beaten Australians Anderson and Emerson (8-10, 6-3, 6-4, 6-4) to get there. Ultimately, Hoad and Rosewall displayed too much power, speed and all-round court ability for Seixas and Richardson, and won by 6-2, 6-2, 3-6, 6-4.

The seedings for the US National singles event at Forest Hills placed Hoad number one, followed by Rosewall, Richardson, Seixas, Fraser and Anderson. Rosewall continued to face American combatants that he had met from previous Davis Cup matches and international events over the last five years. In the quarter-finals he struggled through an arduous five-set match against Dick Savitt by 6-4, 7-5, 4-6, 8-10, 6-1 (a surprising struggle considering Savitt had not played much tournament tennis for almost four years). The American won the third set and then recovered from 1-3 down to win the fourth set—an excited Forest Hills crowd cheered raucously

102 *Sports Illustrated*, 16 July 1956

for the upset of the year, but were finally disappointed as Rosewall gave "a beautiful display of tactics, mobility and finesse"[103].

Then in the semi-finals Rosewall once again destroyed the hopes of Seixas, winning 10-8, 6-0, 6-3. When asked to pose for photographs following the match he quickly sought out a pocket mirror and combed his hair, "just in case my fiancée sees the pictures!"[104]

The semi-final results meant that Hoad and Rosewall played off again in a major international final. Hoad was one match away from his destiny, the grand slam, but it was his childhood rival who crushed that dream by winning the US Championships 4-6, 6-2, 6-3, 6-3. Those watching commented that Hoad might have played better, but even so, he was not far from his best. On this day it was Rosewall's turn to play sublime tennis.

> *[Rosewall] gave one of the finest performances of his career. Outplaying Hoad almost throughout he somehow matched his opponent's power and surpassed him in delicacy of touch and court positioning. He turned apparent winners from Hoad into winners of his own and put drives and volleys past Hoad in the most convincing fashion. Rosewall was supreme in the forecourt. He followed in not only services but also returns of service to smash and volley with a high degree of success.*[105]

It was a day of strong, chilly and gusty winds at Forest Hills, and one of the vital differences between the players was that Rosewall learned how to use the wind to his advantage. "I realised I couldn't win by trying to best the wind," said Rosewall. I concentrated on getting my first serve in and did not worry about its strength, because I knew the wind would swing it around and make in hard to return. Then I ran into the net and cut short his returns."[106] He sounded like a man on a mission, and under this pressure Hoad began to err. Rosewall trailed 0-2 in the third set, but then proceeded to win 12 of the next 16 games: "He was the master—a craft

103 *World Tennis*, October 1956

104 *The New York Times*, 10 September 1956

105 ibid

106 *The Sydney Morning Herald*, 11 September 1956

tailor sewing a garment of defeat for his victim."[107] By the end Rosewall was so in control he lost a total of three points on serve in the fourth set.

> In this match Lew did not play as well as he could. Maybe he never really played his best at Forest Hills—at least apart from those occasions in the 1955 Challenge Round and when we were 17-year-olds back in 1952. It was windy, and I knew I had to take a few risks. This was interesting because it went against my father's advice: 'Keep the ball in play, and play conservatively.' I was getting some help with my serve on the soft grass and I think Lew was probably surprised that I was playing much more aggressively than I had been previously. It was a combination of things—he didn't play as well as he could, while I played well. Plus he was under a lot of pressure as his face was on the cover of *Sports Illustrated* with an article about whether he was going to win the grand slam.
>
> I'm not sure if it mattered to Lew that it was me who prevented him from winning the grand slam. At different times it didn't seem to matter who he lost to. Perhaps that made him different from Frank Sedgman and Rod Laver, because whenever they went on court they wanted to play as well as they could. And I was a bit like that as well. Certainly in the amateur days Lew wasn't like that—and every now and then he didn't give it 100 per cent. It was different in the professional ranks when you had to give it your complete effort all the time—and it took Lew a while to adapt to that.

Gardnar Mulloy wrote about Rosewall's performance in the US Championships in *World Tennis*:

> *The new champion is a true racquet artist. He has a the quickest reflexes and best groundstrokes in the game today and he is unbelievably fast at*

107 Commentary by Bill Talbert quoted in *Sports Illustrated*, 17 September 1956

the net. He has pace, although not the power of Hoad, and he lacks only a big serve, which is almost impossible for a little fellow. Both he and Hoad outclassed every player in the tournament, with the possible exception of Dick Savitt.[108]

There was a lot of pressure on Hoad, and he was described as more moody and petulant than usual. He also smiled bravely in defeat as Rosewall squelched his opportunity to win the grand slam. An interesting footnote is that at about the same time as the tournament was played, a young Rod Laver won the US Championships junior boy's singles, played as a separate event at Kalamazoo, Michigan. In his semi-final, Laver beat Donald Dell, who went on to become significant player-promoter when open tennis was introduced a decade later.

◇◇◇◇◇◇◇

Returning to Australia towards the end of 1956, it wasn't long before Rosewall and Wilma got married. The news was plastered on the front page of the *Australian Women's Weekly* and 2500 onlookers crowded into the grounds of St John's Cathedral, Brisbane on 6 October to see the two 21-year-olds. Extra police were called in to control the crowd—the largest the cathedral had seen since the Queen and the Duke of Edinburgh attended a service during the 1954 royal tour. There were 800 guests inside the cathedral, including the premier of Queensland.

According to news reports a nervous Rosewall commenced to walk from the vestry to the altar 20 minutes early, and a startled clergyman rushed to stop him. There had been problems getting him to Brisbane at all. Rosewall ended having to travel from Sydney by freight plane, after missing a connecting flight, plus two other planes. The young pair honeymooned at Coolangatta, near the Gold Coast.

The wedding was an exciting event. My two grandmothers came up from Sydney. Lew and Harry were there as well as Ted Harris,

108 *World Tennis*, October 1956

> a sports broadcaster and executive for AMPOL, who became a lifelong friend of Kramer's. He had been involved in the talks between Kramer and my father about me turning professional. Wilma's brother gave her away, as her father passed away a couple of years before. Our wedding photographs were on the cover of *Australian Women's Weekly*. I joke occasionally about young people these days selling the rights to their wedding photos for a six-figure sum. We only got three copies of the magazine! There was a lot of interest in the wedding from tennis people, and Wilma was then with me when I played in state tournaments leading up to the 1956 Davis Cup Challenge Round.

In early December Rosewall beat Hoad in a straightforward final of the South Australian Championships, 6-1, 7-5, 6-1, and two weeks later he repeated the feat in the Victorian Championships, staging a magnificent comeback to win 4-6, 4-6, 6-1, 6-4, 6-3. On that occasion, a grumpy Hoad did not even wait about for the trophy presentation.

At the end of the year, American newspapers reported Rosewall had reached an agreement to join Kramer's professional tour as soon as the Challenge Round in Adelaide was completed, with a £22,300 guarantee payment over a 12-month period. However, discussions involving Rosewall's father continued to take place and it was assumed the Australian would give his answer once the Challenge Round matches were concluded.

Assuming the pro arrangements were agreed upon Rosewall was to play a series of matches through Australia and America against recognised pro champion Pancho Gonzales. When told of the proposed match-up, Gonzales apparently told Kramer that he would "blow Rosewall off the court" [109]. Hoad was also approached by Kramer, but he wanted to stay amateur for another 12 months, possibly to have another crack at winning the grand slam in 1957.

109 *The Sydney Morning Herald*, 20 December 1956

◇◇◇◇◇◇◇

On the opening day of the 1956 Davis Challenge Round, Hoad blasted Herbie Flam off the court by 6-2, 6-3, 6-3, while Rosewall posted yet another victory over Seixas by 6-1, 6-4, 4-6, 6-1. It was Rosewall's 11th victory out of 13 matches against the 33-year-old American. He was an irresistible force to Seixas, who was reduced to distraction watching Rosewall's superb groundstrokes pass him cleanly at the net. Exhibiting a sparkling net attack, Rosewall easily won the match in the fourth set.

After the first day Kramer had more or less given up, writing: "As we say in America, 'you can't win without the horsepower' and your team has all the horsepower in this Challenge Round."[110] The Americans also bemoaned the fact they were faced up against top-flight players, who played on a full-time basis: "We can't take boys who play tennis four months a year and expect them to beat rivals who are coached and cajoled the year around. We must set up own assembly line and turn them out like Fords."[111]

In the doubles match Hoad and Rosewall defeated Seixas and Sam Giammalva, 1-6, 6-1, 7-5, 6-4. Despite being an internationally recognised doubles team for four or five years, this was only Hoad and Rosewall's second Challenge Round as a combined team and they were yet to win a match. The doubles victory ensured that the Davis Cup was to remain in Australia for another year. In the return singles matches Rosewall beat Giammalva 4-6, 6-1, 8-6, 7-5 and Hoad crushed Seixas, by 6-2, 7-5, 6-3. In the Rosewall-Giammalva match, the American streaked ahead to a 5-1 lead in the fourth set, only to see Rosewall lift his game and win the next six games in a row. It was a good match to place in his memory bank as his last amateur appearance.

> On this occasion the Americans didn't have a team with a lot of depth. Vic was the main player. The crowds were good as they always were in Davis Cup Challenge Rounds, and I fondly remember my mother and father being there alongside Wilma.

---

110 *The Sydney Morning Herald*, 27 December 1956

111 *Sports Illustrated*, 7 January 1957

CHAPTER 4

◇◇◇◇◇◇◇

WELCOME TO PRO TENNIS KEN!

Rosewall signed a pro contract with Jack Kramer in the dying days of 1956, almost as soon as he and Hoad beat the Americans in the 1956 Davis Cup Challenge Round. The agreement guaranteed him US$65,000 for a 12-month period and he was also entitled to 20 per cent of gate receipts over US$350,000 accumulated during the 1957 tour. If he beat Gonzales over the tour he was entitled to an option on a contract of $25,000 for 1958. If not, the contract was voided.

> Lew and I were asked to turn pro the year before and we both decided go for it, but then had second thoughts when we returned to Australia. It was probably a good decision as the earlier contract wasn't too exciting.
>
> Kramer again approached us early in the 1956-57 Australian season, and I think his plan was to have an American team versus an Australian team match. On this occasion Lew was not interested, but I felt it was a good opportunity. I had just got married, and it meant Wilma and I would be able to travel.

DESTINED TO BE A CHAMPION Ken Rosewall's parents were keen tennis players. His father Robert taught him the fundamental strokes that were to remain almost unchanged throughout his career, while his mother Vera gave him inspiration and encouragement.

At the family home on Bay Street, Rockdale, NSW in 1942, a young Rosewall proudly shows off his first racket with a long handle.

TEEN PRODIGY At 14-years-old, Rosewall dons his tennis whites for a training session with his father, and at 16 he is photographed with his parents at Kooyong in Melbourne; he would soon be travelling the world to compete against the game's best players.

GOING INTERNATIONAL Rosewall embarks on his first overseas trip in May 1952. The Australian travelling team flew directly from Sydney to London, a trip that took three days and two nights, on a Super Constellation flight. Going up the stairs, from left to right, are Lew Hoad, Harry Hopman, Ken Rosewall, Mervyn Rose and Ken McGregor.

CAPTAIN-COACH-MENTOR Having just returned from their first successful trip to America in September 1952, Harry Hopman (centre) was regarded by most of the sporting world as the person to discover the famous 'tennis twins' Hoad (left) and Rosewall. Today, however, Rosewall believes Hopman's contribution to his development was questionable.

A ROYAL ENCOUNTER During a number of exhibition matches in February 1954, Hoad and Rosewall had the honour of having a trophy presented to them by Queen Elizabeth II. One of Australia's greatest players and tennis administrators, Sir Norman Brookes, stands to the Queen's right.

WEDDING DAY On 6 October 1956, Rosewall married Wilma McIver at St John's Cathedral in Brisbane, where the happy couple were photographed with Rosewall's parents (above). The ceremony took place at 5pm in front of 800 people, while police were called in to control the crowds gathered outside. *Australian Women's Weekly* dedicated several pages to the event (top), for which the couple received six copies of the magazine. The reception was attended by several Australian tennis players and officials, including Hoad and the Davis Cup team manager Hopman.

THE GOLDEN YEAR The 1953 Davis Cup Challenge Round was played at Melbourne's Kooyong courts between Christmas and New Year. It was Hoad (left) and Rosewall's winning performances in the reverse singles that secured Australia's victory, after Hoad and Rex Hartwig lost to Americans Tony Trabert and Vic Seixas in the doubles, a selection decision made over the head of Hopman (middle).

SCREEN IDOL Rosewall meets Doris Day in 1956. The actress was a keen tennis player herself, and became a close friend of both Ken and Wilma.

JUST DESSERTS The Australian international touring team in 1956 tuck into sweet offerings from Carnation Milk, one of tennis' early sponsors. From left to right: Ashley Cooper, Rosewall, Neale Fraser, captain Cliff Sproule, Anderson and Roy Emerson. Hoad was touring privately at the time.

KRAMER CUP Taken in the early 1960s, this international event for touring pros attracted tennis greats. From left to right: Pancho Segura, Luis Ayala, British player Mike Davies, Alex Olmedo, Andres Gimeno, French player Robert Haillet. The Australian team of Ashley Cooper, Mal Anderson, Lew Hoad and Ken Rosewall stand behind Jack Kramer and the trophy. Note the height difference between Rosewall and the Americans to the right—Pancho Gonzales, Barry MacKay, Tony Trabert and Butch Buchholz.

KEN TURNS PRO Rosewall and Pancho Gonzales (left), his challenger for supremacy in Jack Kramer's 1957 tour, take time out to be interviewed by Kramer himself (right). The formidable promoter thought it best for Rosewall to make his professional debut in Australia, before his countrymen, and on familiar courts.

A FRENCH AFFAIR At Stade Roland Garros in Paris during the first French Open title in 1968. From left, René Lacoste's son Bernard, Rosewall and Philippe Chatrier. French junior tennis champion in 1945 and a member of the French Davis Cup team from 1948-50, Chatrier was later president of the ILTF.

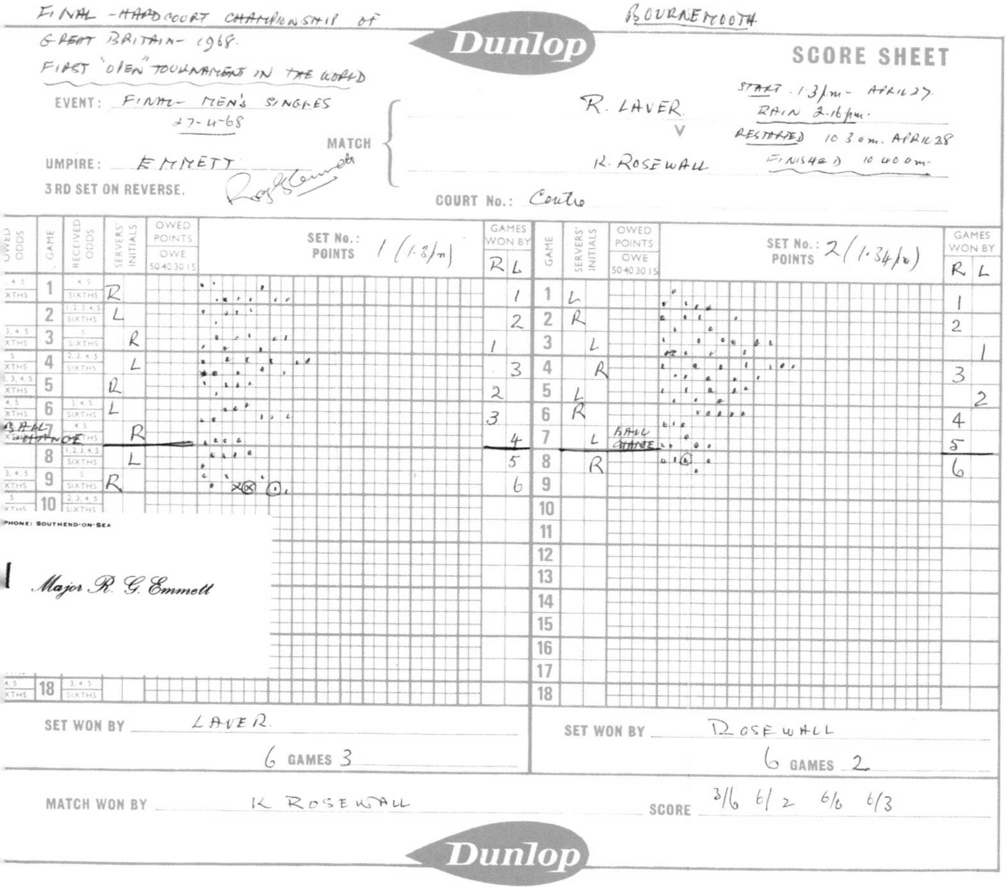

FINAL – HARDCOURT CHAMPIONSHIP OF GREAT BRITAIN – 1968.
FIRST "OPEN" TOURNAMENT IN THE WORLD

BOURNEMOUTH

Dunlop

SCORE SHEET

EVENT: FINAL – MEN'S SINGLES 27-4-68

MATCH: R. LAVER v R. ROSEWALL

START 1.3 pm – APRIL 27. RAIN 2.16 pm. RESTARTED 10.30 am. APRIL 28. FINISHED 10.40 am.

UMPIRE: EMMETT

3RD SET ON REVERSE.

COURT No.: Centre

SET No.: 1 (1.3 pm)

GAME	SERVERS' INITIALS	GAMES WON BY R	GAMES WON BY L
1	R		1
2	L		2
3	R	1	
4	L		3
5	R	2	
6	L	3	
7 (BALL CHANGE)	R		4
8	L		5
9	R		6

SET No.: 2 (1.34 pm)

GAME	SERVERS' INITIALS	GAMES WON BY R	GAMES WON BY L
1	L	1	
2	R	2	
3	L		1
4	R	3	
5	L		2
6	R	4	
7 (BALL CHANGE)	L	5	
8	R	6	

PHONE: SOUTHEND-ON-SEA

Major R. G. Emmett

SET WON BY LAVER 6 GAMES 3

SET WON BY ROSEWALL 6 GAMES 2

MATCH WON BY K ROSEWALL SCORE 3/6 6/2 6/0 6/3

Dunlop

LAVER v ROSEWALL The scorecard from the first open tournament—the 1968 Hard Court Championships of Great Britain, held at the West Hants Club, Bournemouth. The umpire's card is stapled to the sheet, which charts each game in the four-set encounter. Rosewall won 3-6, 6-2, 6-0, 6-3.

ORDER OF PLAY Professional troupe promoter Kramer (top) and Rosewall survey the board at Wimbledon during the 1970 All England championships. When Rosewall met Newcombe in the final he was the oldest finalist since Bill Tilden in 1930. It was a closely fought struggle, which Newcombe won 5-7, 6-3, 6-2, 3-6, 6-1. It was a disappointing result for Rosewall, who believed it was his last chance at the only major title to have eluded him.

MOVING IN CELEBRITY CIRCLES The Rosewall family enjoy time together at the John Gardiner Tennis Ranch in Scottsdale, Arizona in 1974 (below). It was while staying with friends in America that Ken, Wilma, Brett and Glenn had the pleasure of meeting Charlton Heston in the early 1970s (above left) and Jesse Owens in 1974 (above right).

PHOTO CREDIT: EIICHI KAWATEI

I didn't realise what I was getting into when you look at the amount of travel and the tennis I played during 1957. But at the time I wasn't making a lot of money playing tennis. I had a contract with Carnation Milk doing some promotions for them, and I thought it was in my long-term interest to turn professional so long as I stayed injury free.

The negotiations with Kramer were mainly in Sydney, with Kramer and his Australian representative, Bob Barnes. My friend Ted Harris, who later became general manager of AMPOL, was also involved. We knew Ted through tennis and sporting connections and he was a friend of Kramer and his people. My mother and father and Wilma also took part in these discussions. Jack came out to the family grocery shop and we had some of the negotiations there. I was advised to accept the contract.

The announcement was made on 2 January 1957, just after the Davis Cup finished. I asked Lew if he'd reconsider and turn pro but he said no.

"I can beat any player in the world, including Ken Rosewall, and I can beat him in straight sets."[112] So said Pancho Gonzales, Rosewall's challenger for supremacy in the 1957 tour, shortly before their first match-up in the 1957 contest. This first encounter was played on the grass courts at Kooyong before a crowd of 12,000 and ended up being unexpectedly close, with the tall and powerful man from Los Angeles winning 6-3, 3-6, 6-3, 1-6, 9-7. This contest was one of 100 matches the pair would play during the course of the year. The 'elephant in the room' was Hoad, who declined to turn pro in 1957, but was likely to do so the following year. Hoad wanted another chance to score the grand slam of tennis, but that dream ended surprisingly in the Australian Championships when he lost to Neale Fraser in the semi-finals. The blond bomber was also carrying an injury, later diagnosed as a strained ligament in the lower part of his back.

---

112 *The New York Times*, 15 January 1957

Kramer and others had thought it was best for Rosewall to make his professional debut in Australia, before his countrymen, and on familiar courts, rather than the indoor surfaces in America. As a result the young man arrived in America with the advantage of knowing just what he would face.

Despite organising the series of encounters, it seems Kramer was worried that Rosewall might be eaten alive by Gonzales. He believed Rosewall was "a cute little fellow with a dink serve, who operated mostly from the baseline" and who had fallen into Hoad's shadow in recent times. The promoter admitted that he offered Gonzales an "extra five per cent of the gross"[113], if he found a way to carry Rosewall. Kramer's 'dirty deed' troubled his conscience for many years and arguably placed his contract with Gonzales at risk; it also showed that Big Jake completely underestimated Rosewall.

Gonzales was the established professional champion through most of the 1950s, his career a volatile mixture of boom and bust. He won the US Championships singles as a 19-year-old in 1948, when he was number 17 in the US national rankings, and backed this up by winning the following year. As a young man he only ever played at Wimbledon in 1949, and lost to the Australian Geoff Brown in an early round. He did, however, win the doubles event with Frank Parker at Wimbledon in 1949.

It was interesting that Kooyong, the stadium run by the Lawn Tennis Association of Victoria (LTAV), was used for the event. The LTAA did not want Kooyong to be used by the pros as the Australian Championships were being held there later the same week. Don Ferguson, the new head of the LTAA, felt the pros were a threat to amateur tennis and the Davis Cup, and the organisation's view was that Kramer was dipping into amateur ranks and robbing Australia of its tennis power. Eventually, the LTAA council decided by a majority of 7-5 that Kooyong could be used, rejecting the president's position.[114]

Initially there were two matches played at Kooyong—Rosewall won the second encounter by 7-5, 6-4, 14-12. However, in their third

113 J Kramer and F Deford, *The Game—My 40 Years in Tennis*, pages 260 and 228

114 LTAA council minutes, 7 January 1957

match, Rosewall was overwhelmed by Gonzales' tremendous power and succumbed 6-2, 6-4, 6-0. In the following weeks there were matches played in Sydney, Brisbane, Auckland, Wellington and Christchurch.

Gonzales took the tour extremely seriously and by the time the players arrived in Adelaide in early February he had streaked to a 7-1 lead in the head-to-head contest. This didn't mean some of the matches weren't close. One match in Brisbane, played at the Milton courts in subtropical temperatures, lasted three-and-a-half hours with Gonzales winning 3-6, 6-3, 11-9, 1-6, 15-13. At the end the big American claimed it was one of the toughest matches he had ever played.

> Playing Pancho was quite a challenge. I had never really seen him play and senior Australian players didn't tell me much about him—I know that Sedgman, McGregor and Hartwig had played him quite a lot. That first match at Kooyong, on the grass courts and under lights, was quite an experience. I had not played important matches under lights before and I was a little nervous. I played reasonably well and don't know if Pancho was a bit tired for the second match, but he was 29 and reasonably fit. He was the sort of player who won a lot of long matches because he was able to keep himself in the game. Part of this was his serve, and the fact that he was an intimidating character.

No one was prepared for the drama that took place in Adelaide at the AMPOL Tournament of Champions the following week. In a match at Memorial Drive, Rosewall rallied to defeat Gonzales 4-6, 4-6, 6-3, 9-7, 6-1. The crowd sat quietly during the first two sets, but then started heckling the American, as Rosewall gradually worked his way into the match. Normally Australian tennis fans are respectful enough, but they had been affronted by Gonzales' comments about Rosewall struggling to keep the ball in play and predicting he would continue to beat him every night. When Rosewall won the 16-game fourth set, the crowd started jeering the American, and he responded by turning and hurling his racket at a microphone close to the umpire's chair. The racket struck with such force that it bounced into the stands. After that, it almost looked as if Gonzales threw away the final set, although he claimed Rosewall's tennis was the best ever played against him.

The taunting of Gonzales during that match caused him to walk towards the crowd and call someone in the stands 'horsehead'. Later, in his defence, Gonzales said he identified one of the crowd that was heckling, and asked him "politely" to come on the court and repeat his comments. "Of course, the guy didn't move."[115] At home in Los Angeles, Gonzales' wife said that if she knew her husband, he called the heckler a worse name than 'horsehead', to which Gonzales responded: "Well, I admit I thought of a worse name, but I didn't use it."[116] In spite of all this disruption, Gonzales certainly got the crowds in.

> Pancho was ahead of me in that Adelaide match and looked like he was going to have an easy win. There was a lot of crowd support for me, and it was a big crowd. I can't remember what the calls from the crowd were about, but he certainly gave the microphone a bit of a whack. He went through these moments and got himself extremely upset, but could also forget about it and be back to normal the next day. He was a strange character.

In spite of Gonzales' early comments, the challenger in the 1957 tour had great respect for Rosewall, saying:

> *His stroking was flawless. He was exactly what the instructor ordered. He played the game literally the way it was taught. His backhand, slightly undercut, looked stronger than his forehand. But that was deceptive. He took his forehand shots nicely on the rise with pace. His serve held no terrors. Yet it was effortless and well placed ... Every time he returns a well-placed first service it amazes me. He ought to be an inspiration to all the small players in the world.*[117]

---

115 *Washington Post*, 6 February 1957

116 R Gonzales, *Man With a Racket*, page 180

117 ibid, pages 175 and 181

The 1957 pro tour of Australia was enormously successful—the crowds applauded their Davis Cup hero's every move, but greeted the American with silence or mild contempt. Arthur Daley nevertheless commented that Australian fans were true sportsmen: "By the end of each match they were so consumed with admiration for Gonzales' craftsmanship that they accorded him a noisy acclaim. The big power hitter from Los Angeles kept his somewhat volatile temperament under control [at least until one of the final matches of the tour]."[118] In Gonzales' biography written shortly afterwards he claimed that tennis players were a bit like actors, and nobody criticised them for temperamental outbursts. Some years later, Joe McCauley wrote of the contrast in personalities between Rosewall and the big American: "Gonzales was a maverick with a piranha mentality and would skin alive a rookie pro given half a chance. Not only that, he was arrogant with it. Rosewall on the other hand, was a quiet humble man, the antithesis of Gonzales."[119]

◇◇◇◇◇◇◇

The success of the Australian tour made Kramer wonder whether open tennis (regular tournament play between amateur and professional players) was just around the corner. He now had seven of the best players with signed pro contracts. The only major absentee was Hoad.

The contrast between Kramer's moves towards professionalism and the view of amateur officialdom was there for all to see at the Annual Interstate Tennis Conference held in Melbourne in January 1957, where several delegates urged state associations to stop cooperating with the touring pros.

A special committee of the United States Lawn Tennis Association (USLTA) recommended holding an open tournament, but its report was rejected by the association's executive committee.

Rosewall played the opening match in his American tour New York's Madison Square Garden on 17 February 1957 and was blown away by a masterly performance of Gonzales by 6-2, 6-4, 6-2, before a crowd of 11,500 fans. The match was played on a canvas court stretched over

118 ibid, page 181

119 J McCauley, *The History of Professional Tennis*, page 74

ice, as the arena was used for the New York Rangers hockey team in the evenings. The surface was 25 per cent faster than the canvas court Rosewall had practised on at the Brooklyn arena and, perhaps as a result, Gonzales adopted an unconventional style of play. Despite playing with a punctured cyst on his racket hand, serving at three-quarter pace and merely blocking the ball during rallies, Gonzales convincingly outplayed the Australian. He had lost their last two meetings in Australia, and was in no mood to show any mercy. His serve was loaded with spin and aimed at the Rosewall forehand, and the little man's errors on that side cost him the match.

> I was not aware of Pancho's injury. But he was never one to complain. You'd never know there was anything wrong with him. We practised in Brooklyn Heights because it was the only court available. Using Madison Square Garden as a venue meant there would always be a court strung out over ice at that time of year. This suited Gonzales; he was a good athlete and it enabled him to use his strength. He was able to serve and volley, and he was much too good for me under those conditions. Lew had a better chance when he played him in tour matches the following year, because of his physical strength.
>
> Wilma did not make it to New York for that match. She was staying in Honolulu with Kramer's wife, and the plan was that we would meet up again in California about a week later.

This New York match was the first in a tour of Kramer's professional group that would play in approximately 50 American cities, before heading to Europe and Asia. The key feature of the tour was the match-up between Gonzales and Rosewall, a contest that was the best-of-100 matches, and after the encounter at Madison Square Garden, Gonzales led 8-3. Before the primary contest each night there was a supporting one-set match-up between the wily Pancho Segura of Ecuador and the 36-year-old Australian teaching pro, Dinny Pails.

After New York the Kramer tour travelled to California where Rosewall registered two successive victories over his powerful rival. Newspapers of the time report that Gonzales increased his ascendancy over Rosewall as they travelled to: Phoenix, Arizona; Corpus Christi, Dallas, Fort Worth, Houston, Lubbock and Odessa, Texas; Kansas City and St Louis, Missouri; Chicago, Illinois; Washington; Lynchburg, Virginia; Muncie and Evansville, Indiana; Ann Arbour, Michigan; and Montreal, Toronto and Ottawa, Canada. By this stage Gonzales led the individual contest with Rosewall 29-13.

Occasionally conditions were highly unsatisfactory. In Fort Worth the players were forced to play on a court that allowed only eight feet behind the baseline, and in St Louis there was a pall of smoke hanging over the Washington University Fieldhouse court. It was a difficult initiation for Rosewall. In Princeton, New Jersey he told reporters:

> *Pancho just doesn't seem to have any bad nights. It's not human. He's not human. He's always tough. I have to work like crazy in every match, and it's only when I am playing extremely well that I'm able to pull off a win. Somebody ought to define and spell the word 'slump' for Pancho. I don't think he understands it.*[120]

We often played in university venues with a shorter run back, and it was sometimes difficult for the canvas court to be properly tightened. The equipment man used sand bags so the canvas could be pulled tighter.

We had to do all our own driving from place to place, and the roads weren't as good as now. It was tough. I think the longest drive we had was from Winnipeg in Canada to Denver, Colorado, and that took two and a half days. We had Mercury station wagons that stayed with us for the four-month period of the tour.

Kramer was only at some of the matches. Otherwise he was at home doing business developing the tour. Another of his staff—Myron MacNamara—organised promotions. The arrangement was that 60 per cent of the gross earned at these matches came to World Tennis Inc (Kramer's company), and 40 per cent went

---

120 R Gonzales, *Man With a Racket*, page 184

> to the locals organising the matches in different cities. As per the contract I was entitled to my share of the 60 per cent that went to Kramer's company (a 20 per cent share of the gross). In contrast, Dinny Pails and Segura were paid a flat fee.
>
> It was a tough time for Wilma, travelling about in these conditions. She had never been overseas before, and we didn't have much time to enjoy ourselves. Every day would be spent travelling, practising or playing. It was good that Dinny was travelling with us, as he was a lifetime friend of ours from Sydney.

The challenge series was interrupted when all the professional players played off at the World Professional Championships, in Cleveland. Gonzales overcame Frank Parker, Trabert and Segura to win the event. During that tournament Rosewall was beaten by the cagey and sharp Segura who bombarded the Rosewall forehand with his double-handed ground shots, and scored an easy win (6-2, 6-3). At that point it looked like the Rosewall game might be failing under the strain of these 'one-night stand' tennis encounters.

The tour was occasionally disrupted by an ongoing personality contest between Gonzales and Kramer, with the star player continually arguing that he did not have a binding contract with the tour promoter and could walk away at time. The big man spoke of playing out the 1957 tour, but not wanting to play another: "I've been playing continuously for 18 months. I've been playing with a cyst on my racket hand, and I want to give it time to heal." Kramer said he was fed up with Gonzales "popping off". He owed an obligation to all those associated with the tour "and he certainly wouldn't be making the money he is without them", said Kramer.[121]

There was no love lost between Kramer and Gonzales. After losing his first pro tour as challenger to Kramer in 1950, Gonzales felt he was treated as a has-been, because he wasn't given an opportunity to play again until 1954. And then on the 1956 tour he was offered a guarantee of $15,000 compared with the challenger—Trabert—being offered $75,000. Gonzales did not like Kramer or Trabert from that moment on.

121 *Washington Post*, 2 April 1957

There were rumours that Gonzales was cranky as hell whenever he lost to Rosewall. On one occasion he jumped in a tour car immediately after a match and drove off by himself to the next destination. In response to this story, Gonzales acknowledged there was an occasion when he lost, and he hurried everyone along to get moving. He said, "the sooner I got to the next city, the sooner I could avenge my defeat"[122]. Gonzales was a difficult customer, for sure. Trabert later made this assessment:

> *I found him to be unapproachable, a loner who kept all of his thoughts and ideas to himself. Sullen most of the time, with a chip on his shoulder as big as a two-by-four, he rarely associated with us on the road. Instead he'd appear at the appointed hour for his match, then vanish back into the night soon after without saying a word to anyone. We'd all stay around giving autographs to the fans before moving on to the next city. Not Pancho. But on the court he was totally professional—as well as a fantastic player.*[123]

Pancho jumping in the car and driving off to the next destination could actually happen if he won or lost. There were two station wagons shared between the players, but Pancho occasionally had his own car, and sometimes his brother was on the road with him. He even brought his dog sometimes. Often he and his brother would take off at the end of the match, win or lose. The rest of us, Pancho Segura, Pails, myself and Wilma, and Olen Parkes from Wilson sporting goods would share the other two vehicles. Olen was the tour manager. He did a lot of driving, drank a lot of coffee, smoked a lot of cigars, and made announcements on the courts.

Olen played the role of tour manager for all the pro tennis tours from 1953 through to 1963—he passed away shortly after the first open Wimbledon in 1968. All the pros were involved in a charity day in Chicago after his death.

122 R Gonzales, *Man With a Racket*, page 184

123 T Trabert, *Trabert on Tennis—The View from the Centre Court*, page 114

The tour continued on through cities like Rochester, New York; Atlanta, Georgia; Parkersburg, West Virginia; Cincinnati, Ohio; South Bend, Indiana; Lansing, Michigan; and Salt Lake City, Utah. The contest between Gonzales and Rosewall reached 46-25 at one point, and eventually the score stood at 51-26 when the pros played in Bakersfield, California, on 28 May. When this milestone was reached the volatile Pancho announced that he was leaving for a six-week vacation. Later he said he wanted to stay at home, rest and get to know his family again. The overall contest between him and Rosewall was generally considered a success and grossed as much in 70 matches as the tour between Gonzales and Trabert earned in 125 matches the year before.

Kramer's tour then shifted to a short stint of matches through the Caribbean and South America, with Kramer substituting for Gonzales. Even in his absence the testy relationship between the two major figures of the professional game continued. In July 1957 Gonzales accused his boss of trying to be the czar of the professional game. And staged a rebellion by turning up just three hours before Kramer's Tournament of Champions, a round robin event played at Forest Hills in New York, was due to begin. "Let Kramer dictate to the players all he wants to," the star player grumbled, "he's not going to dictate to me. He would do a lot better if he treated the players differently."[124] Now the issue in dispute was that Kramer offered Gonzales the same percentage of gross proceeds on an upcoming tour with Hoad commencing in January 1958 as he received for the Rosewall tour. Kramer believed that a tour between Gonzales and Hoad would break all records. These two were emotionally alike and played the same 'slam-bang' tennis. Gonzales insisted that the payment terms were unfair in the extreme, and in any event he did not have an ongoing contract with Kramer. What was the man doing playing in the Kramer Tournament of Champions, you may ask? "I'm only here because my lawyer asked me to come," offered Gonzales.[125]

---

124 *Washington Post*, 14 July 1957

125 J McCauley, *The History of Professional Tennis*, page 74

> I knew that one of Gonzales's grievances against Kramer was that he played against Trabert in the tour matches in 1956, and won easily, but Trabert received most of the money due to his deal with Kramer. He was anti-Kramer and anti-Trabert.
>
> But there were other issues. During that 1957 tour some of the matches were televised, and Pancho believed that some of the funds from the television stations should go into a kitty where he got his percentage. As players, we were never in a position to check Kramer's figures. We didn't have the right or the know-how to check what moneys were coming in or out. One time Pancho actually came to me and said, 'Why don't we go off and organise our own tour?' I don't know if he said that to anyone else. My response was that my contract was with Jack, and I intended to be loyal to that contract. I thought that Jack was loyal to me in organising the matches. Pancho had a lot of these arguments with Kramer but he didn't actually win any of them.

Hoad signed a contract with Kramer immediately after winning the 1957 Wimbledon Championships singles, and was offered a US$125,000 guarantee against a 25 per cent gross for a two-year contract. This was the largest amount ever guaranteed to an amateur tennis player to join pro ranks. Gonzales hadn't been so fortunate—his request that Kramer grant him 30 per cent of the Hoad 1958 tour fell on deaf ears. At that point Gonzales was the pro champion, yet he was being paid less than the challenger for this upcoming tour (as happened during the 1956 tour against Trabert).

Hoad travelled to Los Angeles to sign the pro contract, meaning he would not be able to defend the Davis Cup later in the year, much to the annoyance of the LTAA. Did Hoad's departure from amateur ranks mean the Davis Cup was no longer the world's top tennis fixture? "How can the Challenge Round be the test of the world's tennis supremacy when hardly any of its contestants are among the world's top 10," questioned Harry Gordon of the *Melbourne Sun*.

In contrast, the professional Tournament of Champions at Forest Hills in July 1957 was described by some as the toughest tournament in the history of tennis. On this occasion Rosewall was dealt out stern defeats, reminding him that he was now in the big league. He lost to Trabert on the first day, but on day two he scored a victory in a five-set encounter against his tormentor Segura (Rosewall won by 13-11 in the deciding set). Unlike the 'crash-bash' approach of some of their contemporaries, Rosewall and Segura treated tennis as a game of carefully considered chess-like moves. A day later Rosewall was soundly beaten by Gonzales by 6-2, 8-6, 6-4, with the big man's overpowering service doing most of the damage. Gonzales remained undefeated throughout this round-robin event, and confirmed his status as the world's professional champion.

There was some irony when it was Rosewall who handed out Hoad's first defeat as a professional, beating him 6-3, 9-7, 4-6, 6-3 at the Tournament of Champions. The match was played on the same court where Rosewall had won the US National Championships against Hoad the previous year. A *New York Times* writer praised Rosewall's play, saying it "showed a control of the ball equal to any test of his virtuosity in shackling speed with marvellously wrought ripostes"[126]. The Rosewall service had also strengthened considerably since joining the pro ranks, and Hoad (the recently crowned Wimbledon champion) was kept on the defensive throughout the match.

Following New York, a similar professional round-robin tournament was played in Los Angeles, and Rosewall again defeated Hoad 6-3, 6-4. Here, Rosewall also beat Gonzales in a two-and-a-half hour match with the score of 22-20, 1-6, 6-2, while Hoad suffered debilitating losses to his middle-aged countryman Pails and Segura. Eventually Gonzales recorded wins over Hoad, Pails and Sedgman, and took first place in the Los Angeles tournament, with Rosewall coming third. Hoad suffered the indignity of losing six matches in a row to finish in last place. One reporter claimed he played like an amateur, and some of his fellow professionals questioned whether he justified the $125,000 investment made in him by

126 *The New York Times*, 19 July 1957

Kramer. Gonzales argued that the mangling Hoad received from fellow pros in these 1957 events had taken the edge off the 1958 tour. Why sign up Hoad before the US National Championships and the Davis Cup, he asked? Gonzales explained, "Jack's eyes were on the turnstiles."[127]

◇◇◇◇◇◇◇

The pro tour group of Rosewall, Segura, Hoad and Kramer (without Gonzales) then travelled though Europe in a series of exhibition matches. In one event at Cannes more than 3000 spectators turned out, and there were fights between fans as they jostled for seats.

> I played a lot of times against Lew during that trip through Europe. The real headache at the time was that very few of the matches had been properly set up. The year before Fred Perry had organised the pro tour in Europe, but in 1957 Kramer had him organising matches in the US, and little was done to arrange matches in Europe. Eventually it meant that Pat Hughes from Dunlop in London was called in to help organise these events, and he became Kramer's agent in Europe until Trabert took over this role some years later.

The 1957 London Indoor Professional tournament at Wembley—a 14-man knock-out event—was a prestigious event for the pros. Kramer entered various contracts with British promoters on the basis that Hoad would play and the event saw the return of Gonzales. It was here that Rosewall claimed his first major professional title, and £425, when he beat Segura in a five-set final (1-6, 6-3, 6-4, 3-6, 6-4).

Hoad—the reigning Wimbledon champion—was playing with a pulled groin muscle and made yet another problematic transition to professional tennis when he lost in the first round to Kramer (6-1, 6-3).[128] For Kramer

127 R Gonzales, *Man With a Racket*, page 199. Even Kramer later admitted Hoad's performance was "for a quick kill at the gate". J Kramer and F Deford, *The Game—My 40 Years in Tennis*, page 230

128 J Kramer and F Deford, *The Game—My 40 Years in Tennis*, page 232. But according to Joe McCauley, the match went to 10-8 in the second set—J McCauley, *The History of Professional Tennis*, page 79

this was a dilemma—he was entitled to half the gate and his business interests were better served if the Australian progressed further through the draw. Rosewall beat Kramer 6-1, 6-3, 6-2 in the semi-finals and Gonzales was also knocked out at the semi-final stage by Segura (11-9, 12-10, 6-4).

In spite of Hoad's loss, the four-day tournament drew record crowds of more than 45,000. It was now evident that the fans would come out to watch the professionals play, and these were not mere exhibition matches.

Following London, the pro group travelled to South Africa, Asia and then on to Australia. By this time the group of four travelling players was Rosewall, Hoad, Segura and Frank Sedgman.

> Segura was a very underrated player, with two hands on the forehand. He was 14 years older than me. I played my best at 40, and Gonzales and Segura were a bit the same. Gonzales was always in great shape. Kramer was sometimes on his back for drinking too many soft drinks and smoking, but he always stayed in great shape. In South Africa we played 20 matches in 21 days. We had this old aeroplane owned by a wealthy business from Port Elizabeth, who helped out organising the pro tour the year before. I recall the lightest of the players—usually me—had to sit up the front with the pilot.

In a significant match played in their home city of Sydney, Rosewall defeated Hoad (1-6, 12-10, 6-2), followed by another three-set victory three days later. Hoad then showed some improvement in form and managed to defeat Rosewall twice before the end of the year.

> Segura was with us during the Australian leg of the tour, but he was complaining that he had already played his 150 matches for the year—under his flat-rate contract. By the time we got to Canberra, Lew and I had to put in some extra money to make sure he played in the last fixture on the tour.

The 1958 pro tennis tour continued through Australian cities, with Gonzales returning once more after another break of some months from consistent play. By this time, Hoad showed the advantage of experience gained through playing pro matches, and learning the 'percentages' on the world tour with Rosewall, Kramer, Segura and Sedgman. It was Hoad who won a round-robin tennis event played at Kooyong in January, as the only unbeaten player in the event, while Rosewall lost to Sedgman, Hoad and Gonzales.[129]

By the time Hoad was due to play Gonzales at Madison Square Garden in February as part of their pro contest, he led 8-5 in the individual rivalry, based on matches against each other in Australia. Kramer proudly made it known that these encounters broke all attendance records in 10 of the 13 cases, saying the matches blew amateur tennis off the map.

> *They really fought each other. In Adelaide, Gonzales played with bleeding fingers, in Sydney with an aching forearm muscle. Neither would quit. For once in his life, Lew Hoad cared. The thing was so exciting that even he got swept along. We started playing five sets, and invariably it went five sets. We had to kill the doubles finale, the programs went so long. Then I cut the feature back to best-of-three because I was afraid that I was going to kill them both if they had to go five every day.*[130]

During the pro tour through Australia in early 1958 Hoad and Gonzales were the feature match, with support matches between myself, Sedgman and Hartwig. After those matches I stayed in Australia until I joined up with the Kramer tour later in the year. In that period I practised with some of the Australian players, including juniors. I wasn't making any money, although I was still associated with Carnation Milk. They kept me on during 1957 and 1958. I was still under contract to Kramer but not guaranteed any payments after that 1957 tour.

---

129 LTAA council minutes (4 August 1957 and 16 September 1957) indicate that there were ongoing disputes as to whether pros should be entitled to use association courts (like Kooyong). The compromise was that the pros were required to submit an itinerary of events and to comply with detailed obligations.

130 J Kramer and F Deford, *The Game—My 40 Years in Tennis*, page 233

The crowd for the Hoad-Gonzales match at Madison Square Garden was the largest in US tennis history at that time, numbering 15,237. Eventually the series between them ended in June 1958 with Gonzales leading 51-36. Despite Hoad's ongoing sciatic nerve condition, Gonzales spoke of this being his toughest tour, demanding: "Every trick I ever learned, more concentration than was previously required, rigorous conditioning, and lastly, a maximum of determination were needed before Lew was conquered." Gonzales was fond of his rival, calling him a "replica of himself"[131]. Kramer was more concerned with Hoad's overall inconsistency, believing he was "so damn popular with everyone that people in tennis wanted to believe he was better". He went on to say: "Even when Hoad was clobbering Gonzales, Gorgo wanted his friendship and respect."[132]

The contest between Hoad and Gonzales was closer than in previous tours. After the matches in Australia, Hoad extended his lead to 18-9 during stopovers in America, but gradually Gonzales pinned back the lead by the middle of the year. It was difficult contest for the American player, who commented: "I'd replay every match in my mind hours after it was over. Especially those I lost. I'd be mean for days, even scowling at waitresses and strangers on the street. A scowl didn't have much effect on Lew. It's hard to see across the court."[133]

◇◇◇◇◇◇◇

Rosewall returned to America in May 1958, when Kramer set up a number of one-day events as part of the lead-in to the US Pro Championship event held at Forest Hills in June. That was a round-robin tournament, where seven of the top pros faced each other once. There was some novelty about this event as some sessions were played on the grass surface under lights.

Rosewall had wins over Segura and his fellow countrymen Sedgman and Hartwig to remain on even terms. His final round-robin match against Gonzales was postponed for a number of days due to rain but was

131 R Gonzales, *Man With a Racket*, page 204

132 J Kramer and F Deford, *The Game*, page 230. Gonzales was also known as 'Gorgo' to fellow players.

133 R Gonzales, *Man With a Racket*, page 209

eventually played before 8000 people—the largest crowd to turn out during the $15,000 event.

The match was a torrid, exciting encounter (the 36-game opening set alone lasted an hour and 25 minutes) with Gonzales eventually winning 19-17, 5-7, 6-4. At one point Gonzales faced three set points when trailing 6-7, while in the second set Rosewall appeared resigned to defeat at 3-5, but then managed to run off a string of four games. *The New York Times* wrote that Gonzales' victory was due to his "unshakeable fighting qualities and concentration against the entrancing artistry from the little master"[134]. His win guaranteed him the championship.[135]

The grumpiness between Gonzales and Kramer was once more on public display at the US Pro Championship. Kramer told the press: "I'm fed up with Pancho's gripes, his constant demands and repeated holdouts. I can't find out what he wants. I can't make schedules or commitments. I told Pancho that he could buy [his] contract himself if he wanted it at a reasonable price."[136]

The following week a similar round-robin contest took place in Los Angeles, with a similar pattern of results. Rosewall lost to Gonzales 10-8, 0-6, 12-10, but then won relatively convincingly over Hoad 6-4, 6-2 (Hoad failed to win any of his six matches). The surprise was 37-year-old Segura, who had the best win-loss record and ended up winning the tournament.

After Los Angeles the professional troupe travelled to Europe to play tournaments in France, Austria and the United Kingdom. One remarkable match was Rosewall's defeat of Trabert in the final of a tournament at Eastbourne. Rosewall eventually won the match 6-0, 6-2, 6-8, 2-6, 7-5, but it was a dreadful day for Trabert. In the fifth set he took control and led 5-4, 40-love on his serve. On those three points Rosewall hit a clean passing shot, followed by a lucky winner off the wood, and then Trabert dumped a volley into the net. After that run of good fortune, the little

134 *The New York Times*, 23 June 1958

135 The day after losing to Gonzales, Rosewall defeated Hoad (6-2, 9-7), meaning he had a string of victories over Hoad at Forest Hills, including the 1956 US National Championships and 1957 Tournament of Champions. During the course of the 1958 Tournament of Champions, Hoad defeated Gonzales 13-15, 6-3, 6-4.

136 R Gonzales, *Man With a Racket*, page 212

Australian took complete command. A dispirited Trabert fell apart and double faulted on the final point.

After these preliminary tournaments there were major international professional tournaments in Paris and London. The Paris tournament, played on slow, red clay, saw Rosewall beat Sedgman in the semi-finals (6-4, 6-3, 5-7, 6-2), despite holding a poor record against his compatriot. Then he proceeded to defeat Hoad (who beat Gonzales in the semi-finals) in the final by 2-6, 6-2, 6-4, 6-0.

In the 1958 London Professional Indoor tournament, played on indoor boards at the Wembley Empire Pool, saw Rosewall lose to Trabert in the semi-final (7-5, 1-6, 6-1, 1-6, 7-5). The result shows the topsy-turvy nature of the encounter, and it was possibly some recompense for the match played at Eastbourne just a few weeks before. Ultimately, the winner of the Wembley tournament was Frank Sedgman, who beat Gonzales in the semi-final and then Trabert in the final in straight sets (6-4, 6-3, 6-4).

The endless pro tour then resumed with events in Belgium, Sweden, Austria and Spain and a series of tournaments involving Segura, Gonzales, Trabert and Rosewall. At the end of 1958 the top six in the professional rankings were: Gonzales, Hoad, Segura, Trabert, Rosewall and Sedgman.

◇◇◇◇◇◇◇

In late November 1958, after months of discussion and attempts at negotiation, the LTAA voted to bar the Kramer tour group from using any affiliate clubs and courts during events held in Australia. Don Ferguson, the LTAA president, used his casting vote to decide the matter after a special meeting resulted in a 6-6 deadlock. Ferguson was considered Kramer's number-one opponent, and he insisted that any Australian tennis club allowing Kramer to use its courts was "violating international regulations"[137]. His chief gripe was that Kramer's Australia pro tour grossed something like $392,000 earlier in the year, while attendance at Australian amateur events during this time was at embarrassingly low levels.

137 LTAA council minutes, 17 November 1958

As soon as the 1958 Davis Cup Challenge Round was completed, where America won after technically 'employing' the services of Peruvian player Alex Olmedo[138], the two best Australian amateurs—Mal Anderson and Ashley Cooper—became members of the Kramer professional tennis troupe.[139] The professional players commenced their Australian tour with matches in Cairns, Townsville and MacKay. On two of those outings Rosewall scored victories over Gonzales.

> The LTAA ban preventing professionals from using regular tennis stadiums meant that matches on the 1959 pro tour meant were played at Marks Athletic Field in Sydney rather than White City, and the Olympic Cycling Stadium in Melbourne rather than Kooyong. In Brisbane we played at the Exhibition Centre and in Adelaide at the velodrome. The matches played on 6 January 1959 in Sydney were a testimonial benefit for Jack Crawford, the 1933 Wimbledon champion. However, the tennis association wouldn't let us use White City. If it had we would have got even more people and raised more money for Jack Crawford.

Another necessary change was that professional matches were played on a portable plywood court (built by Ralph Symonds, the 'Plywood King' of Australia) that was transported to each of the successive venues. It seemed a good idea, but the court came in various sections and took a full day to set up, and up to three hours to dismantle. Reg Ansett, the father of Ansett Airlines, stepped in to arrange transport of the court about Australia, partly because he felt that Kramer was given a rough deal by the LTAA.

> At this time, the Australian amateur circuit was not doing well. There were some good players, but very few overseas players. There were no Europeans because they did not like playing on grass. Our crowds were good and Kramer's group was making

138 Olmedo had been at a college in the US for four years and therefore able to be recruited to the American team. He won both his singles matches, and was a member of the winning American doubles team.

139 Mervyn Rose, the holder of the French Championships, signed on 20 November 1958

> money, but the LTAA was in poor shape. It was always a full house when either Lew or I played Gonzales, and even years later when Laver turned pro. Us not being able to use the LTAA's facilities probably cost the organisation a lot of money. I assume the 60-40 rule applied where 60 per cent went to the Kramer organisation and 40 per cent to the organisers (for example the state associations). Kooyong members were able to get two seats for the price of one ticket.[140]

During the 1959 Australian tour Rosewall suffered losses to Cooper and Segura, but he hit top form in late January beating Gonzales in the semi-final of a pro event in Brisbane by 6-3, 13 -11, 6-3. He followed this up with a five-set victory over Trabert in the final. That event was followed by events in Perth, Sydney and Adelaide, where there were reports of matches played on 11 February being hampered by an invasion of flying ants. Rosewall defeated Segura that evening, but the open-air wooden court was swarming with insects and the players kept slipping on the nasty intruders. Hoad defeated Rosewall in a close three-set encounter 5-7, 7-5, 6-4, in that tournament.

The five principal Australian tournaments used a points-based system, the outcome of which was: Hoad 13; Rosewall 12; Sedgman 11; Gonzales 10; Cooper three; Trabert two; and Segura two.

◇◇◇◇◇◇◇

Rosewall took a break from play in the first months of 1959, in the lead up to the birth of his and Wilma's first child—Brett, born 9 May 1959—but returned to the pro circuit in June.

> The US tour in 1959 was Hoad and Gonzales, and Cooper and Anderson. This took the form of a round-robin. Even though Lew beat Gonzales more times than he lost to him, he lost a few matches to Anderson and Cooper. On the other hand, Gonzales

140 A matter of dispute between Kramer and the LTAA—council minutes, 20 October 1958

did not lose at all to those players. This meant he was still top player at the end of the 1959 series.

Rosewall entered events in Los Angeles (a round-robin where he beat Gonzales, but lost to Hoad 6-4, 2-6, 6-4[141]) and Toronto in the lead-up to Kramer's 1959 Tournament of Champions in New York. In this hotly contested eight-man elimination tournament, Gonzales and Hoad were the fancied players—the blond, powerful Australian had won 15 out of 28 matches against the American on the 1959 circuit to this point.

In his first match, Rosewall beat Segura in straight sets, showing that the Ecuadorian no longer held fears for him at this level, while Hoad beat Anderson. This meant semi-finals were played between Hoad and Rosewall, and Gonzales and Trabert. Unlike Hoad, who had been touring throughout the year, Rosewall had seen limited competition and was eager to score a victory over his childhood rival. While Hoad eventually won 5-7, 6-4, 7-5, there were trying moments throughout—for example in the first set when Hoad led 5-3 and 40-0, Rosewall scrambled back to prolong the contest. In the final set Hoad trailed 2-4, before being assisted by a vital net cord on the final point of the seventh game. He then won four games in a row to go through to the final. It was nevertheless an excellent performance by Rosewall, and there was no time that Hoad could take anything for granted, despite the superiority of his serving power and groundstrokes. After watching the match Allison Danzig wrote that Rosewall was:

> *One of the cleverest and most knowing of players. Quick as lightning in his reflex action and afoot, he is master of the lob and the dropshot, is highly skilled in volleying from the backhand, and is possessed of the most beautifully fashioned groundstrokes in tennis.*[142]

In the final Hoad blitzed Gonzales 6-1, 5-7, 6-2, 6-1. The 16-minute first set was described as "an opening assault of electrifying violence"[143].

141 Gonzales captured the event, beating Hoad and posting a 5-1 record.

142 *The New York Times*, 28 June 1959

143 *The New York Times*, 29 June 1959

Joe McCauley wrote that it was "Hoad's Rubicon—the zenith of his career"[144]. The Australian had established himself as the king of the pros.

The Tournament of Champions event was now regarded as the main showcase of the pro tour, and Kramer announced that he intended to negotiate with the Professional Lawn Tennis Association for it to be officially recognised as a national championship.

Shortly after Wimbledon that year, a committee of the International Lawn Tennis Federation (ILTF) was established to study open tennis—the result of a proposal by Jean Borotra, the French delegate and former Wimbledon great, who thought the terms 'amateur' and 'professional' should be scrapped. Instead, players were either 'registered' or 'non-registered', with governing national associations remaining in control of the game. According to the proposal, it would be possible for open tournaments to take place with amateurs competing against professionals, a decision that would leave a professional promoter like Kramer out in the cold as top amateur players would no longer have an incentive to shift into pro ranks.

◇◇◇◇◇◇

In the second half of 1959 the pros played the usual series of events throughout Europe, now termed a European professional grand prix (Gonzales, who remained in dispute with Kramer, was absent). The major event was the 1959 London Indoor Professional tournament at Wembley, where Rosewall lost in a semi-final match to Anderson (7-5, 2-6, 4-6, 6-3, 6-4). Anderson, the new boy in the pro ranks, went on to defeat Segura in the final and score his first professional tournament victory. Anderson said he was playing pro tennis so he could buy a farm, and that the £1000 prize money would go towards this dream. Eventually, however, it was Sedgman who won the most matches throughout the 1959 grand prix series in Europe to take first prize. The players returned to Australia in December 1959 with professional rankings issued by the French sports paper *L'Équipe* almost matching Kramer's personal rankings for 1959[145].

144 J McCauley, *The History of Professional Tennis*, page 93

145 *L'Équipe* = Gonzales (number one), Sedgman, Rosewall, Trabert and Hoad.
Kramer = Gonzales (number one), Sedgman, Rosewall, Hoad and Trabert.

◇◇◇◇◇◇◇

In early January 1960 a professional tournament was staged at Kooyong, with Hoad and Rosewall competing in the final (Hoad won 6-3, 10-8, 4-6, 15-13). Going into the Kooyong event Hoad and Gonzales were dead-level in their 1959 series of matches, but Gonzales gave up any chance of winning their contest by choosing to return to the US on New Year's Eve. Therefore Hoad took the overall prize in his one-to-one contest with Gonzales for the 1959 tour. It was at this time that both Hoad and Rosewall entered new seven-year professional contracts (these were in fact verbal agreements) with the Kramer organisation, with any guarantee being based upon the number of tournaments they played.

The politics of open tennis commenced in earnest. The 1960 USLTA annual session at Scottsdale Arizona voted unanimously against the creation of a new class of 'authorised' player, which would permit an amateur to compete for cash prizes. This was a rejection of the Borotra proposal, which hoped to end the hypocrisy of amateurs being paid under-the-table expenses by playing in tournaments[146]. Borotra wanted this new category of authorised player to be a professional in all senses of the word, and yet retain amateur standing and be eligible to play in amateur events and the Davis Cup. Conversely, the USLTA believed that the concept of authorised players made a mockery of the distinction between amateurs and professionals.[147]

With the French proposal approved by a special committee of the ILTF, the USLTA had bought into a serious argument about the future of the game. The association also came under fire when it supported the suggestions that there be a limited number of open tournaments during 1961.[148] If the USLTA failed in its bid to prevent the category of authorised players, there was significant concern that it would withdraw from Davis Cup matches, or else seek an injunction to prevent this category of player from competing in cup matches. American administrators took the view

146 R Gonzales (*Man With a Racket*, page 168) referred to the difference between professional and amateur tennis as "related to a phantom table" with amateurs receiving money under the table, professionals over it.

147 The LTAA considered authorised players as professionals in disguise, council minutes, 3 February 1960

148 Tournament committee head Perry T Jones recommended eight open tournaments sanctioned in various countries in 1961, with the possibility of an additional five. At its annual meeting the USLTA voted that a maximum of 13 open tournaments should be held throughout the world in 1961.

that problems facing the amateur game should not be resolved by the ILTF abandoning its principles and standards. And, unsurprisingly, Kramer was fuming about the proposal, which he regarded as a set-up to take control of the game away from him. To make the Davis Cup a purely amateur event, according to Kramer, would be "like Harvard playing Cambridge, unless they open it to the professionals"[149].

The USLTA's position on open events also played into Kramer's hands. The principal pro promoter now had almost a dozen of the world's leading tennis players under contract, and he indicated that he and his players expected to share in the proceeds of these open tournaments, and to have a say in selecting dates and sites for tournaments.

These developments in America sent reverberations around the tennis world. By early February 1960 the British Lawn Tennis Association (LTA) and the LTAA had voted to support the open tennis proposal. The Australian association's position was that it was cautiously in favour of a limited number of open tournaments being held on a trial basis.

◇◇◇◇◇◇◇

In February, a world professional tennis tour commenced involving Gonzales, Trabert, Olmedo, Rosewall and Segura. Matches were played throughout the US and Canada until the end of March, followed by matches in Australia in May, when Hoad joined the troupe. An interesting aspect of some of the matches was the use of the 'one-bounce' or 'three-bounce' format, used to prevent the dominance of serve-volley players and to guarantee longer rallies. The server was not allowed to approach the net without first taking the return of serve from a bounce at the back of the court, and the receiver was required to hit the shot following his service return off the ground. It was a plan to stop tennis developing into a monotonous spectacle where the server summarily finished off the point when volleying behind a cannonball service.

Anderson and Cooper were not asked to play in the US tour in 1960, while Olmedo had been the best amateur player in 1959

149 *The New York Times*, 4 February 1960

> [and winner of the Wimbledon event]. Pancho [Gonzales] played as well as the others under this new format, even better. He changed his strategy and served bigger. Then he got a weaker return and was able to come to the net after the next shot. For me it was different as I had a slower, softer serve, and depended on the return. It was hard for Olmedo who was a serve-volleyer, and joined the tour only to be faced with these new rules.

Throughout the US matches Gonzales maintained his dominance with a win-loss record of 28-2. Rosewall's record was 16-14. In Australia, Gonzales repeatedly told the press that this was his last tour with the Kramer group. He said he wanted to limit any future play to tennis tournaments and open tennis, if the latter arrived. The American actually withdrew from the final tournament in Melbourne, labelled the 'world title', and Rosewall won the event defeating Hoad in a closely fought final by 6-3, 9 -11, 8-10, 7-5, 6-3. Hoad was not at his best—he suffered a neck sprain during the week and experienced difficulty serving at his best, he also foot faulted 15 times.

Throughout the week the crowd attendance at matches held at the Olympic swimming stadium had been disappointing. On some occasions there were less than 2000 in the 5500-capacity arena. It was true that Melbourne was experiencing a patch of cold, miserable weather, but others wondered whether Australians had seen too much of the pros over recent years. Or was it the absence of Gonzales, whose withdrawal deepened the feud with Kramer, especially when he proceeded to enter another event for a rival promoter in the US.

In June the players took part in a series of events leading up to Kramer's $15,000 Masters Round Robin tournament played at Los Angeles Tennis Club. It was an opportunity for Rosewall to establish his supremacy among the pros and in successive weeks he beat Hoad in a tournament in San Francisco (7-5, 7-5), and then again triumphed over Hoad in Los Angeles (10-12, 6-3, 6-4). Hoad did win against Rosewall at the Santa Barbara Championship (6-1, 4-6, 6-3), while Kramer's keynote event at Forest Hills (previously called the Tournament of Champions) was not held due to poor crowd attendances in previous years.

The ILTF backed away from the tentative moves towards open tennis as the year progressed. At a meeting in Paris it narrowly defeated a motion to stage open tournaments within major countries if they wished[150], even though the US, Britain, France and Australia all supported the proposal. It would now be another seven years before this dream would ultimately be realised. Kramer writes unkindly about that ILTF meeting, stating that one man who was committed to open tennis went to the bathroom when the vote was called, and the USLTA effectively brought about the defeat of the proposal, by voting one way yet lobbying the other.[151]

The major professional events in 1960 were an international pro championship in France (played for the first time at Stade Roland Garros—the famous home of the French Championships), and the London Indoor Professional tournament at Wembley, both played over successive weeks in September. The crowds in Paris embraced this new event, with 6000 turning out to watch the final, where Rosewall beat Hoad 6-2, 2-6, 6-2, 6-1. The result meant that Rosewall had won six of his last seven matches against Hoad. The event was also helped by the fact that Trabert, now a partner in Kramer's tour promotions, had set up residence in Paris, with the aim of strengthening professional tennis in Europe. In 1960 French, Spanish and British players turned pro[152] so the game started to acquire a more international feel.

Another change for pro tennis was the establishment of the International Professional Tennis Players' Association in the middle of the year. This was the first time there had been a working organisation for the pros, along the lines of the Professional Golfers Association. The association's intent was to promote tennis as a 'world game' and it immediately established the Jack Kramer Professional Cup, played between professionals along the lines of the Davis Cup. This arrangement immediately sent the ILTF into apoplexy, who believed it would compete with the Davis Cup.

---

150 Open tennis needed 139 votes out of 209; it got 134.

151 J Kramer and F Deford, *The Game*, page 253. The Turkish delegate had been instructed to vote in favour of the motion and then mistakenly voted against it (*World Tennis*, January 1961). The proposal failed to achieve the required two-thirds majority, partly because "some key voters were either asleep, on the toilet, or booking the evening's entertainment"— C Gorringe, *Holding Court*, page 43

152 Players included Alex Olmedo (Spain), Robert Haillet (France) and Mike Davies (Britain).

Rosewall was voted in unanimously as treasurer of the association, possibly because of his reputation for having "short arms and long pockets"[153]. In the letter pages of *World Tennis* magazine Sedgman sought to refute the assertion that there was a direct link between Kramer and the association. That was fine, responded Gladys Heldman, the feisty editor of the magazine, but what Sedgman's letter did not explain was that every member of the association was actually "an active participant in Jack Kramer's Pro Troupe"[154].

> The players' association was set up partly because Jack started to reduce his financial responsibility for the tour around this time. Trabert became executive director of the association and there was a committee of players involved in decision making. Kramer didn't step away from organisational matters but he wasn't responsible for contracts or anything like that. At the same time we introduced the idea of the Kramer Cup. The proposal was that players would devote their time to this event and any profits would go to the association to help us get other events going.

Rosewall won the 1960 London event at Wembley, which now placed him at the forefront of the professional game, especially in the absence of Gonzales. In the semi-finals he destroyed Alex Olmedo (6-0, 6-0, 6-3) while the crowd "fidgeted embarrassingly"[155] on the Peruvian's part, and then in the final he beat Segura 5-7, 8-6, 6-1, 6-3. The description of the play at Wembley suggested that the gap in standards between amateur and professional games was widening. Even though there was a downward trend in attendances everywhere, *The Times* correspondent suggested there was still a market for professional lawn tennis in Britain—there were crowds of more than 8000 for each of the finals nights at the Wembley event. John Barrett recalls the semi-final match against Olmedo when Rosewall won the first 15 games. One of Barrett's colleagues commented

153 J McCauley, *The History of Professional Tennis*, page 107

154 *World Tennis*, February-March 1961

155 J McCauley, *The History of Professional Tennis*, page 103

to Rosewall: "That was amazing! Do you realise you only made four errors the entire match?" "Three," Rosewall quickly corrected, and proceeded to list them.[156]

Later in the year the pro group played in events throughout Asia, and in Tokyo a crowd of more than 12,000 enthusiastic fans (and on one evening the Crown Prince and Princess of Japan) turned out to watch Hoad and Rosewall belting the ball back and forth. In that match Hoad prevailed, 6-2, 0-6, 3-6, 6-1, 13-11. In the final set there were no service breaks until Hoad finally broke to take a 12-11 lead. There was revenge for Hoad as he had taken second place to Rosewall in most recent encounters. Regrettably, however, this hard-fought final caused Hoad's back problems to recur, and he was unable to play in the final tournament of the year in Manila.

> During 1960 Wilma and I moved from the home unit where we were living in Neutral Bay up to the north shore and Pymble. We found a little colonial house in Maryvale Lane and we lived there for six years. Later, we moved to another house in Pymble close to the golf course, which was the main place the boys grew up.

◇◇◇◇◇◇◇

In early 1961 Kramer fired cannon shots at the state of the amateur game, pointing out that there were less than 100 spectators at a semi-final match of the Australian Championships doubles in Melbourne. He commented that administrators were prepared to give their players anything to keep them amateur, and this surely made the top amateur players pros. Having pretty much cornered the market on the world's best players, it was now Kramer who was the principal advocate for open tennis, and the nature of the concept changed because of his involvement (as this may have meant him controlling the game).

Allison Danzig observed that Kramer probably wanted more than prize money for his players, and this included commitments about additional open tournaments. The veteran journalist counselled that Kramer would

156 Interview with author, 11 June 2012

be unwise if he insisted on a schedule of open competition that wrecked amateur competition. He was highly critical of Kramer by this point, suggesting he was effectively destroying the game with his view that open tennis was his salvation, and therefore going to any lengths to achieve it.

As it turned out, Kramer cancelled a proposed Australian tour with his pro troupe in February 1961, mainly because the players were again banned from using amateur facilities. On this occasion it was a new president of the LTAA, Norman Strange, who cast the deciding vote against Kramer, citing the promoter's decision to sign leading European amateurs and a concern about the impact of the Kramer Cup on the amateur game. It was an odd decision considering the LTAA and state associations stood to benefit from the rental of their facilities. Strange subsequently justified his position by saying that he was being challenged for the LTAA presidency later in the year, and he needed to vote with Queensland and New South Wales delegates to ensure their support for his presidency ambitions.

By mid-1961, there was a recognised state of crisis in the amateur game. One day only 25 spectators turned up to watch the French Championships, and the crowds at events during the Australian season were abysmal. Kramer argued that the amateur administrators were destroying the game by seeking to control tennis and refusing to sanction open tournaments. On the other hand, his ongoing attempts to sign-up the best players from across the globe made him persona non grata among national associations. Australia, which supported the open tournament proposal in 1960, now indicated that it would fight the same proposal scheduled for discussion in Stockholm in July 1961.

It was interesting to see just how disliked Kramer had become with Australia's tennis officials. The president of the Queensland Lawn Tennis Association (QLTA), 'Big Bill' Edwards, included an attack on Kramer in the official program for the Queensland Championships in 1960:

> *There was a time when there was plenty of room for both amateur and professional, but the professionals appear to be bent on killing the amateur game, and as they have thrown down the gauntlet, we must*

pick it up. Professional tennis at one time contributed approximately £25,000 to amateur associations from their gates (today they would only bring £6000), but the damage that has been caused to the amateur game by the professionals far outweighs any financial benefits from matches. Professional tennis has lost its appeal and can no longer draw the crowds some of the players with big amateur names attracted in the past, despite their policy of attempting to denude the amateur ranks of players. Whilst the professional circus was limited to six players, we had a chance to develop up and coming players and this kept both games well in the public eye, but the latest moves of the professionals appear to be designed to harm the amateur game. Players have been taken from a number of countries and the latest approach to Laver and Fraser, and the introduction of the Kramer Cup, appears to be intended to hurt amateur tennis. The professional players seem to forget that it was the amateur game that gave them their start and made them famous personalities. The way they are going, however, they could end up with a lot of players and no courts.[157]

Edwards believed that the pros were out to crush the amateur game, and he made it known that he would fight Kramer tooth and nail. 'Big Bill' was an interesting character. Weighing more than 300 pounds, when he visited Sydney to watch the tennis they made special arrangements for a chair in the stands, which on all other occasions seated two people.

The USLTA (together with Britain and France) continued to support the idea of open tennis, and spoke of holding up to nine open events including five national championships in 1962. The LTAA's belief that Kramer was out to control the game was not helped when he spoke about major open events having to conform to his schedule, requesting he be consulted about seedings, and that there be minimum prize money of $10,000.

In 1961 Rosewall took a period of leave from the professional tour and did not return until the European events played immediately before the fifth annual French Pro Championships (a tournament on hard courts) in the second half of the year. There were no Australian professional events

157 *World Tennis*, February-March 1961

as the amateur officials steadfastly refused to allow the pros the use of their courts. Between November 1960 and August 1961, Rosewall relaxed at home in Sydney and did not play tennis at all.

◇◇◇◇◇◇◇

Once again the Kramer professional tournament at Forest Hills was not staged in 1961, so the major pro events for the year were the French Championships and the London Indoor Professional tournament at Wembley. The French tournament was again played at Stade Roland Garros in mid-September, and partly under lights. The finalists were Gonzales and Rosewall, after Gonzales beat Trabert (6-3, 6-0, 6-4) and Rosewall beat Segura (4-6, 6-1, 6-4, 7-5) in the semi-finals. Gonzales was at his most ruthless in his match against Trabert, refusing to relax, concede a shot, or crack a smile. According to Robert Daley of *The New York Times*:

> *Gonzales never smiled. Instead he told off ball boys, photographers and linesmen respectively. Once, though Trabert had not won a game for 20 minutes, Gonzales rushed the umpire shouting: 'Don't you call it, let the linesman call it.' The crowd—it numbered more than 10,000 outdoors on a very hot, sunny day—booed and hissed him. He never acknowledged the crowd in any way, nor Trabert either, except to blast the ball even more viciously across the net. When the match ended Gonzales posed 20 seconds for photographers, then snapped: 'That's enough' and stalked icily into the dressing room. He never addressed a word to Trabert. He has long been feuding with the Jack Kramer organisation of which Trabert is the European representative. The feud is obviously deep and real.*[158]

The final was uphill work for Rosewall, who lost the first set 2-6, but then won the next three 6-4, 6-3, 8-6. In the first set Daley wrote that Rosewall looked like a little boy as he was talking to himself and giving himself pep talks as Gonzales thumped the ball past him. But when Rosewall broke the big man's serve in the second set Gonzales began to

158 *The New York Times*, 17 September 1961

snap angrily at the linesmen, ball boys and also the crowd. Gonzales' shots, which before had clipped the lines, began to miss while Rosewall stepped up and began to hit magnificent passing shots. It was all a bit much for the 35-year-old Gonzales who gradually wilted with fatigue. McCauley wrote the Australian's "nimbleness made the great Gonzales look positively pedestrian by comparison"[159]. As soon as the match finished, Gonzales announced his retirement from pro tournaments, saying he was going to coach tennis at a resort in the Bahamas, but would possibly return to play in *open* competitions. The Paris event was a wonderful success for Rosewall and professional tennis. There were 35,000-40,000 spectators through the turnstiles in four days.

At the 1961 Wembley tournament the following week Rosewall won the final over Hoad by 6-3, 3-6, 6-2, 6-3, in what was his third victory in this major event. Again the world's top professionals had to adjust from slow clay to indoor boards in a matter of days. Hoad played a marvellous semi-final to beat Gonzales 4-6, 13-11, 6-3, 6-2, and it was always going to be difficult to recover his full mobility within 24 hours for the final. After his victory Rosewall spoke of wanting to see the fledgling sport of professional tennis firmly established in major international centres, and that included doing whatever he could to get the game properly developed in Australia.

Winning the two major professional events that year meant Rosewall now supplanted Gonzales at the top of the tree of pro players. *L'Équipe* rankings for 1961 were Rosewall, Gonzales, Hoad, Trabert and Segura.

> In 1961 the pro tour in the US was between Barry MacKay and Butch Buchholz, and Gonzales and Andres Gimeno. Hailing from Spain, Gimeno had recently joined the group, and also Luis Ayala from Chile. We were getting more players. I was at home for most of 1961 as Wilma had our second child in August. I then left home to play in Europe, including some Kramer Cup matches in Barcelona and South Africa. This cup event saw players competing in four zones: Segura, Olmedo and Ayala

159 J McCauley, *The History of Professional Tennis*, page 111

(South America); Gonzales, Buchholz and MacKay (North America); Gimeno, Mike Davies and Robert Haillet (Europe); and myself, Hoad, Anderson and Cooper (Australia). The final was held in South Africa. People criticised pro tennis, but South Africa developed an interest in the game mainly because of the professionals touring there.

None of the players got paid for their participation in the Kramer Cup, and we even paid for our own trophy. Trabert organised for a gold trophy to be made in Paris, which cost $6000—Hoad, Segura, Sedgman, Kramer, Trabert and I put in $1000 each. We got our money back from the association's funds, and the competition lasted another two years.

Sadly, the trophy ended up in my house from 1963 until 1970. Then in 1970 Mike Davies, who by that time was working with Lamar Hunt of World Championship Tennis (WCT), rang and told me that WCT was going to have a championship event and needed a trophy.

It was probably one of the worst decisions I ever made handing over that trophy! I mean Lamar was worth millions and millions. Also that was when gold was worth $39 dollars an ounce. It's now worth about $1600 an ounce. So Lamar Hunt got the trophy that came from our little association (which was already defunct by then). I was actually a great supporter of Lamar and WCT. But I regret that I didn't talk to some of the other players about what we were going to do with that Kramer Cup trophy. There's not much use crying over spilt milk I guess! The same trophy is now in the International Tennis Hall of Fame at Newport.

The semi-finals of the Kramer Cup were played in Barcelona, and resulted in victories to the Australian and the North American zones—the final was played in Johannesburg, South Africa, where Australia beat North America by three matches to two. Around 4000 South African fans attended matches in the brand new Ellis Park Stadium on the first night in spite of threatening weather. As the match between Hoad and MacKay commenced the rain was little more than a drizzle, but after 40 minutes it was pelting down and the players had to quit.

> *The crowd held their seats, and 40 minutes later the rain stopped. Ground crews promptly went to work with the stadium's newest and proudest acquisition—a water-sucking vacuum cleaner. Thirsty as it was, however, the vacuum couldn't devour all the water that lay on the special all-weather court. As the ranks of impatient spectators began to thin, one of the officials had a sudden inspiration. Grabbing a microphone, he issued a plea to everyone in the stands with a pocket handkerchief. If, he begged, each man would just mop three-square inches they would soon have the whole court dry. Within seconds 400 or more tennis fans were on their hands and knees mopping industriously. Ten minutes later the court was dust-dry—and then it began to rain again.* [160]

After that everyone called it quits for the night. During the next two days rain threatened but somehow held off. In five matches of sometimes superb tennis, the Australian team of Hoad and Rosewall defeated the Americans—Trabert, Buchholz and MacKay (Pancho Gonzales finally did retire)—to become the first winners of the Kramer Cup. But after the big mop-up of the first night it seemed almost an anticlimax.

Later in 1961 the pro circuit travelled to events in Europe—including Russia for the first time—before returning to Australia in mid-December. At around this time there was an opportunity for the LTAA to remove its ban on pros using association courts and facilities. Three major states, New South Wales, Victoria and South Australia, were in favour of removing the ban and sporting commentators suggested that the ban was a complete farce: amateur tennis by this stage was not a major spectator sport and the revenue generated from leasing the facilities could only have assisted the struggling associations.[161]

At about this time it was reported that Rod Laver and Roy Emerson, Australia's recently victorious team in the Davis Cup Challenge Round

160 *Sports Illustrated*, 20 November 1961

161 The ban was finally removed at a special meeting of the LTAA on 10 November 1962

against Italy, would be offered pro contracts with the Kramer group as the tour commenced its journey through Australia in January 1962. Laver ultimately did not join the tour, and instead the year marked his greatest performances as an amateur and was notable for him winning the grand slam.[162] There was ongoing talk of Laver joining the professional group once Australia had defended the Davis Cup at the end of the year. But in spite of Laver's dominance of the amateur game, it was understood that he might have trouble winning consistently in his first year as a pro. Only Kramer had ever actually won his first series as a pro when he defeated Bobby Riggs in 1948. Other players, like Sedgman, Gonzales, Trabert, Rosewall and Hoad, had been soundly thrashed in their first seasons as professionals.[163]

The pro circuit had a difficult year in 1962. Gonzales had retired and Kramer withdrew from being a full time promoter, shutting down his Los Angeles office and leaving some international matters to be managed by Trabert from Paris. In a discussion with Segura, Kramer said: "I tried everything and nothing ever worked. There's nothing more I can do. I've got to get out or we'll never see an open game."[164] Without these two dominant personalities there was concern the pro game might fade away, open tennis still seemed a long way off and, for the first time since World War II, there was no pro tennis tour in the US.

The year started with three professional tournaments in Australia, and Rosewall won them all. But the absence of any pro tournaments in the US meant the French Championships and the London Indoor Professional tournament at Wembley were the major events in 1962.

> We did play some pro tour matches through autumn and winter in Europe with myself, Lew, MacKay, Olmedo, Buchholz and Anderson. Once again these were organised by Pat Hughes of the Dunlop organisation.

---

162 Laver was the first male player since Don Budge in 1938 to win men's singles events in the championships of Australia, France and the US, and Wimbledon.

163 In these cases the pro tennis tour was a head-to-head contest between the new pro and the reigning champion. Kramer defeated Gonzales 96-27 in 1949; Kramer defeated Sedgman 54-41 in 1953; Gonzales defeated Trabert 74-27 in 1955-56; Gonzales defeated Rosewall 51-26 in 1957; and Gonzales defeated Hoad 51-38 in 1958.

164 J Kramer and F Deford, *The Game—My 40 Years in Tennis*, page 258

In the final of the French Championships, Rosewall beat Gimeno to win 3-6, 6-2, 7-5, 6-2. He then played in the Wembley tournament with a chance of securing a hat-trick of titles, the first time this had happened since Gonzales in 1950-52. In the semi-final Rosewall won a close match against Segura (6-3, 4-6, 3-6, 7-5, 6-4) even though he was down a match point at one stage[165]. Segura drove players to distraction with his clever, angular game, drawing his opponents out of court, and then finishing things off with a powerful, double-handed forehand. *The Times* described their encounter as a "magnetic affair" that was "full of uncertainty, and still replete with artistry and perfection"[166]. The result placed him in his fourth Wembley final in six years, and third in succession. Just as in 1961, Rosewall met Hoad in the final. And, as in the previous year, he won the match against Hoad by 6-4, 5-7, 15-13, 7-5. McCauley describes the match as "one of the all-time great finals"[167].

> There was some very good tennis played at Empire Pool [built for the 1938 Empire and Commonwealth Games], where the Wembley tournament was played, even though the surface was not all that good. We played across the boards not with the boards, and sometimes the boards warped. Also, because the boards were on top of a pool the game was not as fast as if laid on a flat surface. I always played well there, and Sedgman and Gonzales played a great final there in 1956.
>
> They had established a pro tennis tournament at Wembley from before World War II and Tilden, Budge and Perry played, although it was mainly exhibition in those times. It was Kramer's idea to make the game more competitive.

In the dying days of 1962 the pros returned to Australia and the Kramer Cup was played once more, this time in Adelaide. On this occasion the

165 In Rosewall's quarter-final match he just recovered from 2-5, 0-30 down against Cooper in the deciding set.

166 *The Times*, 21 September 1962

167 J McCauley, *The History of Professional Tennis*, page 119

Australians defeated a South American zone team of Segura and Olmedo in the final.

There was little question that Rosewall had now established himself as the best professional player in the world as he won seven of eight tournaments held during the year. Descriptions of his play refer to the "little master" playing with "the clinical accuracy of a surgeon", with his shots angled to "the last refined inch"[168].

168 *Washington Post*, 4 February 1963

CHAPTER 5

THE 'ROCKET' TAKES OFF

The slowdown in events during 1962 seemed to signal the demise of the pro game and was the reason why Rosewall and Hoad made a personally guaranteed offer to Rod Laver encouraging him to move into the pro ranks in 1963. This move was more or less a direct result of Kramer's decision to depart from pro tennis management, leaving the scheduling of tournaments to the fledgling International Professional Tennis Players' Association. It was clear that if pro players wanted to tempt a leading amateur into their ranks they had to chip in themselves. Big Jake remained on hand to help out in some specialist events and Trabert continued to oversee arrangements from his base in Europe.

Rosewall and Hoad offered Laver $110,000 for 13 months pro play, and while he expressed some concern as to whether the pair could make good on their personal guarantee, or whether he would have even held them to it, he said: "Their sincerity impressed me, as well as their belief that if we could just keep it going some day pro tennis would thrive as a significant sport."[169] Ultimately, an agreement was reached with Hoad and Rosewall taking a reduced cut of gate receipts in order to make way for Laver.

Laver's amateur status during the 1962 Davis Cup was possibly compromised when large billboards appeared in Sydney advertising his professional debut against Rosewall, while his name was printed in the official program of the International Professional Tennis Players' Association and a Dunlop racket bearing his autograph was manufactured.

> The plan was for Laver to play professional matches in Australia in January 1963, and then be part of the American professional tour commencing in February, however, 1962 had been a delicate year. We had some help organising pro tournaments in Australia from Dinny Pails, but we weren't making much money.
>
> At this stage Gonzales wasn't playing because he had gone off to a coaching position, although that did not last all that long. We all knew we had to get Rod involved. There were some negotiations with him during the year. At one stage we were playing in France and Rod was playing in an event close by and I went to see him.
>
> Rod was quite interested. He felt that he had won everything in amateur tennis and wanted to play against Lew, myself and Gonzales before we all got too old. It just probably went from there. It was more or less a 'shake-hands' thing, although we provided him with a contract when we got back to Australia. I committed to play a lot of tennis in 1963, while Lew played matches in Australia and we made a lot of money out of that.

In Australia, at the outset of his pro career, Laver was unable to match the skills of the experienced pros and lost three times to Rosewall and twice to Hoad. Commenting on a 64-minute match[170] Rosewall said: "Laver's contract demands that he be in the best physical condition, and that he concentrate entirely on tennis. I think he has spent too much time recently

169 Max Roberston (ed), *The Encyclopaedia of Tennis*, page 65

170 Rosewall won the first match against Laver by 6-3, 6-3, 6-4

playing golf. He had better stick to tennis from now on, if he wants to realise his possibilities."[171]

Perhaps these results showed the difference between the level of tennis at amateur and professional levels, and the disservice amateur officials were doing by depriving the spectators of the opportunity to see open tennis. Why continue to allow the artificial and hypocritical 'amateur' distinctions, asked some papers. Like most first-timers the Rocket was having trouble catching up with his pro rivals—the term 'Rocket' was initially coined by Harry Hopman, who actually said he was anything but a rocket, although he was willing to work harder than most other players. Trabert explained the difficulties Laver was experiencing:

> *Laver had perhaps one or two tough matches a week when he was an amateur, and [that] caliber of competition could not compare with what Laver is getting now. In this tour every match is a tough one. But Laver will catch on, as Gonzales, Sedgman, Hoad and Rosewall did.*[172]

Finally Laver broke through his 'duck' record as a pro when he defeated Rosewall in a match at Kooyong before 15,000 people on 19 January 1963. He won 6-3, 3-6, 7-5, 6-2 after suffering eight successive losses to Rosewall. During those matches in January, Laver won only two out of 17 contests against Hoad and Rosewall (with both wins being against Rosewall). When the pro circuit reached America and matches commenced on the east coast, Rosewall told the press he was convinced Laver would improve, just as he himself had: "Since 1956 I must have improved at least 25 per cent over what I was as an amateur."[173]

Laver started to become concerned about the catastrophic start to his professional campaign. In what was dubbed the 'American World Series of Tennis' at Madison Square Garden in February, Laver lost three successive matches, including a 12-10 pro set loss to Rosewall. The red-headed grand slam winner apparently lost five pounds from worry, and was distressed by the ongoing losses. He commented:

171 *The New York Times*, 15 January 1963

172 *Washington Post*, 6 February 1963

173 *Washington Post*, 8 February 1963

This is a different game entirely. The conditions are strange to me in almost every way. For instance at Boston [the match] was played on a floor that was uneven and we got bad bounces. At Philadelphia [it] was played on canvas stretched over ice and I thought my legs from the knees down would freeze. And at the Garden some fans started fighting in the balcony and the distraction was terrible. These are things the other fellows are used to. I am not. I'm not complaining. I just say it is going to take time to adjust.[174]

I don't remember Rod being affected by stress quite like that. When you're playing you lose weight because it's hectic.

It was during this tournament at Madison Square Garden that a watchman stopped Rosewall as he was about to enter the arena and asked him who he was. "I'm Ken Rosewall, one of the tennis players," said Ken. "Ok then, but you're awful small to be a tennis player," the guard replied.[175]

◇◇◇◇◇◇◇

Things did improve for Laver. By mid-April 1963, he held second place on the US circuit after Rosewall. The circuit now comprised a number of other players like Barry MacKay, Butch Buchholz, Andres Gimeno and Luis Ayala[176]. The playing conditions were getting more consistent—during the North American tour a canvas court was transported and installed at each site, meaning that the bounce of the ball was pretty much the same wherever they played. In May the pros returned to Madison Square Garden for a play-off series of matches that was part of the national tour. This was also part of the 20-match contest between Laver and Rosewall for first prize money of $35,000. By the time they reached New York, Laver had won three out of 10 meetings with the professional champion.

The match itself was a remarkable turnaround in form as Laver crushed his fellow countryman 6-0, 6-3. In the first set Rosewall appeared listless,

174 *Washington Post*, 12 February 1963

175 Recounted in P Rowley, *Twenty Years at the Top*, page 100

176 By this time there had been approximately 35 stops on the US circuit. Hoad was not participating in 1963.

with little answer to the slashing topspin drives of Laver. The first set took just 13 minutes, with Laver conceding only nine points. It was something of a wake-up call for Rosewall as Laver now appeared fully focused on his pro tennis career. Rosewall won the next four of their contests to clinch the pro tennis championship[177]. On some occasions the matches were played before a trickle of tennis fans, like when Rosewall beat Laver 6-1, 6-3 at Medford, Oregon, before a paltry audience of 300.

During 1963 Rod played a lot, even when he was injured to some degree. I committed to play all the US circuit and also through Europe, which meant it was a busy year for me. Rod was great for the pro game, and he played a lot of matches against me, Hoad and Gonzales.

The pro circuit in the US was now organised by Trabert, as the executive director of our group, and Kramer was out of the picture, at least in a financial sense. He remained fully involved organising tournaments and committed to the growth of the pro game. There were six players playing matches against each other in cities across the US. After a certain number of matches during the pro circuit the bottom two were eliminated (MacKay and Ayala). Then, after 20 or so more matches, Rod and I played off for first place; Gimeno and Buchholz played for third and fourth.

I wouldn't say the 1963 tour was a complete success. In those days you had to pay all your own expenses and it was still a case of jumping in a car overnight to get to different destinations about the country. With no sponsorship, the money in the kitty all depended on the number of tickets sold. Olen Parkes was on hand as the court announcer, and we had an equipment man to help the locals lay and dismantle the court.

In the middle part of the year, after the pro circuit was over, Wilma came to America with the boys: Brett was about four and Glenn was one and a half. We were able to spend some time

177 Defeating Laver 6-2, 6-2 in Eugene, Oregon (22 May 1963) giving Rosewall an 11-4 lead on the US tour.

> together at the John Gardiner Tennis Ranch in Carmel Valley, California. It was the first of the live-in tennis ranches to be successful and we were able to stay there for a couple of weeks before the summer tournaments.
>
> After the pro circuit Kramer once again became involved in organising the US Professional Grass Court Championships at Forest Hills. There were further issues with Gonzales at this event, including him being paid appearance money by the organisers. That didn't sit well with the rest of us who weren't getting paid this fee. Then there were the problems with the draw.

Both Gonzales and Hoad returned for the 1963 US Professional Grass Court event, and it marked the return of the pros to Forest Hills—they had not been there since Kramer staged the last of his promotions in 1958. The event, with 12 participants, was an elimination tournament, rather than a round-robin.

The volatile Gonzales arrived in New York in a swell of controversy. He was annoyed that the draw for the event had been remade (promoters had apparently made up the draw without seeking the agreement of the players), with him being shifted from Laver's half into Rosewall's side of the draw. Trabert, the head of the professional organisation, told the press that his suggestions about seeding had not reached the promoters before the original draw was made and, as a result, a new draw was made. Gonzales, however, believed this was all part of a conspiracy against him by Trabert. The fiery American player had just lost a court case against the Professional Tennis Association, after he and Segura entered a contract to make a television series about coaching tennis that was in competition with a series being made by the association.

Gonzales, who was not in 'match-fit' condition, lost his first encounter in the Forest Hills event to Olmedo (10-8, 2-6, 6-0, 6-1). Hoad was another first round loser—beaten in straight sets by Buchholz. That week in June 1963 was a hot and unpleasant week in New York, and the crowds stayed away. One newspaper referred to "fewer than 1000 looking on apathetically"[178] as Rosewall defeated Trabert 6-2, 6-2, 6-2 in one early match. By this time it was acknowledged that Rosewall and Laver were the best professional players, and it was fitting that they played off the final. Fortunately, the crowds did pick up for that match. Allison Danzig wrote that 5000 people endured sultry, threatening weather to witness "an unforgettable exposition of the art, science and vigor of lawn tennis at its finest". This was Rosewall at his best as he sliced and chopped the Rocket to pieces. The final score was 6-4, 6-2, 6-2. Danzig, always one of Rosewall's great admirers, wrote:

> *The match was no contest after the first set, with Laver's mighty strokes reduced to ruin as his confidence was destroyed and his touch fled. The authority and almost infallible precision with which the calculating Rosewall disarmed the youth who completed his grand slam on the same turf as the world amateur champion, exerted a fascinating spell, however.*
>
> *It was one of the most harrowing, unhappy days Laver has known. Rosewall kept him under merciless, continuing pressure that brought his game to the point of almost total collapse.*[179]

There was not a happy ending to the match financially for either of the players, when they discovered the cheques they received had bounced due to insufficient funds.[180]

> The only one that got any money from that event was Gonzales, because he received his $5000 appearance fee!

◇◇◇◇◇◇◇

The last time the Kramer Cup was played was in Dublin in September 1963, when an Australian team of Rosewall, Laver and Sedgman (who played doubles with one or other of his stellar compatriots), first beat North America and then South America (Olmedo and Ayala) in the final.

---

178 *The New York Times*, 29 June 1963

179 *The New York Times*, 1 July 1963

180 *The New York Times*, 27 November 1971

After that match the trophy ended up in a cupboard in Rosewall's house for a number of years, before Rosewall handed it to Lamar Hunt of WCT.

The following week Rosewall and Laver reached the final of the French Pro Championships after a journey that clearly demonstrated their growing rivalry and ongoing superiority over rivals. By the end of spring 1963, Laver was able to beat Hoad most times, and also managed victories over Rosewall. He won professional events in Cannes, Kitzbühel (Austria) and Noordwijk (Holland).

Rosewall had won the Paris event the previous two years on clay at Stade Roland Garros, but this year the tournament was shifted indoors to Stade Coubertin, a stadium used primarily as a basketball arena. It provided "an intimate kind of tennis"[181] with spectators perched close to the action. The noise of the battle was exaggeratedly loud and the ball bounced low and fast. This was another victory to Rosewall. It was an extraordinary five-set match, with Rosewall succeeding by 6-8, 6-4, 5-7, 6-3, 6-4. But just setting out the score in this way fails to indicate the struggle Rosewall put up as he came back from 1-4 in the fifth set.

> Well, I don't actually remember this match! I can remember matches when I was leading in the fifth set against Laver and lost. That happened once in Paris and once at Wembley.

In September 1963 Trabert announced that he planned to abandon tennis, both as a player and as a promoter, because he had obtained a business position and wanted to spend more time with his family, but newspaper reports also spoke of there being trouble with other pros.[182] Trabert's decision was effective from 1 November 1963 and once again the Professional Tennis Players Association took over management of the tour with Rosewall named acting manager.[183]

181 *The New York Times*, 15 September 1963

182 *The New York Times*, 17 September 1963. Trabert later wrote that he appreciated Gonzales' tennis ability, but never came to respect him as a person. "Too often have I witnessed him treat people badly without a cause" *Trabert on Tennis—The View from the Centre Court*, page 113

183 According to Butch Buchholz, Trabert's decision meant arrangements were made to assist in the management of events. Frank Sedgman played a role in Australia and Pat Hughes in England. Later, Barry MacKay and Buchholz took on management roles in the US. Interview with author, 30 May 2012

For Rosewall the 1963 London Indoor Professional tournament was the icing on the cake. He won the event for the fourth successive time, defeating Hoad in the final, 6-4, 6-2, 4-6, 6-3. *The Times* wrote that two things were clear after the match—while Rosewall might have been the undisputed reigning champion among the professional players, it was Hoad who was the popular favourite of the rank and file. Nevertheless, the result shows that Rosewall won this most lucrative of professional titles for the fourth year in succession and the fifth time overall. He had now outdone anything Gonzales achieved at Wembley. At the same time some picky and critical commentators wondered whether the tennis crowds had ever really warmed to a person they described as "an unobtrusive little man", notwithstanding his obvious genius. "Perhaps he has been too disciplined, too exact, too coldly clinical, lacking the comforting human frailties of Hoad and others. But there is no denying that he is the supreme surgeon."[184]

◇◇◇◇◇◇◇

The pro tennis players played through the Australian summer in January and February 1964, with Rosewall and Laver being the most successful players. The most important early tournament in the American season was an event in May at the Westchester County Center in White Plains, New York, billed as the United States Professional Indoor Championships. This proved to be the only appearance of the professional players in the metropolitan region of New York City during the year. It was an elimination tournament with 12 players, including Rosewall, Hoad, Gonzales and Laver, and Kramer had some involvement with management of the event. On this occasion Gonzales was better prepared—he defeated Laver and then Hoad to qualify for the final against Rosewall.

Gonzales was now to face the man who had assumed his position as the world's leading tennis player. Somewhat ridiculously, this notable encounter was played before a crowd of fewer than 500. It was a remarkable match, lasting three hours and 11 minutes. At one stage Gonzales trailed 5-7, 3-6, and 1-4 in the third set. He was down two service breaks in that set, but the turning point came in the next game. The big man from Los Angeles

184 *The Times*, 23 September 1963

thumped back a succession of strong service returns, while Rosewall carelessly missed a number of apparently easy volleys to drop his service. From that point on, Gonzales appeared to relax, while Rosewall retreated into himself and was unable to break the American's service. Eventually the American secured a victory, 5-7, 3-6, 10-8, 11-9, 8-6.

> During 1964 Kramer helped us run a lot of other tournaments—even though he had been out of the game for a year or so. We had a lot more players and were able to have a 14- or 16-man tournament. We wanted to build up a circuit, and we were helped out by the New England Merchants Bank in Boston and their PR man Ed Hickey. He went to Jack and said he would put up $10,000 prize money and $2500 in expenses to organise a tournament at Longwood Cricket Club, outside Boston. It was then that Jack and the players organised other tournaments. Buchholz planned a tournament in St Louis, his hometown; John Gardiner organised an event in Monterey that was held in a fairground; Jack organised an event at the Los Angeles Tennis Club; and there was another one in Milwaukee.
>
> These tournaments were all run along the same lines, with $10,000 prize money, and played in the lead-up to the event in Boston (the US Pro Championships at Longwood Cricket Club). This was the first year you could say we had a proper circuit of pro events, but we couldn't follow it up the following year.

At the tournament at the Los Angeles Tennis Club, organised by Kramer and played as a round robin, Rosewall defeated Gonzales 4-6, 6-2, 6-4. He then beat Sedgman in the final match by 6-2, 6-4. The same thing happened in St Louis—Rosewall defeated Gonzales in the semi-final before beating Sedgman in the final. Those results confirmed Rosewall's status as the leader of the pack on the tour. It was at around this time that Gonzales started telling crowds that the reason for the Australians' success was that they drank "kangaroo juice"[185].

185 *St Louis Post-Dispatch*, 14 June 1964

In July 1964 the US Pro Championships was played at Longwood Cricket Club. This same tournament went broke when staged at Forest Hills the year before. Here, Laver upset Rosewall in the semi-final to earn himself a place in the final against Gonzales. Laver called this his first 'big' win over Rosewall, and even makes some allowance for the fact that Rosewall was suffering from food poisoning on the day. Laver also believed Rosewall was cross, partly because the tournament winner was to receive $2,200, a huge prize at the time. The final was played out in a continuous drizzle, and a sopping wet gallery of 2,300 watched on rather uncomfortably as Laver defeated Gonzales 4-6, 6-3, 7-5, 6-4.

At around the same time there was an ILTF meeting in Vienna, where the LTA and the All England Club asked that the Wimbledon Championships in 1965 be conducted as an open tournament. This was possibly the start of the British leading all future moves towards open tennis.

Rosewall's run of ill fortune continued in a follow up event played in London. This was called the Golden Racquet Professional Tennis Tournament, and Rosewall lost a semi-final match to Hoad (played in a professional format) by 8-1. Here Gonzales beat Laver in their semi-final 8-5, and then proceeded to defeat Hoad 0-6, 6-4, 9-7. The tournament had some interest for pro tennis as the sport came under royal patronage for the first time, with the Duke of Edinburgh on hand to present the winner's prize.

◇◇◇◇◇◇◇

The players' association selected Buchholz to direct a series of pro tournaments in the US during April, May and June 1965, having successfully managed the Volkswagon Championship of St Louis. Throughout this period Rosewall had been at the forefront of the players' association, and Kramer spoke of him as the best organisational man the pros had ever had. He did not insist on a bigger share of association earnings for himself and this made eight-man tours and 12-man tournaments possible. Kramer also referred to Rosewall as the hardest worker in the pro group: "He handles all the finances accurately and diligently, and he can tell you just how every penny has been spent."[186]

186 *World Tennis*, April 1965

Things improved for Rosewall in Paris in September when he won the final of the French Championships against Laver (6-3, 7-5, 3-6, 6-3). The match of the tournament was said to be Rosewall's semi-final battle with his old adversary, Gonzales. That was a three-hour encounter, which Rosewall finally won 4-6, 6-2, 5-7, 7-5, 6-2. At one point Gonzales hurt himself when chasing down a Rosewall return. The little Australian showed no mercy and proceeded to "run him ragged"[187]. It was his fifth successive triumph in Paris.

The players then returned to London for the Wembley indoor event. Here, Rosewall reached the final after beating Sedgman, while Laver beat Gonzales in the other semi-final match. It was a great opportunity for a showcase match between Rosewall and Laver: the world's champion and the chief pretender to the throne. Rosewall was also seeking his fifth Wembley title in succession and sixth overall. In fact, he had never lost a *final* match at the Empire Pool.[188] But Laver's record during the course of 1964, at least until the Paris final, had arguably been better. The red-headed Queenslander had performed well on the Australian circuit, and beat Rosewall in two finals on the American tour.

The five-set match on the wooden surface at Wembley was described as "one of the great matches of a lifetime"[189] and, arguably, it saw Laver overtake Rosewall as the world's professional champion. The doughty Rosewall actually led 5-3 in the fifth set before finally succumbing in a two-and-three-quarter hour epic by 7-5, 5-7, 4-6, 8-6, 8-6.

Writing in the *Daily Mirror*, the pipe-smoking, ever-thoughtful Peter Wilson stated:

> *Look at that score. Not a one-sided set in the five. Laver—at 26, nearly four years the younger—has more inspiration, Rosewall the greater consistency. So at six-all in the fifth set, who do you pick? Beforehand, during the struggle, and up to the match point, I wanted to pick Rosewall. My companion wanted to do likewise. Neither of us would change.*

---

187 J McCauley, *The History of Professional Tennis*, page 128

188 Wembley Arena was originally known as the Empire Pool

189 *The Times*, 19 September 1966. According to *The Sydney Morning Herald*, English tennis writers called it "the greatest game of tennis ever played in England." (27 September 1964)

In the end with the score at 30-all, in the 62nd game, with Rosewall serving, one net cord broke his rhythm and gave Laver match point. And that, in sober truth—ONE NET CORD—was all that was between them in two hours and 40 minutes of superlative, sporting combat, in which Laver won 32 games to Rosewall's 30, with I'm sure, the points relatively as close.

After the match, and over a bottle of beer, Laver told me he thought he had played as well as he had ever played in his life. A dark, gaunt Rosewall—close up, how incredibly thin his arms are—said he thought he should have won, if he was going to win, in four sets. He thought his return of serve was a little below its peak, and opined that Laver had the greatest backhand ever produced by a left-hander.[190]

Who was the best professional player in the world in 1964? Laver declared he was not ready to assume the mantle:

I've still got plenty of ambitions left and would like to be the world's number one. Despite this win, I am not that yet—Ken is. I may have beaten him more often than he has beaten me this year but he has won the biggest tournaments except here. I lost to other people but Ken hasn't.[191]

After the Wembley event we went down to South Africa again. By that time Owen Williams, a former Davis Cup player from South Africa, became the promoter for our matches. He was a good operator down there, and finished up being the organiser of the US Open in 1969.

At the end of the year, Rosewall was involved in negotiations with Roy Emerson, the reigning Wimbledon champion, about joining the pro ranks. When offered \$75,000 by Rosewall, he asked for a guarantee of \$100,000. The offer was subsequently increased to \$85,000[192] but this was rejected.

190 *Daily Mirror*, 21 September 1964

191 J McCauley, *The History of Professional Tennis*, page 128

192 Emerson did not join the pro ranks, and would again win the Wimbledon crown in 1965.

◇◇◇◇◇◇◇

The pro players toured Australia in January and February 1965, and Rosewall suffered a number of losses to Laver and Gonzales, raising more questions about his ongoing dominance. Then in April 1965 professional tennis returned to New York City for the first time in two years, with the US Indoor Championships event[193] being played at the Seventy-First Regiment Armory on Park Avenue and 34th Street. This tournament, plus an event at Newport Casino in July, and the US Pro Championships at the Longwood Cricket Club were all part of the US professional circuit, together with tournaments in six other major centres. In the New York indoor event Gonzales easily beat Rosewall in a semi-final to set up a final against Laver. This final match saw Laver at his best, as his clever angles and placements caught Gonzales out of position time after time, and he won with ease 6-3, 6-1.

Mal Anderson wrote an article in *World Tennis* magazine at this time suggesting that Rosewall was overwhelmed by his responsibilities running the players' association, while trying to hold on to his number one ranking. Anderson wrote that Rosewall had taken on too much:

> *He was treasurer, vice-president and director of the association, and had to make decisions and play matches. When he wasn't playing he was answering the phone; when the matches were over, he checked the tickets and counted the money. He was doing the work of two men and trying at the same time to maintain his position as the world's best player.*[194]

Anderson also wrote that whenever Rosewall was playing on tour he was often afflicted with a nervous rash on his ankles, legs and arms. Rosewall's tennis commitments meant he had little opportunity to spend time in Sydney with Wilma and the boys. During 1964 he managed to spend four months in Sydney, and in 1963 it was only two. Later in 1965 some of the organisational responsibilities for the American pro tour were taken on by Barry MacKay, who was termed pro tour director.

---

193 This was the event played at Westchester County Center in White Plains, New York in 1964

194 *World Tennis*, July 1965

I was born with the skin problem and as I grew older I started to suffer with allergies. As a kid my parents took me for tests. Like millions of other people I was allergic to pollen, grass and bed mites. I had to live with that, although I suffered with it at different places around Australia—on visits to Melbourne I found I had difficulty with the different pollens and grasses.

When I started travelling overseas my hayfever was occasionally a nuisance. You would come off planes and sneeze about 30 times. In those days it was something you just lived with. The skin problems came when I was a junior. I can remember a match I played against Lew when I was a kid, and I was having problems with my skin. I went to a specialist to get some help, and on the day of the match I was loaded up with cortisone because of my skin. That day I was a bit sleepy and not active, and didn't play as well as I thought I might have. My parents were worried about the drugs so they went back to the specialist and got me off the treatment. Over the years I have had to have cortisone on my skin to try and manage the dermatitis and eczema. It occasionally affected me a bit, and it was probably one of the reasons I wasn't taken into national service, even though they said that was more because of my flat feet than anything else.

The sensitive skin and allergies are something I have lived with all my life—they play up every now and then depending on the weather, or nervous stress or whatever. I suffered with hayfever throughout my tennis career, without making any excuses. In Houston, one time during WCT days, I had to go to hospital to get injections to make sure I could keep going, and another time in Charlotte I ended up losing to Vitas Gerulaitis after being in bad shape the day before with my allergies.

Throughout the American circuit Rosewall continued to lose matches to Gonzales and Laver, and suffered the indignity of being seeded third in many of the events. He did win an event in St Louis, beating Laver 6-1, 6-4 in a semi-final and Andres Gimeno in the final.

In July 1965 the first professional tennis event to be held at the Newport Casino, the home of the United States Tennis Hall of Fame, took place. That round-robin event was also of interest because it adopted the Van Alen Simple Scoring System (VASSS), where sets of 31 points (or occasionally 21 points) were played, rather than the traditional six games. In addition, the serve was delivered from a line three feet behind the baseline—presumably to thwart servers charging to the net. On the very first day a major surprise was sprung when Laver was stunned by Luis Ayala 31-25. Such an upset made it difficult for Laver to be at the head of his group in this format (the top two in each group progressed through to the semi-finals). That same day, Rosewall made mincemeat of Ayala, running him all over the court.

> As I recall the tournament winner would receive $10,000, but we had to play by Van Alen's rules. He was pushing for sudden death tie-breaks and wanted a nine-point system (the first to five), meaning that one player served the last three points.
>
> We played there for three years and each year the rules were different: one was table tennis scoring; another was the three-bounce rule; and there was the rule about serving from three feet behind the baseline.

Gonzales narrowly won his first match against the Australian, Mal Anderson 31-28. The big man was in an unhappy frame of mind, and fell heavily on the turf at one point as the grass courts were slippery due to the fog rolling in from the ocean. The service restrictions also had a particular impact on the Californian's game. Rosewall won his second match against Pancho Segura in easy style 31-12, but again the fog played a role in the encounter. It was so thick at times that it was difficult to follow the ball.[195] Rosewall lost two of his matches in the round-robin (including a 31-21 defeat to Laver), but still managed to qualify among the final four.

195 *The New York Times*, 10 July 1965

> We had night matches to get more people in, and that's when it got foggy. It also meant the courts were slippery.

There was a lovely description of the Newport event by Barry MacKay:

> *Let me describe a typical match. Rosewall is playing Segura at 10:15pm. The fog is rolling in and you can scarcely see the ball. The scoreboards not only show the points but have dollar signs as well. Both players are wearing spikes. The tournament chairman, James Van Alen, is sitting in a chair accompanied by a dog, whose name is VASSS. His mother, the dowager of Newport, is viewing matches from a wicker chair. The score reads 13-6. You walk in and exclaim, 'What the hell is going on here?'*[196]

Laver won all three of his matches in the final round robin between the top four players (Rosewall, Anderson, Gimeno and himself). The final was played between Laver and Rosewall, with Laver winning a nail-biting encounter 31-28. Laver won that match despite losing 13 of 14 successive points at one stage, and trailing precariously by 25-27.

Maybe the players were relieved when the following tournament, the US Pro Championships at the Longwood Cricket Club, was 'traditional' in nature with players playing in an elimination event, with standard regulations and scoring. They didn't seem to like the VASSS system, at least at the start. According to *World Tennis*, losers griped loudly and one player referred to "Senor Vasseline's goofy system"[197].

Laver and Rosewall again won through to the final of the Longwood event, and the semi-final matches were notable for a series of rain delays, and the fact Rosewall thoroughly overwhelmed Gonzales. It was not a happy day for Pancho, who was unhappy with the slippery conditions and the shortcomings of his service and backhand. In the final Rosewall initially fell behind 1-4 in the first set, troubled by the impact of Laver's thrashing topspin drives. From that point Rosewall gave one of the most masterly performances of his career. He won five successive games in that

196 *World Tennis*, October 1965
197 ibid

first set, and proceeded to win 6-4, 6-3, 6-3. Allison Danzig wrote that "the little black-haired fellow from Sydney gained absolute command of the court"[198] returning serve with nonchalant ease, and transforming the match with his marvellously fluent underspin backhand. Laver's lashing topspin drives were blocked back into play, and Rosewall employed the deftest of drop volleys. Even the apparently innocuous Rosewall serve caused Laver to fall into error.

The victory meant Rosewall won three of the last four tournaments on the 1965 US pro circuit, with the flaw in his record being the round-robin event at the Newport Casino. Laver had won four tournaments on the circuit with prize money of $17,744. Again, it was difficult to separate the two competitive Australians in their quest for dominance.

In September the pair played off in the final of the French Pro Championships, again played as an indoor event at the Stade Coubertin. Laver was seeded first in the event, but was crushed in the final by Rosewall (6-3, 6-2, 6-4). It was Rosewall's sixth consecutive French Pro crown, and it seemed the lightning-fast indoor wooden surface was very much to his liking. Shortly afterwards, however, Laver would win the 1965 London Indoor Professional tournament at Wembley. On that occasion Rosewall was surprised by Gimeno in a semi-final. The Spaniard's lobbing tactics gradually wore Rosewall down and he lost the match, 2-6, 1-6, 6-0, 6-3, 6-3. Similar 'high ball' tactics were of little success against Laver, who belted overheads to all areas of the court and won the final against Gimeno in straight sets, 6-2, 6-3, 6-4.

The red-headed Queenslander was now generally recognised as the leading pro player because he won 12 out of 17 matches against Rosewall during the course of 1965. He was also the leading money winner, even though he had lost in two of the major professional events.

By early 1966 the professional players decided that the best approach to developing their circuit was to engage a professional organiser—Wally Dill. At the time Dill was a sports agent representing golf star Billy Casper.

198 *The New York Times*, 20 July 1965

> We didn't have any new players. Many of the top amateurs were doing too well through arrangements they had with their national associations to want to turn pro. We talked with Roy Emerson, Fred Stolle and Dennis Ralston at that time, but we thought it would be better to have a professional organiser like Wally Dill.

Dill was described as a 34-year-old, blond-haired earnest-type engaged by the pros to act as their commissioner. According to Buchholz the tennis pros decided they wanted someone from outside the world of tennis, and with the skills of a business executive to develop the future of the international game. It was Dill's role to convince promoters that a pro-tennis tournament was a good investment. When he came on board he told players they could be making half a million in purses in a few years, and they all laughed and giggled. Dill continued:

> *But the money's there, all right. It's just that no one had ever gone after it before. You know how organised these guys were? It was as if you and I got together with a couple of other fellows and went up to the YMCA to play skins-and-shirts basketball, and we call ourselves an organisation. Good lord, they didn't even have liability insurance.*[199]

◇◇◇◇◇◇

In January 1966 the professionals played in a series of tournaments in Australia, with Rosewall winning the Australian Pro Championships in a final against Pierre Barthes 9-7, 3-6, 6-2, (Barthes had beaten Laver in the semi-finals of the event). They then returned to Madison Square Garden for a tournament in March. It was the first time since 1963 that tennis was played in this famous inner city sporting venue—the focal point for major sporting events in New York City. The tournament was played on a new rubber mat surface that was a quarter of an inch thick and designed to ensure longer exchanges than the canvas surface previously used.

199 *Sports Illustrated*, 20 June 1966

◇◇◇◇◇◇◇

> With the development of indoor tennis, there were all these new surfaces, and we were almost like guinea pigs on them. The rubber court was slower than canvas, and took a lot more spin. But really, we played on any surface available.

The matches at Madison Square Garden were complicated due to a range of other sporting events being held in the stadium at the same time. The tennis started on Tuesday 22 March, but there was no play on the Wednesday as an ice hockey game was scheduled. On the Thursday the showcase match was between Hoad and Gonzales. *The New York Times* wrote that Gonzales was "courted by promoters, adored by galleries, and merely tolerated by rivals"[200]. Before the match Hoad fancied his chances of beating the grand old man from Los Angeles: "He hits the ball as well as ever, but he doesn't have as much power because he doesn't last as long. It's just a matter of age. I will enjoy beating him if only because of his mean personality."[201] None of this appeared to bother Pancho and he registered one of his finest performances in months as he thoroughly baffled the Australian, winning 6-1, 6-1 in 41 minutes.

The following day the 'aging master' (as Gonzales was now described) lost to a 31-year-old Rosewall in the semi-finals, 7-5, 7-5. It was a wonderful display, played in front of 13,541 fans, full of drama as the score first favoured one player and then the other. Gonzales was a set point down at 2-5 in the first set before fighting back to 5-5, and then led 5-4 in the second. As always a match involving Gonzales was not without drama. He blamed the defeat on flashing photographic lights, stating he would never again play a match with a photographer on the court. On the other side of the draw, Laver reached the final by annihilating Gimeno 6-0, 6-1.

Most expected that Laver would have Rosewall's measure in the Madison Square Garden final, but this was another occasion when Rosewall was

---

200 *The New York Times*, 24 March 1966

201 ibid

simply unwilling to hand over primacy of the game. Perhaps Laver's passage to the final had been too easy. Danzig wrote that "the little 31-year-old 'classicist' from Sydney quelled the devil in Laver's thunderbolts, and won the match in 55 minutes, 6-3, 6-3". The eminent tennis writer recognised the "rapacity" of Laver's shots, but they were nevertheless unable to withstand the "breathtaking ripostes of the player with the soundest, most formidable groundstrokes in tennis"[202]. It was a good pay day for the Australians, with Rosewall winning $5000 and Laver $2500.

◇◇◇◇◇◇◇

The next major professional event was an international tournament played at Forest Hills between 8-12 June 1966. This was the first time the pros had returned to play at Forest Hills since June 1963, in the days of bouncing cheques! The round-robin tournament promised new innovations. It was to be played at night utilising the VASSS scoring system, and the serve delivered from three feet behind the baseline. There were lots of controversies as well. Gonzales was furious when some matches were played to the abbreviated 21 points, rather than 31 points as he expected. He was also unhappy with the artificial lighting and stalked off the court after losing his match to Ayala by 21-18. This was a little embarrassing for the big man as the day before he had told Ayala: "Luis, I could beat you even if I had to play behind the fence."[203]

Gonzales was generally grumpy and felt the tournament lacked organisation. After being booed off the court, Gonzales shouted at Wally Dill: "I hope you're satisfied. You wanted it this way, didn't you? Just don't invite me to these tournaments any more." Dill's riposte was: "Will you put it in writing?" to which Pancho responded: "You bet I will!" All this led him to announce that he was quitting the International Professional Tennis Association, preferring day matches, grass courts and regular rules. In spite of these dramas he made it through to the final four players of this event, together with Laver, Rosewall and Gimeno.

202 *The New York Times*, 27 March 1966
203 *Sports Illustrated*, 20 June 1966

In the final round-robin matches, Rosewall beat everyone except Laver—in fact he lost twice to Laver on the final day of the VASSS-format tournament. Nevertheless the final play-off match for first place was remarkably tense and hard-fought. At one point Rosewall led 29-28, and this was followed by a brisk exchange of rapid-fire volleys at the net, in a point that Laver won. Then Laver was saved with two enormous serves that Rosewall could not return.

> Everyone was a bit tense with this sort of scoring and no one liked it much. But Van Alen persevered with the tie-break system and it was finally adopted by the USLTA in 1970 (and later modified to the current 12-point tie-break system).

In a similar VASSS-style event played at Newport Casino the following month, Rosewall managed to get the measure of Laver in this unusual scoring format and went on to win the tournament. Rosewall defeated Laver 31-23 in the play-off of the final four qualifiers and then defeated Mal Anderson in an eight-point game, as the first player to reach five. The 'Rosewall and Laver show' assembled once more at the US Pro Championships on the grass courts at Longwood Cricket Club in July. As expected they won through to the final of this $23,500 event, with Laver defeating his fellow Australian, 6-4, 4-6, 6-2, 8-10, 6-3.

In the middle of 1966, after an overseas trip with her husband, Wilma spoke about life as part of Rosewall's support team, which involved "living out of suitcases, in hotel rooms. Something I don't enjoy at all." Was Rosewall going to retire anytime soon? "When he turned professional, he only wanted to play for two years," she replied. "But since then they've been taking new players into the troupe, and the 'oldies' are still needed to bolster the 'youngies', and keep the troupe going."[204]

The 1966 London Indoor Professional tournament at Wembley saw another test of supremacy between Rosewall and Laver. Laver was seeking his third successive victory in this tournament, while Rosewall had won

---

204 *Sydney Sun-Herald*, 19 June 1966

the event five times overall. It was a tournament Gonzales and Segura were expected to attend, and they appeared on the posters, but dropped out prior to the event. In the semi-finals Rosewall won a five-set struggle over his old adversary Hoad, by 6-3, 3-6, 7-9, 6-1, 6-4, to earn himself the final match-up against the Rockhampton Rocket. Again newspaper columnists complained of a lack of interest or compassion for Rosewall and his style of play. After the Hoad match one wrote somewhat unfairly: "It is curious how Rosewall, with all his efficiency, continually fails to generate sympathetic warmth. The crowd seems to be unable to become involved or identified. It is almost as if he were some mechanical Ernie, some automaton."[205]

> I am not sure about this sort of comment. I actually think I was pretty lucky with the level of crowd support I got wherever I played. This might have been because of the way I played, or my size, or because I looked so insignificant. The crowd seemed to be on my side throughout my career.

The journalist's comment does seem unfair considering the contrast that existed whenever Rosewall and Hoad appeared on a tennis court. Hoad's style was always going to be described in more stirring terms—one writer referred to his "brilliant, violent game" being back at its "most intoxicating and exasperating"[206], but this didn't mean the greatness of the little master was unappreciated. Hyperbole aside, there must have been something exciting (even memorable) in Rosewall recovering from 0-3 to win the final set in the match against Hoad.

The score in this 1966 Wembley final suggests that Laver was just too good, as he won the match (which lasted little more than 75 minutes) by 6-2, 6-2, 6-3. It seemed Rosewall was "now unable to raise his game to close the gap which Laver in his prime has created"[207]. Two weeks later the pair, who had now established a considerable superiority in pro ranks, met again in the final of the French Pro Championships, where

205 *The Times*, 16 September 1966

206 *World Tennis*, December 1966

207 ibid

Rosewall won 6-3, 6-2, 14-12. Some new faces were needed to enhance the Laver-Rosewall act, or else the sport's amateur administrators needed to support the move to open tennis.

> We had developed a competitive rivalry, but Rod and I always got on. We travelled together. We'd be at the same hotel, and quite often have dinner together. Rod was a good guy in terms of what he did on court and how he behaved. His country boy upbringing made him someone who everyone was happy to be with.
>
> Of course, you might have had some disappointments, depending on how you played. You might end up going back to your room before the others. But we were all together and we knew we had a job to do.
>
> Sometimes it was hard for people to realise how much competition there was in the pro circuit because we were travelling together, carrying one another's bags, and so on. Everyone kept going because we thought it was important to keep the circuit going, and we all hoped that open tennis would soon be introduced. Laver turning pro at the start of 1963 was important to us. He was ambitious, and he was determined to be the best: to win against me, Hoad and Gonzales. That kept pro tennis going.
>
> The big problem we had at this time was that some leading amateur federations were willing to pay their players money to stop them turning pro.

◇◇◇◇◇◇

The 1967 New York City indoor event was held at the 71st Regiment Armoury once more, and the draw was made by Mrs John V. Lindsay, wife of the mayor, described as "green-eyed, honey-haired, and a three-time a week player"[208]. Rosewall elected not to play in the event for personal reasons, which generally meant spending time at home.

---

208 *The New York Times*, 24 February 1967

His return to tournament play was marked by a London professional indoor event in April, when he defeated Dennis Ralston (a recent recruit to pro ranks) in the final by 6-4, 6-2.[209]

Major developments in pro tennis took place in the first half of 1967. In early May it was announced that there would be an annual professional tournament at Madison Square Garden, with plans for other events at major arenas in the US, Canada and Mexico. This was part of a five-year agreement struck between Madison Square Garden and the professional players' association. The deal involved a $25,000 tournament at the Garden in June 1967, with plans for increased prize money in future events. The parties behind these deals were the members of the professional association's executive committee: Wally Dill, acting as association director; Buchholz; Mike Davies; and two businessmen—Joseph F. Cullman (third), board chairman of Philip Morris Inc, and Ed Hickey, vice president of New England Merchants National Bank.

The pro tournament in June at Madison Square Garden involved 14 of the top pros. Rosewall arrived to play in New York after he had ended Laver's invincibility throughout the season in two tournaments in California. Prior to this Laver won seven tournaments in a row[210] but Rosewall finally beat him in matches at Los Angeles (a $25,000 event that Rosewall won 6-2, 2-6, 7-5) and Berkeley—the final of which was especially quirky as Laver led 5-3 and 40-0 on his serve in the final set, but then lost 6-8, 7-5, 8-6. Laver recalled the match in his autobiography written four years later. It wasn't just because of the Rosewall recovery, but it was another occasion when there wasn't any prize money for them at the end of the day!

> *Muscles wasn't rattled. I couldn't rattle him—ever. Three unbelievable backhand returns he hit to get himself to deuce, and then two more for the game. I was stunned, and by the time I got with it again it was time to shake hands. He'd won the next two games and the match. As it turned out that was the minor stunning. The major problem occurred when the*

209 In the semi-finals Ralston beat Laver 10-7, and Rosewall defeated Gonzales by the same score.

210 Including a victory over Rosewall in the final of the French Pro Championships (6-0, 10-8, 10-8).

> *tournament promoter told us our pay was applause. He hadn't collected enough at the box office to meet expenses. This was the big league?*[211]

It would again be a Rosewall-Laver encounter in the final of the Madison Square Garden tournament. The two Australians overcame their opponents in the semi-finals with devastating ease. Laver beat Ralston 6-1, 6-3, and then in a 40-minute match Rosewall beat Gimeno 6-3, 6-2. Rosewall and Laver had played each other four times during the year and stood at two apiece; but Rosewall had won the two most recent encounters. The final of the Madison Square Garden event was described as a "lacklustre, error-filled match before a crowd of 8,000"[212], where Laver stamped his authority by winning 6-4, 6-4.

◇◇◇◇◇◇◇

Through June 1967, Rosewall had ongoing success in professional tournament play. He won the US Professional Hardcourt Championships by defeating Gimeno in the final, and then reached the final of the $25,000 event at Newport Beach, California, where he beat the Rocket 6-3, 6-4. This gave Rosewall an impressive tally of three tournament victories in his last four tour events.[213]

In mid-July the professionals played their major American event—the US Pro Championships—but here Rosewall was upset in a semi-final match against Gimeno, losing 7-5, 6-2 after holding three set points in that first set. From here the Australian gradually weakened, and the tall man from Barcelona was able to record his most stirring victory on the pro circuit. The Spaniard was on an impressive run, having also beaten both Rosewall and Laver in Cincinnati the previous week. For a time it looked as if this run of upsets would continue in the Longwood final. Laver lost the first set before finally winning the match, 4-6, 6-2, 6-4.

---

211 R Laver with B Collins, *Education of a Tennis Player*, page 106

212 *The New York Times*, 11 June 1966

213 The tournaments were followed by professional events in Oklahoma City and Cincinnati. In Oklahoma City, Laver defeated Rosewall in the final match, 6-2, 3-6, 6-4.

At around this time, Wally Dill, the executive director of the International Professional Tennis Association, gave his assessment of the state of the pro game in *Sports Illustrated*, 24 July 1967:

> *I admit we've got a long way to go, but consider this. We've got 12 touring pros now. Three years ago there were four. And it wasn't too long ago that a couple of guys would play for $200 and expenses in a supermarket parking lot. When I first got into this 18 months ago, there was no real tournament circuit, and prize money amounted to nickels and dimes. Now we make 19 stops in the US alone, and we're playing here at Longwood for $25,000.*

After the US Pro Championships the players moved on to the annual VASSS tournament staged at Newport. Here Laver (despite an opening round loss to MacKay), Rosewall, Gimeno and Buchholz reached the qualifying round. This was another occasion when Laver demonstrated that no one was quite as proficient under these VASSS 'sudden death' conditions as he was. He swept aside the other three qualifiers to win the event, including scoring a relatively straightforward victory against Rosewall by 31-20.

In among all this professional tournament play perhaps the most significant development during 1967 was the All England Club's announcement that it would stage a professional tournament on its hallowed courts in late August. The club was a firm believer in open tennis, and this was its way of leading the world in that direction, or perhaps it was just thumbing its nose at the ILTF and their anti-open stance. The BBC agreed to put up a singles purse of $35,000, and Wimbledon provided a doubles prize of $10,000, making it that largest prize money event to that date.

By now the LTAA had reconsidered its position on open tennis, although this had not come without acrimonious debate. By a vote of 8-4 the LTAA council accepted open tournaments throughout the world, on a two-year trial basis. The alternative view was that any open tournament should be restricted to Wimbledon.[214] A subsequent ILTF vote in July 1967 concerning open tennis moved by Britain was rejected. On that occasion the voting was 83 votes for and 139 against, with four countries (holding 24 votes) abstaining. To be effective the proposal required a two-thirds majority. The USLTA adopted a strange position of announcing that it instructed its representatives at the ILTF meeting to vote against the proposal at the July meeting, but also gave out messages that the matter remained under consideration. Other important tennis nations like Italy were firmly opposed to open tennis.

In August 1967 eight pros returned to the centre court of Wimbledon to play in an elimination tournament. The nostalgic event, held over a bank holiday weekend, saw Rosewall and Hoad return to the All England Club turf for the first time in 10 years. In one first round match the bulky, slightly overweight Hoad (described as a "reluctant competitor"[215]) outlasted the great champion of yore, Gonzales, by 3-6, 11-9, 8-6. The two former *wunderkind* of the early 1950s, Hoad and Rosewall, then played off one semi-final, with Rosewall winning 6-2, 6-2. On this occasion Hoad's inconsistent form was described as "splendidly imperfect"[216]. In the other semi-final, Laver thumped Gimeno 6-3, 6-4. As had now become almost inevitable in pro events since 1965, it was Rosewall and Laver who met in the final, and Laver defeated Rosewall 6-2, 6-2, 12-10 before a crowd of 12,000. Laver "systematically dissected" Rosewall during the first two sets, but was forced to recover from a 2-5 deficit in the final set. The pleasing aspect of it all was that the professional event was an "absolute smash". Matches sold out every day, television ratings where high, and it provided a stark contrast with the amateur Wimbledon singles final played two months before, when the 21-year-old John Newcombe defeated West

214 In spite of this vote, the president of the LTAA ('Big Bill' Edwards) claimed that the matter was the subject of ongoing review, suggesting that the vote needed only one state to change its mind for a 3-3 deadlock. If that happened he would exercise his casting vote against open tennis: *World Tennis*, August 1967. Later, Edwards wrote a personal letter to all state associations requesting that they reconsider their vote in favour of open tennis: *World Tennis*, September 1967. During 1967 Edwards' position on open tennis had become a laughing matter for the world's tennis media. Peter Wilson of the *Daily Mirror* referred to some of the his statements as "all round gallimaufry of poppycock!": *World Tennis*, April 1967

215 *World Tennis*, December 1967

216 David Gray in the *Guardian*, quoted in J McCauley, *The History of Professional Tennis*, page 139

German Wilhelm Bungert in "three dull sets"[217]. Arguably, it was the Rosewall versus Laver final that made the British tennis establishment believe in the idea of open tennis and David Gray wrote that the two Australians showed how good first-class lawn tennis on grass can be:

> *Either Rosewall or the occasion brought the best out of Laver. The quality of the returns of service, Rod's fierce backhands, Rosewall's elegant passing shots and Laver's serving in the first two sets was superb. Having grown used to margarine, it was good to be reminded of the taste of butter.*[218]

> Kramer was heavily involved in the Wimbledon event because he arranged financial backing through the BBC. Going back there was not something we thought would happen. But then if the public supported the event, there was a chance open tennis might happen. Although I was aware of how close things had come before and failed.
>
> It was exciting to be back at the All England Club, especially for previous winners like Rod and Lew. The eight of us had all played there often and I am sure Rod wanted to show how much he had improved. I actually don't think I played all that well on the day of the final—losing those first two sets 6-2, 6-2! But the English spectators had always supported professional tennis, and the event worked out well.

The professional event was a harbinger of open tennis at Wimbledon.[219] Just a month or so later the council of the LTA indicated that it was prepared to defy international rules and invite professionals to compete in an open event. This was in blatant defiance of the ILTF decision in July 1967, when it rejected Britain's call for open tennis.[220]

217 J Kramer and F Deford, *The Game—My 40 Years in Tennis*, page 260

218 *World Tennis*, November 1967

219 John Barrett doubts that open tennis would have happened but for the 1967 pro event. "That was the final pistol to the head of the ILTF saying, 'Here we go'." Interview with author, 11 June 2012.

220 The LTA council announced that it would put this proposal to the LTA "whether or not it meant going it alone in 1968": *Sydney Morning Herald*, 6 October 1967

After a trip through South Africa, sponsored by Coca-Cola, the pros returned to Europe for tournaments in mid-October. After an unbeaten seven-year record in Paris, Rosewall was beaten in the semi-finals of the French Pro Championships by Gimeno, losing disappointingly in straight sets, 6-2, 6-3, 6-4. Laver went on to win the event. Soon after the pro tour shifted to London to play the 1967 Wembley tournament. On this occasion Laver won the event for the fourth straight time, defeating Rosewall in the final 2-6, 6-1, 1-6, 8-6, 6-2. Oddly perhaps, it was a match when Rosewall looked the better player throughout, but Laver managed to establish control in an exciting fourth set, and then romp through the fifth.

◇◇◇◇◇◇◇

There were a number of factors affecting the game at the end of 1967. As with the previous year, the crowds at the Wembley tournament had been disappointing. Did this show some lack of interest in the pro game? Many of the professional innovations—like a new scoring arrangement (such as VASSS), the three-bounce rule, and limits on server positioning had been tried and abandoned. So just where was pro tennis headed at the end of 1967?

The players' professional association had fallen apart, and there were now two different promoters who had entered the field: Dave Dixon, a sports promoter from New Orleans (with financial backing from Texas oil millionaire Lamar Hunt and his nephew Al Hill junior), set up a group called 'the Handsome Eight', and signed Newcombe, Roche, Barthes, Buchholz, Ralston, Cliff Drysdale, Nikola Pilic and Roger Taylor; and former US Davis Cup captain George McCall, who retained some of the long-term pros like Laver, Rosewall and Gimeno under contract. This meant there was a split between the most important elements of the professional troupe—the players themselves. It was uncertain what would happen from this point. Another point to note, of course, is that there was not much left of amateur tennis as most of its stars had shifted across into the pro ranks.

> There was just so much bickering at the end of 1967, with most countries lined up against the British, except for the French. In the pro ranks, there were also the differences that existed in McCall and Dixon's groups.

The LTA continued to move towards open tennis and voted overwhelmingly in favour of it on 14 December 1967. The proposal it had taken to the ILTF earlier in the year was for experimental open tournaments to be held for a limited period and under strict controls, but this was rejected and the LTA threatened with suspension. Now the Brits decided to go it alone! The pressure was now on organisations like the LTAA to show where it really stood on this issue and the future of the game. However, the LTAA refused to discuss the possibility of an open Wimbledon at its October meeting, even though the matter was listed on the agenda.

The position taken by some leading figures in Australian tennis was to oppose the very idea of open tennis. Harry Hopman, the Davis Cup captain, said he was 100 per cent behind the ILTF and would be keeping faith "with the 90-odd other countries affiliated with the international body", drawing attention to the fact that America, Britain and Australia might have voted in favour of open tennis at the ILTF meeting in July 1967. 'Big Bill' Edwards spoke about another city, like Paris or Rome, becoming the new centre for amateur tennis. On the other hand, Alf Chave, the president of the Queensland Lawn Tennis Association (QLTA), was contemptible in his response to the suggestion that there could be any replacement for Wimbledon. In his view, it was only a matter of time before the rest of the world followed Britain's lead.

> Most of the tennis administrators in Australia were against open tennis, and there was a lot of influence from Harry Hopman there. Harry didn't like the idea of pro tennis, and had always been against players entering contracts with Kramer. Bill Edwards was dead against anything to do with professionals.

In spite of the stance taken by Hopman and Edwards, other administrators wanted a more moderate compromise. At a major national interstate tennis conference in early 1968 there was support for the position taken by Sweden calling for a special ILTF meeting in Paris at the end of March, and moves "to abolish amateurism and pay players openly *while retaining control*"[221]. The LTAA liked the reference to retaining control and Edwards used his casting vote to pass a resolution underlining his respect for the ILTF. Frank Rostrom, an English writer, commented that Australian officialdom seemed to be "well out of step with its own players and the public"[222]. Watching all the shenanigans, *The Herald* (Melbourne) wrote:

> *Reversing its policy once again, the Australian LTA voted overwhelmingly in favour of abolishing the distinction, often hilarious, between amateurs and professionals. But it will not support the open tennis it says it wants until the International Tennis Federation blesses the change. Most people bewildered by such manoeuvring, will be pleased when the great moguls of tennis finally admit it is unreal to keep pretending the tattered old concept of amateurism still survives.*[223]

It was always going to be a difficult process achieving consensus when the president of the national association regularly spoke of Australian tennis being 'bled dry' by the professionals.

The cause of open tennis was pushed along when the annual meeting of the USLTA declared that it was prepared to follow the British lead. A British journalist wrote that beneath the cleverly drafted language of the association's resolution "there lurked nothing more or less than an ultimatum to the ILTF. In effect it said, 'Change your rules and end *sham*ateurism or we will get out and join Britain in her bid for honesty.'"[224] What was resolved was that the USLTA could secede from the ILTF if it thought fit, when it attended the special meeting of the ILTF in March 1968.

221 *World Tennis*, May 1968 (emphasis added)

222 ibid

223 Quoted in *World Tennis*, May 1968

224 ibid

After much dithering and uncertainty the LTAA decided that it was prepared to support a proposal for a limited number of open tournaments to be conducted during 1968, under the control of the ILTF. This was the motion that was ultimately accepted at an extraordinary meeting of the ILTF on 30 March 1968.

CHAPTER 6

◇◇◇◇◇◇◇

ARRIVAL OF OPEN TENNIS

Open tennis finally 'arrived' in 1968. It had been spoken of back in the 1930s with Sir Norman Brookes acting as an early advocate, so long as the national associations remained in charge. It had *almost* been accepted by the ILTF in 1960, but now it was a reality. Of course, it was likely to take some time for the concept to be fully accepted. Who was in control—was it the national associations or the promoters? This was the subject of discussion and debate during the first two years of open tennis (1968-70), during which time Rosewall won the first and last major open events—the French Open in 1968 and the US Open in 1970.

The pro tennis tour was now split into two separate bodies. Rosewall, together with Laver, Stolle, Gonzales, Stolle and Gimeno (and now Emerson) were part of George McCall's 12-player group—the National Tennis League (NTL). McCall was an experienced operator on the tennis circuit and former captain of the US Davis Cup team. In competition was World Championship Tennis (WCT), initially managed by Dave Dixon, but later taken over by his backers Lamar Hunt and Al Hill junior. WCT had its troubles at the start. By March 1968 there were already rumours that the group of eight players was carrying losses of $100,000.

Nevertheless, Hunt—a wealthy oilman from Dallas—was always confident that professional tennis could be sold to the public.[225]

> We all moved across to having formal contracts with McCall when he decided to set up the NTL. Kramer and Trabert were out of it by this stage. Over the previous couple of years we had worked on our own through Wally Dill, where we would get a percentage of the gate, but now we went back into a contractual arrangement. Wally had moved back into insurance.
>
> When NTL was established McCall did not want all the players. WCT set up its 'Handsome Eight' group, and they were all new pros beginning in 1968, except for Buchholz, who went across from our previous group. McCall sold the NTL package for events that comprised Laver, Emerson, Gonzales, Gimeno, Stolle and myself, and four women players—Billie Jean King, Anne Jones, Rosie Casals and Françoise Dürr.

It was only in late March 1968 that the ILTF finally endorsed open tournament tennis—or at least allowed for a limited number of open events during the 1968 season. It was not open competition between all classes of player for prize money—but it allowed for different categories of player. What had been achieved was a compromise, one that did not meet the terms of the British proposal.

It did not take long for Laver and Rosewall to establish their superiority under the new arrangements. In April 1968 the world's first open tournament was played at West Hants Club, Bournemouth, on the south coast of England—at the British Hard Court Championships. It was an odd sort of week as there were many enormous upsets with seasoned pros falling to amateurs, despite only a few of the world's best amateur players actually turning up. It was also a British player, Mark Cox, who did most of the damage with victories on successive days over Gonzales, and then Emerson. One might have expected Gonzales to be extremely unhappy

225 In early 1968 Dixon sold his interest in WCT to Al Hill junior and Lamar Hunt. The administrative manager of the organisation was Mike Davies, a former British touring pro.

with that result, but he said that it was great to be playing in the sunshine again after years of playing indoor matches in smoke and under lights![226]

Rosewall and Laver won through to the final, and on this occasion Rosewall simply smothered his rival 3-6, 6-2, 6-0, 6-3. The match was played over two days because of constant rain interruptions, the first day's play was finally called off with Rosewall leading 3-0 in the third set—it seemed playing outdoors had its disadvantages after all!

It was an occasion when Rosewall was "merciless", and flawless in his volleying, while Laver "fretted and floundered", failing to play at his best.[227] Laver said Rosewall loved "the salmon-coloured clay courts" at Bournemouth: "I didn't play badly. Once in a while I missed a shot; he never did." It was a great win for Rosewall, who believed the notoriety of winning the first open event was worth more than the money due to its "name value and prestige"[228]. He asked for a copy of the historic score sheet and the umpire, Colonel Roy Emmett, obtained the document explaining to Rosewall he would be provided with a photocopy, but after some persuasion it was handed on to the victor. An article by Jack Kramer in the *Sunday Telegraph* referred to it as a document Rosewall wanted to show to his children and their children when they came along, so he could tell them all about the first open tournament![229]

> I had never played in Bournemouth before. It was an arrangement made by McCall, who secured funding for our six male players and four women. WCT players did not compete. It was a clay court event, with slippery courts, and the weather was average, but it created a lot of interest because of those surprise results caused by Mark Cox when he beat Gonzales and Emerson.

The ups-and-downs of pro competition were on display the following week in the final of an indoor tournament played on boards at Wembley stadium

226 *The Sydney Morning Herald*, 29 April 1968
227 *The New York Times*, 29 April 1968
228 R Laver with B Collins, *The Education of a Tennis Player*, page 89
229 *Sunday Telegraph*, 28 April 1968

when Rosewall suffered the worst loss of his pro career to Laver, losing by 6-0, 6-1, 6-0. It was all over in 48 minutes. Rex Bellamy of *The Times* could not quite believe what he was seeing, describing Rosewall as "pathetically lethargic" and playing as if he were drugged, or "like someone who had suddenly had bad news". Rosewall was embarrassed by it all: "I was in a fog. My reactions were just dead … I'm just sorry for the public."[230] The contest between the pair was much closer at a pro event played at Madison Square Garden a week or so later with Laver coming from behind to beat Rosewall 4-6, 6-3, 9-7, 6-4.

That event in London was a small pro event that Jack Kramer helped organise. I played awful after receiving news from home that Wilma was unwell. Not taking anything away from Rocket, but I didn't have any momentum at that stage. There was a logical excuse for me but I feel sorry for the paying audience.

After that I was back in America playing in some pro events. McCall was trying to organise events for the NTL group. I can remember being in New York at that time and Bobby Riggs suggested I spend a week with him before playing in the French Open. At that time he was starting to take more interest in his tennis. He was about 50 and there was talk of a senior circuit being set up. He said, 'We will just have a nice relaxing week.' On the first day we drove out to his home, which was a very nice place on Long Island. As soon as we got out there he said, 'Ok, let's go have a hit.' He wanted to put some money on it, but I said, 'No let's just play.' Anyway I beat him that day.

I was there for another five days, and on each day we drove into New York to play tennis at an indoor centre, which had previously been used as a place for servicing steam engines. It was huge with two courts end to end. Bobby had organised sets with some of his friends, and they were all handicap matches, with everyone putting some money down. He said he would

230 *The Times*, 8 May 1968

> take care of me if we lost, but I don't think we actually lost a set, even with the handicaps.
>
> At the end of the day he said, 'Ok, let's you and I have a set of singles. And we'll play for $100 a set.' I replied, 'No I don't want to play for any money.' Bobby says, 'No we've gotta play that way, but you have to give me a handicap.' He went on, 'You gotta give me 30-0 start in every game.' I won that set.
>
> Next day we went through the whole process again, and finally he said, 'You have to give me two games start, plus 30-0 start in each game.' Again I won that time. The following day it was a handicap with me on 0-30 and him on 30-0 in each game, plus a two-game advantage! Somehow I won that. And the next day it was the same, but he started with four games in the set. I was obviously playing pretty well because I managed to win that, too.
>
> I think the last handicap I got down to was me only having one serve, plus everything the same, with him on 4-0. And he might have been able to play the doubles alleys as well. Anyway after all that, I lost the last set. I think I had been $700 ahead and I lost it all in the last set.

The next major 'open' event was the 1968 French Open Championship in Paris, played at the same time as a general strike in Paris, during the spring of student riots. A grand slam event, it allowed entry to the top pros, but Joe McCauley writes that it would be wrong to suggest that the French administrators were committed pioneers of the open game. They had "dithered", while it was the British who took the lead in the matter. The industrial conflict in Paris meant there was no public transport or taxis, but huge crowds managed to somehow find their way to the tennis, probably because there "was little else for them to do!"[231]. The players actually had great difficulty just getting to Paris, with the city in a state of anarchy. Rosewall was the first of the contract pros to arrive, travelling from New York and landing at a military airfield.

---

231 J McCauley, *The History of Professional Tennis*, page 146

For the 33-year-old Rosewall this was a satisfying return to Stade Roland Garros, where he last won the French Championships in 1953. He struggled past Gimeno in a five-set semi-final by 3-6, 6-3, 7-5, 3-6, 6-3, in what was described as the match of the tournament, while Laver easily beat Gonzales 6-3, 6-3, 6-1 on the other side of the draw. In spite of riots on the streets, and with almost no available transport, there were record crowds for the final match. Parisian tennis fans walked to the stadium and watched as Rosewall beat Laver 6-3, 6-1, 2-6, 6-2. It was a day when the victor "mesmerised Laver with his immaculate length and tactical nous"[232]. "The idea was to keep him [Laver] away from the net," said Rosewall, "You can't afford to have Rod coming up too often."[233]

> Fortunately I wasn't anywhere near the riots, but I can remember it all. I was staying with Philippe Chatrier during the tournament, a French tennis player I knew very well. He was a good friend of Kramer's and had always been a help to us during the early professional days before he became president of the French Tennis Federation. With all the strikes and demonstrations I can remember him saying he had to be there to witness it, because it was part of French history. So he went off on his own to watch. The city was in turmoil but there was still an interest in the tennis. The field was good, except that the WCT players were not there once more.

The US Pro Championships took place at the Longwood Cricket Club between the French Open and Wimbledon. It was another unusual event, marked by a week of unpleasant rain, which ultimately meant the final was postponed until September. This was one of the few occasions during 1968 when members of WCT and the NTL actually played against one another. Dave Dixon had prevented his troupe of WCT players from entering tournaments where the NTL was represented, so arguably the new sport of 'open' tennis was not fully shown off by the previous tournaments

232 R Bellamy, *Game, Set and Deadline: A Passion for Tennis*, page 147

233 *International Herald Tribune*, 10 June 1968

in Bournemouth and Paris. Rosewall didn't manage the wet conditions all that well in his match against Tony Roche, and fell at an early stage. Roche and Newcombe were both colourful, young representatives of WCT, and they played in one semi-final match, which Newcombe won, 6-2, 6-3, 8-10, 11-13, 6-4. This placed him in the postponed final against NTL rival Laver.

Rosewall's return to Wimbledon in June 1968 was not entirely satisfying. He survived a thrilling five-set match against Charlie Pasarell, which Rex Bellamy called the "first great match of the open Wimbledon". The Australian finally won, 7-9, 6-1, 6-8, 6-2, 6-3, and brilliant wordsmith Bellamy wrote that the players "took us to the mountains yesterday—and the air was like wine". He went on to say:

> *The actors came from different schools. Rosewall is a quick and quiet man, so cool, so calculating, that even his strides between rallies seem to be measured to an inch. Pasarell, splay-footed, repeatedly hitching up his trousers, walks along the baseline as if strolling up to a bar and looking for trouble in an old-time western.*[234]

Rosewall's scrapbooks include a telegram from Charlton Heston after the match: "Saw you beat Pasarell on television from Devon. Thought you played brilliantly. Good luck in the next one!"

> Chuck Heston was always a great supporter of the pro game. Many of us had got to know him during the early 1960s. He was also a good player himself. He often helped us setting up events, and even organised matches playing in the streets in different cities. That happened in Johannesburg on one occasion.

Unfortunately there were not to be too many victories at this Wimbledon. Rosewall played badly to lose quite easily in the fourth round to Roche. The score, 9-7, 6-3, 6-2, was more decisive than Roche's victory at Longwood a couple of weeks previously. Some of the news reporters wondered whether

234 R Bellamy, *Game, Set and Deadline: A Passion for Tennis*, page 64

Rosewall was past his prime. One report spoke of the "gentlemanly figure of Rosewall, in his cream flannel shorts and white shirt, hair combed flat like a bank clerk", looking old fashioned against the "tough, no-nonsense airiness" of Roche. The same commentator wrote that Rosewall was clearly finished at the end of the match, and "it was sad to see the little man in defeat losing what must be his last chance to win the title as a professional"[235]. Most of the news coverage was full of sentimental descriptions of Rosewall's place in the history of the game, while some commentators spoke of Rosewall visibly wilting in the scorching heat. After an English summer marked by dismal, drizzly days, the temperature climbed during the second week of Wimbledon. On the day of the Rosewall-Roche match, 539 of 14,000 fans at Wimbledon fainted in the heat.[236] Prior to that day, ongoing delays meant the tournament was 200 matches behind after four days, which did not help Rosewall in his preparations, or to play at his best.

> By this time Tony had lifted the level of his game, not that I had played against him a lot. He played well in that match. And Laver played well at Wimbledon in 1968. He had the wood on most of the players at that time. I was aware of some of the journalists writing stories about me being past my best. You can't help picking up the papers sometimes. I didn't feel very comfortable playing at Wimbledon that year, even though Wilma was with me—one of the few times she travelled to England. Fred Stolle and I did pretty well in the doubles, reaching the final against Newcombe and Roche.
>
> Wilma and I were staying at the same hotel in London as Rod and Mary Laver, and travelled out with them to the tennis a few times, including the final day. I think I recall even warming him up for the final match.

In the final of the Wimbledon event Laver took exactly an hour to beat Roche in straight sets, 6-3, 6-4, 6-2. *The New York Times* wrote that Laver

235 *Times of India*, 2 July 1968

236 *World Tennis*, October 1968

was "a mild little man with the look of a drowsy cockatoo off the court" but a terror on it.[237] The Rocket's serve was not broken throughout the match, while he broke Roche's delivery on four occasions. It was a nervous Roche who was faced by the pressure of an 'open' Wimbledon championship final: "As [Laver] stepped up the pressure, his opponent's game crumbled and there was no place for him to hide on the centre court. It was a demolition job by a supreme champion."[238]

During the championships the ILTF met and passed controversial motions allowing for the participation of 'registered' players, but barring professionals from playing Davis Cup. This proposal was moved by the LTAA's 'Big Bill' Edwards and passed by a vote of 24-8, barely overcoming the two-thirds majority requirement. This category of registered players appeared on its face to be specifically designed to remove commercial promoters from the game, and place control of the sport in the hands of the amateur associations making up the ILTF. Rosewall fumed: "We've pioneered the open-handed money in the sport and now we're locked out."[239] His compatriot Sedgman stated that the ILTF had turned a blind eye to professionalism, and the decision looked like the body was out to get rid of outside promoters completely.

There was now a "formless distinction"[240] that existed between professional and amateur players. Registered players could compete in open events for prize money, without becoming professionals. They were eligible for Davis Cup play while 'contract' professionals (like Rosewall, Laver and Gonzales) who were contracted to a promoter, could play only in *open* tournaments, plus events created by their promoter.

> My problem with the registered player issue is that the decision was made by the ILTF, and we really didn't have a voice. We could play our professional events and open tournaments, but we couldn't play Davis Cup. The registered players could play

237 *The New York Times*, 6 July 1968

238 J McCauley, *The History of Open Tennis*, page 152

239 *The New York Times*, 5 July 1968

240 *The New York Times*, 7 July 1968

> in open events, but they were allowed to play Davis Cup. It seemed like it was pushed though by the US because they had become a force in Davis Cup—with Arthur Ashe. The Americans thought they could win the Davis Cup for a long time. It wasn't until 1973 that the ILTF allowed the best Australian players—who had been contract pros—to play once more in Davis Cup.

There were other difficult transitional issues as open tennis was 'bedded down'. There was also no great affection between Lamar Hunt and George McCall—the two professional promoters—with talk of Hunt wanting to drive McCall out of business

Perhaps in a more satisfactory world only prize money would be offered—with no appearance money—and then only the deserving would earn their keep. *World Tennis* magazine referred to stories of a well-known international player being offered financial inducements by USLTA officials to play the US Open as an amateur, rather than a registered player. Life was getting very complicated in the world of open tennis.[241]

The week after Wimbledon the pros were again playing on clay in Paris in the French Pro Championships, held once more at Stade Roland Garros. In the final Laver easily beat Newcombe, after what was a highly successful clay-court tournament for the younger man. He beat Segura, Rosewall and then Stolle to reach the final. The victory over Rosewall was something of a feather in Newcombe's cap considering that this was a man who won eight French professional singles titles in the nine years between 1958 and 1966. On this day Newcombe won a classic quarter-final match by 6-4, 6-1, 5-7, 1-6, 6-4. It also meant that Rosewall had failed to reach the semi-finals in three successive major events, and was in need of a short break at home in Australia before returning for the US Open at Forest Hills. At around this time Rosewall gave a candid newspaper interview to Dave Anderson of the *The New York Times*, commenting on the greatness of his rival, Laver, and comparing him with Gonzales:

---

241 *World Tennis*, October 1968

In comparing them both at their peak, Gonzales was a better player on his surface, meaning an indoor surface over a series of matches, but on different surfaces, Laver is the equal of Gonzales at his best.

Rosewall suggested that left-handed Laver's repertoire of strokes was almost infinite compared to some of the other top players:

Potentially he has twice as many strokes as I do. I'm an orthodox player. But with Laver, he has tremendous natural ability, and he's more unorthodox. His iron-clad wrist enables him to hit a topspin backhand like nobody else. Gonzales can hit it, but not successfully in competition ... He has the gift of coordination and timing—the ability to make contact on the run.[242]

The New York Times interview with Rosewall took place during the early stages of the first US Open in 1968. Perhaps it was ironic that while Rosewall may have praised the remarkable abilities of his countryman, Laver was actually defeated in the last 16 of the US Open by South African Cliff Drysdale. In fact it had not been a happy time for Laver since Wimbledon as he lost early in four straight tournaments, troubled by wrist problems. In another last 16 result, the 40-year-old Gonzales, described as "gray at the temples", and "sometimes producing a winner from memory"[243], ousted Roche by 8-6, 6-4, 6-2.

Everyone was excited about this first US Open played at Forest Hills. There were always problems with scheduling because of the weather, and the grass courts were never much good. The facilities were outdated and there were so many more players taking part. It was about this time that the USLTA started thinking about a new facility. They knew the game would grow and there would be more television interest.

242 *The New York Times*, 1 September 1968

243 *The New York Times*, 5 September 1968

> The grass at Wimbledon was always quicker, meaning the game played was quicker. The turf at Forest Hills was softer, and it broke up more quickly. It was affected with the serving rules that applied then, because players had to keep one foot on the ground when serving. The servers dragged big chunks of grass out of the back of the court, and generally the courts wore quicker than at Wimbledon.
>
> I think I was able to adapt, and it probably helped me on my serve. By this time I was trying to play more aggressively. At Forest Hills I certainly had my share of good bounces that helped upset my opponent. Generally, I played well there.

Eventually the list of upsets meant Rosewall was the only Australian in the semi-finals of the first US Open. Not only that, but Rosewall was the only professional player among the last four, after it was reported that the pros had trouble coping with the poor quality grass. One semi-final was played between Rosewall and Tom Okker of the Netherlands (the game's first registered player), with the other between Arthur Ashe and Clark Graebner, both amateur—at this time the USLTA did not allow American players to become registered players.[244] Peculiarly, this meant that whoever won the Rosewall-Okker semi-final was entitled to the $14,000 first prize for the tournament. Questions about 'registered' players being entitled to prize money were a matter of contention for Rosewall: "I have never lost to an amateur, and I'm not going to", he stated after his quarter-final. Now he would be faced with a match against a 'registered' player (or 'amateur' in disguise). It was a disappointing match for Rosewall as he lost to "the Flying Dutchman", by 8-6, 6-4, 6-8, 6-1. After watching the match, Bud Collins wrote that the two played almost completely the same: "They skitter around the court liked souped-up rats, getting everything back. But on this occasion Okker was just too quick and strong."[245]

---

244 *The New York Times*, 16 October 1968

245 R Laver with B Collins, *The Education of a Tennis Player*, page 141

The way the 1968 US Open panned out did not reflect any credit upon the sport's administrators and policy makers. It was the American Ashe who won the men's singles event 14-12, 5-7, 6-3, 3-6, 6-3, but runner-up Okker took home the money prize. It was clearly hypocrisy on the part of the ILTF. How was it possible to describe Okker as anything other than a professional in these circumstances? An anonymous donor made Ashe a gift of 100 General Motors shares (then valued at $8,912.75), based on his view that it was unfair that Okker walked away with first prize in the event. As this 'gift' could be termed an unsolicited, independent gesture, it was not subject to the USLTA's rules governing amateur tennis. Another feature of the US Open in 1968, which dogged professional tennis for the next few years was that the USLTA granted the two contract pro groups a guarantee amount (or appearance money) of $40,000 for their players to participate in the event. Consequently, it was disappointing that none of the contract pros actually made the final, but it also set a precedent that the major events paid these amounts to the promoters. All parties squabbled about this issue for the next few years.

◇◇◇◇◇◇◇

There were some interesting results in the Pacific South West open tournament played in Los Angeles a couple of weeks after Forest Hills. Rosewall defeated Gonzales 11-9, 6-2 in a quarter-final, and then won over Ashe in the semi-final by 6-3, 6-2. This was significant, as it was the American player's first loss in 30 matches played during the American amateur summer circuit. Speaking of the loss Ashe said that Rosewall returned serves better than Laver and was harder to play because "you learn not to expect many errors". In the final, Rosewall squared off against his pro rival Laver once more—the latter winning 4-6, 6-0, 6-0. On the other side of the net Rosewall "could only hold his head in despair as he was repeatedly passed by heavily topspun backhand winners"[246].

In mid-November there was an announcement of a head-to-head battle between the two pro groups (WCT and NTL) at Madison Square Garden.

246 J McCauley, *The History of Professional Tennis*, page 154

This marked a greater involvement of Madison Square Garden itself in the promotion and sponsorship of tennis, as it had been a joint sponsor of the first US Open played in September. Although there was now some accommodation between the two pro groups, there were ongoing issues between the players and the USLTA. The professional players announced they wanted a greater voice in the distribution of prize money in open events, and threatened to boycott open tournaments planned by the USLTA in 1969.

The open tournaments at Forest Hills and Los Angeles had been largely successful and the USLTA planned seven open events in the US in 1969. But the category of registered players remained a matter of dispute between the amateur officials running the sport, and professional promoters. Neil Amdur of *The New York Times* spoke of the arrangement being "the comfort zone for players seeking the best of best worlds", and reported that both the NTL and WCT threatened to bypass all open events if the registered player concept was not revised or abolished.[247]

The Wembley British Professional Indoor event was played in late November 1968 and renamed the Jack Kramer Tournament of Champions. Rosewall beat Newcombe in a four set final by 6-4, 4-6, 7-5, 6-4. The winner's prize of $12,000 (£5000 pounds) was the largest purse offered a player in Britain. It was also described as one of the best matches ever seen in Britain, between "the combative, relentless Newcombe" and "the greater touch and consistency of Rosewall"[248]. The number-one seed, Laver, suffered a first round loss to his fellow Queenslander, Emerson, by 6-3, 9-7.

A week later there was an eight-man invitational tournament at Madison Square Garden including both pro groups. On this occasion Rosewall lost to old foe, Gonzales, by 7-5, 5-7, 6-4, in what *The New York Times* described "as probably about the 300th time these two had played"[249]. The results in that Madison Square Garden event were a little unusual all round. Gonzales proceeded to lose to Gimeno in the semi-finals, and Laver lost in straight sets to Roche.

247 *The New York Times*, 6 November 1968

248 J McCauley, *The History of Professional Tennis*, page 155

249 *The New York Times*, 28 November 1968

Despite his post-Wimbledon slump, Laver was ranked number-one player in the world for 1968 on most ranking systems, including *World Tennis* magazine, who put Rosewall in fourth place, after Laver, Ashe and Okker, and ahead of fellow Australians, Newcombe and Roche. The Davis Cup Challenge Round for 1968 was held in Adelaide, and saw an American team of Ashe, Graebner, Smith and Lutz beat the Australians, Bowrey, Ruffels and Alexander by 4 rubbers to 1. In the course of the Challenge Round representatives from the US, Australia, England and France met to canvas the possibility of opening the Davis Cup to professionals—despite Australian representative 'Big Bill' Edwards' fierce opposition there was now general accord between these four nations that the Cup should become an open event, but they needed the support of at least 30 Davis Cup nations (a two-thirds majority). The Davis Cup nations discussed this proposal at a 1969 meeting, where contract pros were once again denied the privilege of playing Davis Cup.[250]

◇◇◇◇◇◇◇

In early 1969 Rosewall played through the Australian summer circuit, where for the first time all state championships and the national championships event were 'open' tournaments. In Perth he lost to fellow professional American Marty Reissen in the final of the Western Australian Open by 6-3, 6-4, 2-6, 2-6, 6-1. The score shows that Rosewall fought valiantly to square the match at two sets all, but then fell apart against his hard-hitting opponent.

This was followed by the New South Wales Championships played in Sydney, an event with all the major pros, Laver and Gonzales included, entered. Here Laver easily beat Newcombe 6-1, 6-3, 7-5 in the semi-finals,[251] while Rosewall was upset by Roche in a three-and-a-half hour marathon, 5-7, 7-9, 6-4, 11-9, 8-6. He led by two sets to love, but he was slowly and surely tiring. Rosewall fought hard in the fourth set, but by then the match was beyond his reach. It was an oppressively hot day in

250 The proposal was submitted by France and seconded by the US and the Netherlands. It was defeated by 21 votes to 19. Not all nations had the same voting power in the ILTF—Australia, the US and Britain had multiple votes; other countries had one.

251 Newcombe had earlier beaten Gonzales in the event, 5-7, 18-16, 6-3, 14-12

Sydney, although spectators recall Rosewall pouring himself a cup of tea from a pot near the umpire's chair.[252] Roche won the final against Laver, giving a much better account of himself than his nervous showing in the Wimbledon final six months before.

The world's top pros descended on Brisbane for the first Australian Open in January 1969, it was a chaotic, badly organised event that turned into a financial disaster. There were complaints about lack of ballboys and linesman; poor condition of the courts, which made for irregular bounces; strange seedings; scoreboards not operating on centre court; and terrible promotion of the tournament. The event was "dead", wrote Billie Jean King. "There were no interviews, no TV coverage, no publicity and no crowds."[253] Only a few hundred spectators showed up for the first two days of competition, partly because the city was struck by a heatwave, with temperatures reaching well over 37°C and oppressive humidity. As a result, organisers began scheduling matches at night under lights in an effort to save the tournament. Not surprisingly, there were some major upsets—Bill Bowrey took advantage of Gonzales' short-fuse, beating him in the second round by 6-3, 6-0, 11-9. Then in the third round Rosewall lost to Gimeno, by 7-5, 6-1, 6-4. According to press reports, the conditions did not suit Gonzales or Rosewall, and they were upset by a decision that balls were changed first after 11 games, and every 13 thereafter. It seemed to be another blunder in the poorly run event. Heavy morning rain drenched the courts the day of the Gimeno match, and Rosewall's groundstrokes lacked their usual penetration.

Gimeno did however last through the tournament to meet Laver in the final, where Laver methodically repeated his Australian Championship victories of 1960 and 1962, to win the first Australian Open by 6-3, 6-4, 7-5. The final result was reasonably straightforward, but the match of the tournament (and maybe the year) was the Australian's semi-final encounter against Roche, which he won 7-5, 22-20, 9-11, 1-6, 6-3. Sadly, there was no one there to watch! At least half the 2000 spectators left before the end because of the scorching Brisbane heat.

252 *The Sydney Morning Herald*, 20 January 1970

253 *World Tennis*, May 1969

The tournament might have attracted great names in both men's and women's events, but it was ultimately a financial debacle. Only 15,250 spectators attended the eight-day (and three-night) event, and officials claimed a loss of $14,700. Newcombe said he was embarrassed at the staging of the tournament, and even though this was Gimeno's most successful performance in a grand slam event, he called it the "bush league" and threatened never to return,[254] citing the day he was told he wasn't entitled to lunch at the courts because he was only there to train and not drawn to play a match.

> That Australian Open was a shemozzle. There just weren't enough facilities to host a major event and a lot of international players. Roche couldn't get any ice for his drink during his semi-final, and it was as hot as hell! I guess because it was the national championships they were committed to having it in January—but that's the hottest time in Brisbane. As well as all this, there were really only two main courts—both inside the centre court area. The outside courts were not very appealing to play any sort of big match on.
>
> It had been easier back in 1956 when I lost to Lew in the final at Milton. But then we only had a 32-player draw. In 1969 everyone was upset with the scheduling, the courts, and the organisation.
>
> I was there for a while during that Laver-Roche match, but I got too bored and went home. One set was 22-20. You just couldn't sit out there and watch it.

These were bad times for the LTAA. During the course of the year it was found that the organisation was in such a poor financial position that it requested all state associations make financial contributions of $20,000. Newspaper columnists criticised the organisation for its extravagance, as it had somehow managed to fritter away "a fortune out of Davis Cup Challenge Rounds since World War II"[255].

254 ibid

255 *World Tennis*, July 1969

After the Australian Championships the top stars (in the absence of Rosewall) played in the New Zealand Open, where Roche once again beat Laver in the final.

◇◇◇◇◇◇◇

In February 1969 the world's first indoor open tennis tournament was played at the Spectrum Arena in Philadelphia, with a field of 32 players. In his first match, Rosewall played and beat the young Romanian, Ilie Nastase (6-1, 6-4). The encounter signalled the pair's first outing in a rivalry, and personality clash, that would span the following years. The semi-finalists in the tournament were Laver, Roche, Rosewall and Okker (who by now had turned pro). By reaching the semis, Rosewall also gained some revenge for his loss in the Australian Open to Gimeno, as he beat the Spanish player, 6-3, 7-5. In another quarter-final, match Roche easily beat Gonzales 6-3, 6-3, and the big man was left to sum up the encounter by saying: "He went through me like a rat goes through cheese, and I was playing well."[256]

Elsewhere, a USLTA meeting reached a decision allowing for a category of 'players' or 'registered players'. Many believed the decision was a perversion of the principles of amateurism, meaning people like Arthur Ashe and Clark Graebner were not exactly amateurs, and not exactly professionals. The 'player' was ineligible to compete in pro events, but could compete in open and amateur tournaments, such as the Davis Cup (and make as much money as they could from tennis). Arthur Daley of *The New York Times* made fun of the new designation: "He's neither fish nor foul, neither pro nor amateur. He's actually a semi-pro who can compete in either group."[257]

The semi-finals of the Philadelphia tournament resulted in Laver easily beating Rosewall by 6-4, 6-2, and Roche defeating Okker. "Roche is the player of the moment," Rosewall said. "He seems to have improved 50 per cent in the last six months."[258] This is not how it panned out in the

256 *The New York Times*, 8 February 1969

257 *The New York Times*, 27 May 1969

258 *The New York Times*, 9 February 1969

final when Laver beat his closest rival by 7-5, 6-4, 6-4. The carrot-topped star of the tour told the press that he thought about staying number one all the time, but this dominance did not come without a cost. Laver was suffering from an ailing back that required liniment before any match, and a chronically sore elbow. Overall, the indoor event was highly successful, and 8,542 spectators braved a snowstorm to watch the final.

The steady departure of Australia's players into the pro ranks had an unpleasant consequence in May 1969, when what had been the world's leading tennis nation since 1950 lost to Mexico in an elimination round of the Davis Cup. Unlike America, whose best tennis players were 'players' and entitled to compete in Davis Cup play, the best Australians (Laver, Rosewall, Newcombe and Roche) were 'out-and-out' contract pros, and not allowed to compete. It was a sad position for the Davis Cup competition to be in, and a regrettable position for Australian tennis.

Rosewall arrived at the French Open of 1969 as defending champion. He was now 34 years old, yet one newspaper wrote that he "glides back and forth along the baseline as if he were on roller skates, and no winner against him is sure until it bounces twice"[259]. Rosewall defeated fellow Australian Stolle in the quarter-finals 12-10, 4-6, 7-5, 6-2, in an arduous struggle lasting two hours and 40 minutes, with the first set alone lasting 70 minutes. His fellow semi-finalists were Laver, Okker and Roche, meaning that the contract professionals imposed their authority over the event.

In the semi-final matches Laver beat Okker 4-6, 6-0, 6-2, 6-4 and Rosewall won relatively easily over Roche by 7-5, 6-2, 6-2. At one point in the first set Roche had led 4-2, 40-0, before Rosewall managed to find his touch and length. The 'scratchiness' of Rosewall's play might have been due to a recent break from the game, but he was also fresh and ready for a fight. It was an unpleasant, chilly and rain-splattered afternoon, but soon the little master's groundstrokes began clipping the lines, and he produced a stream of winners. At the same time Roche had a rare "off" day. There was little he could do to shake the steadfast defensive play of Rosewall. Roche eventually became resigned to defeat, and there was little point for him to try and rush the net on a slow surface like clay.

259 *The New York Times*, 3 June 1969

Regrettably Rosewall's sparkling form was not repeated in the final. On that occasion the Rocket thrashed his compatriot 6-4, 6-3, 6-4. Laver had one of his best days, achieving great length, speed and accuracy on serve, and forcing Rosewall to backpedal on his famed backhand. The Laver groundstrokes were hit so powerfully that Rosewall was unable to get set on his backhand side. Laver later claimed it was the first time he had beaten Rosewall in a big match on clay. The huge crowd at Stade Roland Garros saw Laver playing at the peak of his powers:

> *From the moment we began, I couldn't miss. Usually I was the one on the string as Kenny played me like a yo-yo. Not this time. I had perfect control, and everything I hit was going so deep that Kenny didn't have much chance to do anything but chase and scramble. I could get up to the net all the time, and I was moving quickly either way to cut of his passing shots. I don't know of any match I ever enjoyed more because I just kept better, and the points rolled in.*[260]

> He was always dangerous, and I think he improved a lot during the period he spent with the pros. I think that Laver had just reached the peak of his game when open tennis came in. It's interesting though that at this time, after Paris in 1969, that no one really suspected that he would win another grand slam. Maybe after Wimbledon it was more on peoples' minds. But you also have to remember that Tony's [Roche] game had lifted a lot during 1969, and he had lots of wins over Rod. They were the two best—and maybe Tony was a bit unlucky. And Laver had some luck in the majors in 1969. He was down two sets in a couple of matches. I see Rod says it was about the best he played against me. I honestly can't remember. That particular day it might have been—like a lot of other times he played—that everything he hit went in. That's the kind of player he was. He wouldn't push the ball; he just went for a whack. That's why he

260 R Laver with B Collins, *The Education of a Tennis Player*, page 110

> was so inconsistent in his earlier days, and he learnt over time to control his emotions. He was always good on the court, like Sedgman and Sampras and Federer. I think he learnt to get a lot more control in his game, and that happened after he joined the pro tour.
>
> As an amateur, when he won the grand slam [in 1962], he was lucky to win at least two of the tournaments. But that's the way he played. If he was behind he would just say: 'Well it looks like I'm going to lose, so let's go for broke.'

After Paris the players played in the Wills Open event at Bristol, now the largest prize money event in Britain after Wimbledon. The tournament was stunned when Cliff Drysdale scored a major upset by beating Laver in the quarter-finals. The final score was 4-6, 6-2, 7-5, with Drysdale recovering from 1-4 down, and saving two match points in the final set. While this brouhaha was taking place, Rosewall slowly but surely worked his way through the field. He beat Emerson in the semi-final, and then Pierre Barthes, the Frenchman, in the final. However the following week Rosewall suffered the indignity of losing to American Ron Holmberg in the third round of the pre-Wimbledon tournament at Queen's Club.

At about this time, Wayne Reid, the 31-year-old captain of Australia's Federation Cup team, was elected president of the LTAA. He was the youngest person to be elected to the position and his relative inexperience suggested that the LTAA had chosen to take a new broom from the cupboard, perhaps recognising that the open game demanded a new style of management for Australian tennis. Meanwhile in America, John Newcombe and a number of players were instrumental in establishing the International Tennis Players' Association.

◇◇◇◇◇◇◇

In the 1969 Wimbledon seedings Rosewall was placed fourth, after Laver, Roche and Okker. In fact it proved a disappointing Wimbledon all round for Rosewall, when he lost in the third round. He was involved in the first major upset of the championships when defeated by the college player from

California, Bob Lutz. The American won the four-set encounter (8-6, 7-9, 6-3, 6-2), his "flamboyant serves and volleys" smothering the "watch-like precision" of Rosewall's game[261]. By the end of the second set one observer wrote that Lutz, "with his Robert Mitchum chest looked strong enough to punch his way through a 15-round bar room brawl" while Rosewall seemed to realise that all was lost. Once again, the description suggested that Rosewall's best days were well and truly past him: "He trailed his racket forlornly behind him as he plodded along the baseline between points, and the man who would have feared only Gonzales and Hoad had they been able to play at Wimbledon 10 years before, seemed reconciled to the fact that it was all too late."[262]

Rosewall's old rival from pro ranks, Pancho Gonzales, was involved in an extraordinary match in the first round of the 1969 Wimbledon tournament. He eventually beat Charles Pasarell of the United States 22-24, 1-6, 16-14, 6-3, 11-9. It became the longest match in Wimbledon history (at that time), lasting five hours and 12 minutes, and played over two days.

> It was another year when I didn't feel I played that well at Wimbledon. Lutz was an up-and-coming star but at that time, as I recall, he was better known as a doubles player. Maybe I did have a bit of an excuse that year. I was staying privately with John Barrett, and the night before I was offered a Carlsberg Elephant beer with dinner. I'm just a social drinker, but I ended up having two. This seemed like a very strong beer! I'm using that as an excuse to say that it had an impact on my movement the next day! I can laugh about it now, but that's my excuse. I also didn't think I would be playing the following day, but then when John and I checked the paper the following morning there I was drawn to play Bob Lutz. Fred Stolle and I lost in the doubles as well, so 1969 wasn't a Wimbledon I want to remember. Barrett says he still feels guilty about the events of that evening!

261 *The New York Times*, 30 June 1969

262 *World Tennis*, September 1969

The story of the 1969 Wimbledon was of Laver repeating his victory of the previous year. There were a number of 'stutters' along the way when he lost the first two sets of a second round match to the Indian Premjit Lall, and was taken to five sets by the tall American, Stan Smith. However, after surviving these perils, Laver had the satisfaction of easily beating Drysdale in the quarter-finals, and then recording victories over Ashe and Newcombe to win the event.

> After those close matches early on, by the time Rocket got to the finals he was playing pretty darn well. Smith was a dangerous player, and his game was just starting to come together then.

In mid-July the US Professional Championships was played at Longwood. The most exciting quarter-final of the event saw Rosewall wearing down Gonzales, to win by 7-9, 9-7, 6-2, placing Muscles in the semi-finals alongside three fellow Australians, Stolle, Newcombe and Laver. The match between Rosewall and Laver saw another Laver victory (6-3, 5-7, 6-2, 6-3) with Rosewall having trouble with his serve (ending with 11 double faults) and Laver cleverly playing a number of tricky lobs over Rosewall's head. Laver beat Newcombe 7-5, 6-2, 4-6, 6-1 in the final to achieve his fourth straight victory in this event.

Needless to say the main preoccupation of almost everyone by the time the 1969 US Open came about was whether Laver could secure his second grand slam—winning all four major championships in a calendar year. It would be an enormous achievement, considering he had been closely tagged by Roche early in the season, and was suffering from several ongoing injuries. Gonzales talked about Laver's disciplined approach to the game: "What I admire most in Rod is his determination and concentration. He carries that determination even into practice because he chases every ball as if it were match point in a championship. It's a wonderful habit to get into."[263] Gonzales thought Laver would have difficulty handling his own game when he was younger. He would have had difficulty handling

263 *The New York Times*, 29 August 1969

the Gonzales serve, and didn't like his lobs and dink shots. Laver liked the other guy to hit hard, and was unable to react to a soft game the way Rosewall could.

Some of Laver's closest rivals had their own problems by the time of the Forest Hills event. Ashe had developed a 'hitch' in his first serve and Okker fell by the wayside, losing his first round match to Britain's Mark Cox. Rosewall had some difficulties of his own. In a match against Pat Kramer, a college student working as an assistant teaching pro at the West Side Tennis Club over the summer, Rosewall was down 2-3 and 0-30 in the fifth set. From that point the great champion managed to steady his nerve and win 6-2, 5-7, 6-4, 4-6, 6-4. It was hardly an impressive performance.

Meanwhile the Laver procession continued when he beat the Chilean Jaime Fillol in the round of 16, meaning that he had recorded a sequence of 26 straight wins since last losing to John Newcombe at the Queens' Club Championship. Rosewall came, saw and conquered the two tempestuous Europeans, Nikola Pilic and Ilie Nastase, in order to set up a meeting with Ashe in the quarter-finals. Just reaching the quarter-final stage of the tournament proved an administrative nightmare for organisers, as heavy rain prevented play for almost three days. Gonzales, who was due to play Roche, spoke of sitting around, "listening to his joints rust"[264].

Before play could eventually take place on some of the courts a helicopter hovered above the spongy, grass surface in an effort to accelerate the drying process. The usual practice of covering courts with tarpaulin was only possible for courts within the stadium. Tournament director, Owen Williams from South Africa, estimated that the incessant rain cost organisers something between $80,000 and $100,000. Waiting around to play did not help Rosewall in his preparations, and he lost his quarter-final match to Ashe by 8-6, 6-3, 6-4.

In the semi-final matches Roche beat Newcombe in a close five-set struggle by 3-6, 6-4, 4-6, 6-3, 8-6, while Laver triumphed over Ashe by 8-6, 6-3, 14-12. It was only right that the year's two best players should meet in this climactic match, with Laver's open grand slam on the line.

264 *The New York Times*, 6 September 1969

Newcombe for one rated Roche's chances highly, saying that his doubles partner was the one person Laver did not like to play. Could Laver could stamp his authority on this most momentous of occasions? It ultimately proved to be a relatively straightforward victory for the number-one seed. He struggled a little at the start, but then totally dominated his opponent by 7-9, 6-1, 6-2, 6-2. Playing through continuous drizzle, the final was described as "a test of technique and courage" with Laver managing to play "wonderful tennis under dreadful conditions"[265].

Rosewall and his doubles partner, Stolle, won the doubles event beating the Americans Ralston and Pasarell in the final. However this happened in the most unusual and controversial of circumstances, as Newcombe and Roche, and Laver and Emerson all defaulted.

Three of the four had contractual commitments to play elsewhere, and the tournament had already been delayed because of the rain. It added to the cycle of unhappy events that characterized the 1969 US Open—131 spectators showed up to watch the men's doubles final and they grumbled about the non-appearance of the top Australians. "The pros collect their dough, blow town before it's over, and forget their responsibility."[266] Former circuit player, Herb Fitzgibbon, wrote that the International Players Association lost a great deal of respect when the president, Newcombe, and two leading members, Laver and Roche, chose to default in the second most important tournament in the world, while the editor of *World Tennis* called it an ugly precedent.

> Where's my trophy? I've got my trophy right here. It's a money clip, that says on the back '1969 US Open Tennis Championship Winner', I always carry it with me. The tournament in 1969 was supposed to finish on the Sunday and it ended up finishing on the Wednesday due to delays because of bad weather!

The 1969 Davis Cup Challenge Round was played between America and Romania, with the Americans easily winning 5-0. Again this was a matter

265 *World Tennis*, November 1969

266 *The New York Times*, 10 September 1969

of discussion, as most observers of the game assumed that the Challenge Round was the international showcase of the sport, and yet the game's best players, Laver, Newcombe, Roche and Rosewall were all absent. The position taken by the ILTF was that the professional players would not relinquish six months of playing in professional events and the chance of winning thousands of dollars to play in the Challenge Round. On the other hand, professional organisations felt they had never been asked, or given an opportunity to cooperate on this issue. In Rosewall's case the matter was of particular relevance as his pro contract was due to expire, and he was regarded as a potential Davis Cup player for Australia in 1970.

A sensational quarter-final match between Gonzales and Rosewall took place in the Pacific South West event in Los Angeles at the end of September 1969. It was a close match lasting almost two and a half hours which Gonzales won by 6-4, 11-13, 7-5. At one point Rosewall protested a linesman's call, and the match was actually delayed until tournament director Jack Kramer managed to smooth things over. Gonzales proceeded to win the Los Angeles tournament, beating Cliff Richey in the final. It was a tournament he won 20 years before. Two weeks later Gonzales again beat Rosewall 6-4, 1-6, 6-3 at the Howard Hughes Open. Gonzales' revival of form continued as he then beat Stan Smith and Ashe to win the event. It made the big man of great interest to promoters once more and despite Gonzales saying that he had played his last tournament, promoters wanted to sign him up for a series of challenge matches against Laver.

Most ranking organisations placed Rosewall fifth or sixth in the world that year. Laver was clearly at the head of the pack after securing the grand slam, and then there was a clutch of players including Roche, Newcombe, Ashe and Okker. Laver was considered to be the top name for the year, but it is important to recognise that Roche had a winning record over his countryman in 1969, beating Laver in six out of their nine encounters. *World Tennis* magazine spoke of Rosewall as "one of the fallen heroes of the game"[267], suggesting that his grass court game was vulnerable, and emphasising that he had lost six times during the year to Laver.

267 *World Tennis*, January 1970

Laver claims that 1969 wasn't a great year for Rosewall because his nerves started to wear: "He could still run as well and his reflexes stayed sharp, but the tensions seemed to eat at him a bit more, and he had some very sour patches, which wasn't like Kenny."[268]

◇◇◇◇◇◇◇

The 1970 Australian Open played in Sydney was once again in the financial doldrums, mainly because of persistent rain and a lack of international stars. Laver told organisers back in October 1969 that he would not return to defend his title, and then Rosewall, Gonzales, Emerson and Stolle (all members of McCall's NTL group) could not agree upon financial terms. McCall apparently stated that the reason his players weren't competing in the combined NSW-Australian event was that the prize money of $13,000 was "peanut butter" compared with amounts they could be earning in the US. In fact, at the time the Australian event was being played, all these stars were playing in a big-money invitation event—the Tennis Champions Pro Classic—at Madison Square Garden. Players earned points (and winner-takes-all prizes) at different tour stops, leading to a final four play-off in June, and then a final in July.

Confronted by these difficulties the Australian organisers asked just who was running the international tennis scene? The ILTF or "the millionaires who put on tournaments when and where they like"[269].

> I don't know anything about the kind of arrangements George McCall tried to make with the tournament organisers. I can just remember the prize money for Australian tournaments being very limited, and this led to Dunlop being involved in later events.

The launch of open tennis became even more complicated in early 1970 when both WCT and the NTL rejected plans made by the USLTA for joint cooperation, after which the professional groups indicated they planned to schedule a tournament at the same time as the US Open. The

268 R Laver with B Collins, *The Education of a Tennis Player*, page 109

269 *World Tennis*, December 1969

pros wanted to hold 10 sanctioned events in the US during the year, and refused to guarantee their players for USLTA open events—a policy that could boycott a major event like the US Open.

The promoters of WCT and NTL also sought 50 per cent of gross profits over $600,000 at major events. Gladys Heldman of *World Tennis* wrote that such a demand could mean the loss of major financial contributors to the sport, like US Open tournament Chairman, Joe Cullman, head of Philip Morris Inc, and the loss of US Open tournament director, Bill Talbert. She went on to say:

> *WCT and NTL can be good for the game if their thoughts are not aimed at total control, if money per se is not their sole objective and their goal is to make tennis a superbly popular sport. If they hold out for percentages, if their package deal for players hurts a major championship because some players are withheld and if they ride roughshod over the men who have literally supported tennis by their own personal efforts, they may well find themselves operating alone because their goals have negatively affected the great army of unpaid workers in the game. Perhaps WCT and NTL can do it on their own, paying for services they need and operating on the theory that money in their pockets means the game will prosper. We are inclined to doubt it.*[270]

Meanwhile, Kramer was pushing for a Grand Prix series of 30 or so of the world's major tournaments, establishing a bonus pool for the 20 top overall finishers with no fees to be paid to promoters. One difficult question was whether this concept (with ILTF support) was being used to drive the pro promoters out of business, certainly WCT indicated that it was not greatly interested and already had a fully booked program for 1970.

In early March 1970 tennis was played for the first time in London's Royal Albert Hall, with players from both the pro groups (NTL and WCT) participating in an 'all pro' event sponsored by Rothmans. Rosewall played through to the final, but lost to his occasional adversary Reissen

270 *World Tennis*, March 1970

by 6-4, 6-2. Again, Rosewall was probably not at his best—one observer wrote that his game was "subdued", and his famous backhand "prone to errors which once would never have blemished it"[271].

Even though the pros had not played in the Australian Open, they returned for an event in Sydney titled the Dunlop International in March. In that tournament Rosewall had the satisfaction of beating Gonzales in a quarter-final match by 6-0, 10-8, 6-2, and then won a testing four-set struggle against Gimeno to reach the final against Laver.[272]

Laver won the final in five sets (3-6, 6-2, 3-6, 6-2, 6-3) in a contest that lasted more than two-and-a-half hours and contained skilful long rallies and tactical manoeuvres—the match was described by *The Sydney Morning Herald* as one of the best matches seen in Australia. The encounter had it's fair share of drama off the court, too. Ken's father, Bob, collapsed with a heart attack shortly after the match ended, as Rosewall and Stolle began their doubles final, which they won. Officials at the event chose not to tell Rosewall of his father's illness until the end of the match.

> I am not sure if my father specifically had a heart attack. It was more like a cramp and he fell down some stairs. I ended up taking him to hospital after that doubles match. The Dunlop International was a good tournament, and most of the contract pros came back for the event.

Through May and June 1970 the pros returned for a series of events in America, as part of the Tennis Champions Pro Classic event at Madison Square Garden. One complication was that the semi-finals in New York were scheduled at the same time as the French Open, meaning the top pros surrendered any chance of seeking glory on the clay courts of Stade Roland Garros that year. There was more money at stake in the Madison Square Garden event than ever before. The final match on 16 July carried prize money of $50,000, with $35,000 to the winner and

271 *World Tennis*, June 1970

272 In the semi-final match Rosewall beat Gimeno 6-4, 6-8, 11-9, 6-1. In his side of the draw Laver beat Roger Taylor of Britain, 6-4, 12-14, 6-2, 6-2.

$15,000 to the runner-up. The event was huge, with excited crowds and tie-breaker scoring.

In the first week of June (just when the French Open was winding up) Rosewall beat Emerson in the semi-finals of the Tennis Champions Pro Classic. It was a three-hour classic between the two Australians, with Rosewall winning 4-6, 6-1, 6-4, 4-6, 7-5. The fifth set was finally determined by a 12-point tie-breaker played at 5-5, with Rosewall winning 7-5, after trailing 3-4. The players thrilled the spectators "with strings of placements, exciting rallies, and retrieves that had the fans gasping, then applauding"[273]. Pro tennis had hit the big time, compared to its humble beginnings in the 1950s: "In the old days the pro tennis players piled into a station wagon or beat up Thunderbird and drove from Dubuque to Des Moines for their one night stands. It was a monastic, lonely existence, but the pros were outcasts seeking respectability in their sport."[274]

It was certainly the big time for Rosewall. Aside from the matches being played at Madison Square Garden, he also played several other tournaments. Rosewall's results in the winner-take-all pro classic event meant he earned himself a place in the final of the tournament scheduled in July, after Wimbledon.

While this was going on Jan Kodes of Czechoslovakia beat the Yugoslovian player, Zeljko Franulovic in the final in Paris (6-2, 6-4, 6-0), but the prize money for this open event was not paid to Kodes and instead went to the Czech government. There were 2000 empty seats in the stands when the match was played, a marked contrast with the previous year when the stands for the Laver-Rosewall final were full to overflowing.

> The $10,000 Challenge format was a McCall concept—with the winner-take-all matches. But it clashed with the French Open, which was always regarded as a physically tough tournament and played over two weeks. We probably thought that playing with our group in American was an easier option. Looking back

273 *The New York Times*, 6 June 1970

274 *The New York Times*, 5 June 1970

> I definitely would like to have played in more major events. I missed a few. Sometimes I missed majors because I was at home with the family, but in 1970 I was playing in the US.

In the Wimbledon lead-up at Eastbourne, Rosewall beat South African (albeit former Australian) Bob Hewitt in the final 6-2, 6-1. He was seeded fifth at Wimbledon, after Laver, Newcombe, Ashe and Roche. All the forecasters referred to Laver being in a class of his own, while Rosewall's age of 35 indicated he "may be past this fortnight's gruelling pace"[275]. The bookies favoured Ashe, as he had beaten Okker, Newcombe and Laver in another Wimbledon lead-up event at Bristol.

> In 1970 I probably thought I was in with a chance at Wimbledon. I was playing well on grass. I played well in those lead-up events.

◇◇◇◇◇◇◇

The 1970 Wimbledon sprung its early surprises with Okker and Kodes (the 'King of the Clay'), losing in the second round. On the Wednesday of the first week the great Lew Hoad was scheduled to play a match against Egyptian Ismail El Shafei on centre court. It had drizzled on-and-off all afternoon, but the crowd watched and hoped that Hoad would relive glories of the past. The Egyptian won the first two sets, helped, according to Hoad and the crowd, by some bad calls and fortunate let cords. At one stage Hoad accused his opponent of being a liar when El Shafei failed to accept that one of his serves had clipped the net. According to Richard Evans: "It was not a pretty sight and one that did Hoad less than justice, but afterwards he explained that he had seen El Shafei turn back instinctively to serve again and then stop when he realised there had been no call."[276] Hoad was furious and played his way back to two sets all. That was the end of it, however, as the Egyptian won 6-3, 6-3, 4-6, 4-6, 6-1, and Hoad was forced into submission.

275 *The New York Times*, 22 June 1970

276 *World Tennis*, September 1970

I wasn't with Lew much at this stage of our careers. I was invited to a few extra events later in the year, including Barcelona for their tournament (by this stage the Hoads had established their tennis camp at Figuerola in Spain, close to Malaga). At that time I organised for Wilma and the boys to travel to those events through Europe and Asia.

That was the only time I really saw Lew, or maybe at a tournament like the French Open. So he wasn't really playing much tennis from 1968-69. But he was involved in helping the Spanish Davis Cup team and other Davis Cup players.

I feel sad that Lew's injuries and physical problems meant that he wasn't able to stay longer in the game. He was a big name and that would have helped us establish the pro game.

He died on the last day of Wimbledon, 1994. Wilma and I travelled to Spain for the funeral along with a lot of other players—including Laver, Santana and Orantes.

The Wimbledon quarter-finals in 1970 were eventually between: Roger Taylor and Clark Graebner; Tony Roche v Ken Rosewall; Bob 'Nails' Carmichael v Andres Gimeno; and Roy Emerson v John Newcombe. The missing names were obviously Rod Laver and Arthur Ashe, who had been beaten in dramatic circumstances on centre court in the fourth round. Laver lost in four sets to Taylor, who immediately became crowd favourite for the event, and Ashe lost to Gimeno. It was the first time that Laver had lost at Wimbledon since the final against Fraser in 1960. The surprising name on the list was Carmichael, an Australian who was a French resident and worked as a carpenter from time to time. He beat Zelijko Franulovic and Bob Hewitt in successive days to reach this stage of the event.

Rosewall's last 16 encounter was against the young American Tom Gorman, ranked number 14 in his country. Rosewall won the match 6-2, 6-2, 3-6, 7-5, but those final two sets were described by *The New York Times* as the highlight of the first week's play. The match was delayed when Rosewall failed to show up at the designated start time—thinking the women's match beforehand would not finish quite so quickly he had left to practise with Fred Stolle. He kept Princess Alexandra and Sir Robert Menzies waiting in the royal box until, finally, a somewhat harassed Rosewall was found on an outside court and forced to sprint to centre court.

> It was a pretty silly move on my part. I went to courts opposite the All England Club to warm up. We kept hitting and then realised we should be getting back, where we were hustled to get straight on court. Tom Gorman was waiting there, and I didn't have time to change my shoes, socks, shorts, or anything—or even go to the toilet. I was lucky that the referee was courteous enough to keep the crowd waiting and they allowed me to be late. The match against Gorman was good—he was a big hitter of the ball, in the way that tennis was played in those days.

The 35-year-old Rosewall still had the strokes and desire to win the event. Could he put it together in three successive matches, starting with a quarter-final against Roche? Just 12 months ago Roche had been close to the peak of the game, but was now "bedeviled by tennis elbow" and forced to change his style of play. He was, nevertheless, "an astute manipulator of the ball"[277], with the best backhand volley in the business.

Most of the crowd did not expect Rosewall to win the match. Wasn't he past his prime? Two years before Roche crunched him in straight sets, and the previous year he lost to the American Lutz. These pessimistic expectations continued through much of the first set against Roche: at 3-3 Rosewall unaccountably served three double faults, and then Roche held a set point at 5-3. But once these challenges had been met, Rosewall paid no heed to the hazards of age and time, and was able to weave his magic. After losing the 18-game first set, Roche fell apart for a time, losing the first five games of the second set, and scoring only seven points in the process. One observer wrote of Rosewall: "His anticipation was uncanny for he supported his brilliant reading of Roche's intentions with a turn of speed that was amazing for a man his age. Once when Roche connected with an

277 *The New York Times*, 29 June 1970

acutely angled volley, Rosewall was on to it like a lizard sliding across the face of a rock, flipping the head of his outstretched racket to return it for a breathtaking crosscourt winner."[278]

The eventual score in Rosewall's favour was 10-8, 6-1, 4-6, 6-2. In his description of the first set, Rex Bellamy wrote: "The first set had a gorgeous thrilling beauty. These are players with touch and flair, quick wits and imagination. They spread richly coloured, flowing patterns across the length and width of the court. They played cat and mouse. If they had as much fun as the rest of us, they had the time of their lives."[279] Fred Tupper wrote "the champagne of Rosewall's play on centre court was intoxicating"[280].

> Encounters between Tony and I were generally pretty good. Tennis matches are best when there is a game of opposites, and my game was not as powerful as Tony's. And certainly being a left-hander he was always dangerous. I am not sure when he started having elbow problems. He played through that year, but was then off the main circuit of the game for a while after that.

After that wonderful display Rosewall beat the left-handed Briton, Roger Taylor, two days later. It was a cold and windy afternoon and Rosewall won the match in four sets, 6-3, 4-6, 6-3, 6-3. To be fair, the task was probably easier for Rosewall than Taylor, who had to deal with the expectations of all his countrymen. When had an Englishman last reached the Wimbledon final? And when had Taylor had ever beaten Rosewall? In fact, that second set was the first set he had ever taken from the little master. Rosewall went on to meet his countryman Newcombe in the final as the oldest finalist since Bill Tilden in 1930, who was 37 at the time. This was Rosewall's third final appearance, having previously made it to the final stage of

278 *World Tennis*, September 1970

279 R Bellamy, *Game, Set and Deadline: A Passion for Tennis*, page 74

280 *The New York Times*, 1 July 1970

the tournament in 1954 and 1956.[281] Newcombe believed the crowd's emotions got the better of them and that they strongly supported Rosewall. This makes for an interesting contrast with the Drobny final in 1954, when Rosewall was faced by a wall of support for his opponent.

The final proved to be a closely fought struggle, which Newcombe won 5-7, 6-3, 6-2, 3-6, 6-1. It was called a terrible result for Rosewall, as it might have been his last fling at the only major title to have eluded him. Muscles didn't go down without a fight and it was the first five-set Wimbledon final since the match between Ted Schroeder and Jaroslav Drobny in 1949. The 35-year-old was never going to be a physical match for the six foot, 26-year-old Newcombe, and so he had to rely on his skill set: "a backhand that flashes like lightning, a feathery touch on the lob, and the intelligence and imagination to create openings"[282]. On the other side of the net Newcombe had a bulldozing serve as penetrating as anyone in tennis, and equally solid groundstrokes, plus remarkable court coverage.

Things went awry for Rosewall at two-all in the second set. He produced his fifth double fault of the match to concede his service and allow Newcombe through with a service break at 4-2. Until then he had a slight advantage over his younger opponent. Rosewall did well to fight back in the fourth set. He trailed 1-3, and 0-30, but somehow managed to win five games in a row. From that point, however, Newcombe bore down, harnessed all his power, and gave Rosewall little chance. "I felt sorry for Ken," the victor said. "But not too sorry. I wanted to win the darn thing myself."[283] Newcombe always considered it his greatest moment—a day when "nothing else existed… The court, the ball and Rosewall were the centre of the universe."[284] John Barrett says the court was watered the night before, and this made it a slicker and different surface from the one that Rosewall had played his semi-final match on two days previously, and also the doubles final the day before. His view is that this was definitely to

281 It was also the longest period of time between a player's finals—16 years. Rosewall's compatriot Norman Brookes made his first final appearance in 1905, and another in 1919 (a span of 14 years).

282 *The New York Times*, 5 July 1970

283 ibid

284 T Tinling, *Sixty Years in Tennis*, page 170

Newcombe's advantage.[285] "The best man won," wrote Richard Evans in *World Tennis*. "Not even the most devoted Rosewall fan would have dared suggest he didn't deserve it."[286]

> Looking back on the match I think I probably lost it in the first set. If I had won the first set easier things could have been different. It would have helped me play better in the second and third sets. I don't know if it was nervous energy, or being tired. In those days you played on continuous days if you were playing doubles like we were. Then, the doubles final was played the day before. Newk played well. He reached the final the year before. Grass was his best surface. He liked to be aggressive. He played pretty well the whole match. There was a point in the fourth, when I got a bit of support from the crowd, and won the set 6-3, but he won the last set pretty easily.

◇◇◇◇◇◇◇

The game's politics were again on show at a meeting during that Wimbledon tournament. The Davis Cup nations once more rejected a proposal that the event be open to all players (including contract professionals) and rejected a further proposal that the Challenge Round be abolished and replaced by an elimination contest for all teams, including the holder.

With Wimbledon out of the way, the tennis community focused on the final match in the $200,000 Tennis Champions Pro Classic Final at Madison Square Garden. Rosewall had squeaked through into the final four by defeating Stolle and Okker, and then qualified for the final by beating Emerson. It meant another major final against Laver, and on this occasion there were questions about the Rocket's form, after his early loss at Wimbledon, and whether a change in racket during the year had impacted his game. A preliminary doubles match was played by the two Panchos,

285 Interview with author, 11 June 2012

286 *World Tennis*, September 1970. A week after the Wimbledon final Rosewall had the minor satisfaction of beating Newcombe in the final of the Welsh Open (6-4, 6-4) in just over an hour.

Gonzales and Segura, partnered by a couple of promising young players from the New York area, Steve Geller and Vitas Gerulaitis. A crowd of 10,292 turned out for the final, which proved a little disappointing with Laver winning in straight sets (6-4, 6-3, 6-3). The big money stakes might have affected the caliber of the tennis played that night.

In late July 1970 WCT's Lamar Hunt, the Texas oilman and owner of the Kansas City Chiefs, acquired the pro contracts of Laver, Rosewall, Gonzales, Emerson, Stolle and Gimeno, meaning WCT and NTL had ostensibly merged to form, as *The Sydney Morning Herald* put it, "one big happy family"[287]. It certainly put an end to the sometimes confusing separate tours. WCT, which initially had been "a financial basket case"[288] and involved in occasional disputes with the NTL, was now the most powerful organisation in professional tennis. It had all the major international players under contract, except for some Europeans and members of the US Davis Cup team (Ashe, Smith, Lutz and Pasarell), who continued to be designated 'players' or 'independent professionals'. The American players were still able to play Davis Cup—an entitlement denied contract professionals.

In early August 1970, the US Professional Championships were again at the Longwood Cricket Club as an open tournament with prize money of $50,000. Here, a notable innovation was that all sets that reached six-all were decided by a nine-point tie-break, and matches were played on a slower synthetic court. Overall, it was a week of upsets with Newcombe, who won the Wimbledon title just a month before, crashing in the first round, losing to the American, Graebner (6-2, 6-4) and Rosewall losing a match to Drysdale, decided on the final point of a nine-point tie-breaker. In the semi-finals, Laver thumped Drysdale (6-3, 6-0, 6-1), while Roche won a tough match against Emerson (2-6, 6-1, 6-4, 6-3). In the final match Roche again displayed his occasional mastery over Laver, winning in five sets (3-6, 6-4, 1-6, 6-2, 6-2).

In late August, Rosewall lost in the semi-finals of an open event played at South Orange, New Jersey, when he was beaten by 'Nails' Carmichael.

287 *The Sydney Morning Herald*, 2 August 1970

288 *The New York Times*, 29 July 1970

From an observers' point of view, this run of losses on the American circuit suggested Rosewall was not at his best. What chance did the 35-year-old have in the 1970 US Open? This 1970 tournament was somewhat special, with 10 former US National champions competing for the $20,000 prize in the men's singles—these were Gonzales (1948, 1949); Trabert (1953, 1955); Seixas (1954); Rosewall (1956); Emerson (1961, 1964); Laver (1962, 1969); Manuel Santana of Spain (1965); Stolle (1966); Newcombe (1967); and Ashe (1968). Laver was seeded first in the event, followed by Newcombe, Rosewall and Roche.

The major match of the first week of the tournament was a thrilling fourth round encounter between Laver and Ralston, where the red-headed 'Rocket' was once more knocked off his perch by 7-6, 7-5, 5-7, 4-6, 6-3. It seemed Ralston managed to thwart a typical Laver comeback from two sets down. It had been an unusual year for Laver. He won more money than anyone, but failed in the major events.[289]

The quarter-final matches at Forest Hills lined up Rosewall against Stan Smith; Ashe against Newcombe; Richey against Ralston; and Roche to play Brian Fairlie of New Zealand. Given Rosewall's patchy form prior to the event he played remarkably well and beat the 6' 4" American 6-2, 6-2, 6-2. "You have to teach these young kids a few things," said Rosewall after the match, and there was little Smith could do but smile.[290] Newcombe also managed to recover some of his Wimbledon form when he beat seventh-seeded Ashe in a match filled with exciting tie-breaks by 6-1, 7-6, 5-7, 7-6. This meant Rosewall and Newcombe were placed in a semi-final against each other, with Roche versus Richey in the other.

On a sun-drenched day, and before a sell-out crowd of 14, 481, Rosewall reminded everyone of his remarkable skills when he picked Newcombe's game apart and won their match in straight sets 6-3, 6-4, 6-3. There might have been some who thought it slightly sad that he hadn't managed to summon up the same skills during the Wimbledon final two months before. On this occasion Rosewall demonstrated why he was a great favourite of the tennis aficionado. He might not be able to overpower other players, so it

289 Although he had not played in the Australian or French Opens

290 *The Sun* (Baltimore), 11 September 1970

was necessary to depend on other qualities—an impeccable return of serve, graceful groundstrokes, consistent if unspectacular volleys, depth and angle on the overhead, and deft touch. It also helped that the Forest Hills grass was soft and spongy, quite different from the slick surface at Wimbledon. Watching the match Neil Amdur of *The New York Times* observed:

> *Rosewall's service return is the finest in the game. His angled return, particularly down the line, forced Newcombe to stretch for the first volley rather than punch it for a winner. On the court, [his] trudging gait, stooped shoulders, and often slow, mechanical movements disguise his intensity and determination. When he wants to remind himself to concentrate, he will slap his hips a few times or stare at the ground before serving.*[291]

> I played as well as I could in that match. Sometimes the grass courts at Forest Hills upset the other players, but I found it helped my serve. Newcombe doesn't talk much about this match! [In fact, Newcombe does not mention this match in his memoirs.] I was playing well. I played him a lot of times in the earlier days, and in previous tournaments. I always felt confident against him. It was that tournament that introduced the sudden death tie-breaker–and a lot of matches were decided on the 'ninth' point–which meant it was four-all, and it could be match point for one player, and set point for the other!

Occasionally Rosewall has said that one reason he played better in this match was that he knew the season was almost over, and he was heading home to Wilma and the kids straight after the tournament.

He certainly seemed to be in a good position—the win over Newcombe placed Rosewall in the US Open final against his compatriot Roche, who he had beaten five times out of nine in previous encounters. His age and diminutive build immediately made him a sentimental favourite of the crowds and *The New York Times* was quick to pick up on the difference

291 *The New York Times*, 13 September 1970

in style between the two finalists being "as contrasting as that between a blacksmith and a cellist".

The final required Rosewall to fight back after losing the first set, and then survive three set points and a tense tie-breaker in the third set, before finally winning 2-6, 6-4, 7-6, 6-3. He also had to deal with the anxiety of cracking the frame of his favourite wooden racket during the match,[292] which he continued to use because of its special "touch". Fortunately, it didn't seem to matter. In this match Rosewall played with variety and a delicate touch, and barely missed a ball. The tactics used against Roche had to be different than the match against Newcombe. Rosewall had to negate Roche's raw power by keeping him from the net. He had to return deeply, and commandeer the net himself. He would force Roche into playing a retrieving game.

> *[He] was all over the net, covering shots like a man with twice his reach and teasing his opponent with his feathery touch. Roche swung his south-paw service about, hoping to break up Rosewall's rhythm, but the backhand was tuned to perfection, whistling softly over the net at outrageous angles; the forehand, although less reliable, picked off more winners than Roche could afford.*[293]

The win meant Rosewall received the largest prize money purse ($20,000), in a tournament event in the open era and drove away from Forest Hills in a new Ford Pinto motorcar. The runner-up, Roche, was again left without a major grass court championship to his name. "That's what happens when you do Muscles a favour" he offered after the match. "I did his laundry for him yesterday, and look what he does to me."[294]

> I was staying at a hotel in the city, while Tony and Newcombe stayed with friends out on Long Island. The night before the final

292 This description appears in newspaper commentaries, although Rosewall states that the racket was old, rather than cracked, and strings had been replaced in the centre: P Rowley, *Twenty Years at the Top*, page 135

293 *World Tennis*, December 1970

294 *The New York Times*, 14 September 1970

> I had dinner with Barry and Margaret Court. I can remember going out to Forest Hills on the train the day of the final. I think Margaret went out by taxi or car as her final match was played immediately before the men's final.[295]

The US Open event was not free of the type of politics that now constantly bedevilled the sport. For its part, WCT announced that it proposed to establish a $1 million circuit called the World Championship of Tennis in 1971. The circuit comprised 20 $50,000 tournaments in America and eight other countries, involving 32 of the world's best players. Almost immediately, in another early morning press conference, the ILTF stated that it would be setting up its own $1.5 million Masters circuit the following year (based on the Kramer Grand Prix bonus pool concept). It looked like war was brewing between these two forces. There were also questions as to whether WCT had the organisational manpower to manage a 20-city tour across America. There were some fundamental issues at stake—who should be running the game, and what players should actually be playing for? Was it limited to prize money? Or was an organisation like WCT entitled to negotiate 'appearance money' and other benefits?

The ILTF believed that players should only be playing for prize money, but that wasn't the view of WCT—which believed it was entitled to expenses to cover the cost of transporting its players about the world. The ILTF and national associations believed the contract pros were bad for tennis, and that an individual like Lamar Hunt was too powerful and out to wreck the game. Instead they embraced Kramer's Grand Prix concept as a way of driving Hunt's WCT out of business. This would be no mean feat now that the WCT had fixed its own circuit in place. The Grand Prix circuit was set up in 1970, and would have full ILTF backing in 1971.

Shortly after the US Open, three of the leading American players, Ashe, Lutz and Pasarell announced they had signed five-year pro contracts with WCT.[296] "I didn't sign for the money," stated Ashe, "I thought the

295 Margaret Court defeated Rosie Casals of the US to win the grand slam of four major titles for the calendar year of 1970 in this match.

296 The only leading American players without contracts to WCT were Smith, Graebner and Richey.

time had come." It was a major decision on his part as he was no longer eligible for Davis Cup play, but when making his announcement Ashe was cautiously critical of the USLTA, speaking of the organisation being bound by "antiquated rules", and not wanting "to assume a role of leadership"[297].

All this led to the USLTA adopting an extremely hardline approach. In November 1970 it announced that its administrative committee was considering whether all contract professionals should be banned from USLTA-sanctioned prize money tournaments during 1971. If this was approved the USLTA planned to seek support from other national associations, with the intent of banning contract pros from major international events. The USLTA's concern was that the WCT's proposed tour of 20 cities in 1971 conflicted with various USLTA-sanctioned events.

It was unclear whether the USLTA would carry out its recommendation and this made for exciting times in the tennis world. At a subsequent meeting in Cleveland in November 1970 the USLTA deferred making any final decision. Instead it embarked on a series of meetings with British and French officials to reach some sort of 'united front' in its battle with the professional organisation.

The ILTF indicated it would suspend players who competed in WCT tournaments. It did not appear to be a hopeful situation at first, and later became the subject of secret meetings in London and Dallas between the ILTF and Mike Davies of WCT, with Ted Tinling, the fashion designer, enlisted as a mediator. In spite of all the drama there was still some hope that the world's best players would compete in the major tournaments in 1971, with a single Grand Prix circuit established on both sides.

◇◇◇◇◇◇◇

There was a pleasant honour for Rosewall in November 1970 when he was named the Martini & Rossi player of the year, chosen by an international panel of tennis writers. The tribute placed him ahead of Laver and Newcombe for his achievements in 1970. In January 1971 *World Tennis* magazine placed Rosewall second in the world rankings after Newcombe.

297 *The New York Times*, 17 September 1970

PHOTO CREDIT: EIICHI KAWATEI

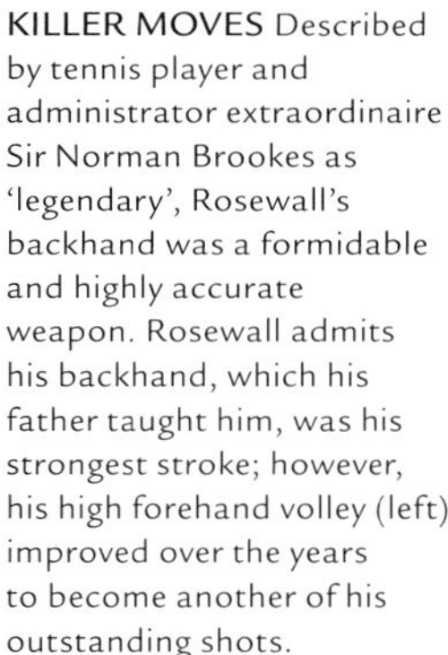

KILLER MOVES Described by tennis player and administrator extraordinaire Sir Norman Brookes as 'legendary', Rosewall's backhand was a formidable and highly accurate weapon. Rosewall admits his backhand, which his father taught him, was his strongest stroke; however, his high forehand volley (left) improved over the years to become another of his outstanding shots.

PHOTO CREDIT: EIICHI KAWATEI

TAKING ON THE INTERNATIONAL SCENE This commemorative photo of Ken Rosewall—one of Australia's Tennis Legends—was released in 1975, at which time he had been part of four Davis Cup victories (1953, 1955, 1956 and 1973) and was the US Open Singles Champion (1956, 1970), Australian Open Singles Champion (1953, 1955, 1971, 1972) and French Open Singles Champion (1953, 1968). He was also four times runner-up at Wimbledon (1954, 1956, 1970, 1974). He is holding the WCT trophy, which started life as the Kramer Cup and was purchased by Rosewall, Hoad, Pancho Segura, Sedgman, Kramer and Trabert for $1000 each.

THE GREATS The 1973 Australian Davis Cup team that beat the United States 5-0. Left to right: captain Fraser (his face slightly obscured by the cup); Colin Dibley (who once held the title for the fastest serve in the world at 148mph); Laver; Rosewall; Newcombe; and Geoff Masters (Anderson is not shown). Although he was a major reason for bringing the team to the peak of its brilliance, Rosewall did not play, perhaps explaining his slightly sad smile.

PHOTO CREDIT: EIICHI KAWATEI

TIME OUT FROM TENNIS TOURS Some of the game's movers and shakers enjoy a round of golf at Mt Washington Hotel, Bretton Woods, New Hampshire in 1969. From left to right: Laver, Stolle, Rosewall and Emerson.

Host Roger Climpson shakes hands with Rosewall after the tennis star's appearance on *This Is Your Life* in 1977. From left to right: father Robert Rosewall, Ken's wife Wilma, and sons Brett and Glenn.

'TENNIS TWINS' Hailing from Sydney, the two star players Rosewall and Hoad enjoy an off-court drink together.

ROYAL RECOGNITION In the Queen's Birthday Honours of 1971, Rosewall was appointed a Member of the Order of the British Empire (MBE). The family joined him in receiving the award at Government House in Sydney. Also present are TV stars Bob and Dolly Dyer (centre).

AUSTRALIA v UNITED STATES The two teams face each other once again at a competition in Flinders Park in 1988. From left: Rosewall, Stan Smith, Newcombe, Marty Reissen, Roche, Tom Gorman, Fraser, Bob Lutz, Sedgman, Olmedo and Anderson.

CHEERS KEN! Still winning events in the 1990s. Rosewall takes part in an ATP Seniors Tournament in Germany.

A SPORTING REUNION Tennis greats gather in the early 1990s, from left to right: Rosewall, Anderson, Laver, Fraser, Sedgman, Newcombe, Emerson and Stolle.

Taken in 2005, Ken and Wilma Rosewall, and Frank and Jean Sedgman take a tram on Newport, Rhode Island, where Rosewall had been inducted into the International Tennis Hall of Fame in 1980.

PAYING TRIBUTE Newcombe speaks at a testimonial evening celebrating Rosewall's sporting achievements. Muscles himself poses for the camera in front of a playing shot of himself.

Ken's induction to the Australian Sports Hall of Fame as a 'Legend' in Melbourne on 8 October 2009. He is pictured with his family Brett, Wilma and Glenn.

This was predominantly because of Newcombe's Wimbledon victory, but the magazine acknowledged that the margin between the two players was minute. For example, Rosewall's record was 11-5 against other top 10 players, while Newcombe was 7-9, but *World Tennis* justified its number-one spot on the grounds that Wimbledon had a greater status than other events. Laver had been stripped of all his titles in 1970, and fell to number four in the rankings, but paradoxically he won more money than he had in 1969.[298]

The following week the players descended on London for the Embassy Indoor Tennis Championships at Wembley. Here, Rosewall cruised to victory against Gonzales in the quarter-finals (6-2, 6-3) and in scenes reminiscent of matches on the pro tour a decade before, Gonzales became grumpy with the noise of fans dining at courtside. In the semi-finals Rosewall lost 7-5, 6-2 to the fast-improving American, Cliff Richey, who then lost in the final match to Laver 6-3, 6-4, 6-4.

Richey's performances in the Wembley tournament guaranteed him a share of the first prize in the ITF Pepsi Cola Grand Prix Circuit (the competition championed by Kramer). The series comprised players' results in 20 different tournaments during 1970, but leading pros like Laver and Rosewall had not played in all of them. This was a huge prize money event, and the heavy sponsorship of Pepsi Cola signalled the start of significant commercial sponsorship in the sport.

The final tournament of the year was the Pepsi Cola Grand Prix Masters (similar to the current Masters play-off) played in Tokyo. This was a round robin event between the top six (rather then eight) finishers on the Grand Prix circuit, as both Newcombe and Richey were absent. During the course of the event Laver beat Rosewall 5-6, 6-3, 6-5, but he was relegated to second place as he suffered an earlier loss to Smith during the tournament. The round-robin match between Rosewall and Smith resulted in a 6-4, 6-5 victory to the American, with the contest going until 7-5 in the second set tie-break. It had an odd conclusion in the second set when Smith was serving for the set at 5-4, only to have a piece of the carpeting surface of

298 It could be argued that Laver's relegation to fourth was unfair because he had a superior record to the three players ahead of him throughout the year, despite holding a less impressive record in the major events.

the court come loose on Rosewall's side of the net. This caused a delay in proceedings. Later Smith admitted that Rosewall was within his rights to have the court properly taped down, but for a time he lost concentration and found himself behind 3-5 in the tie break. He was worried Rosewall was going to take control of proceedings, but that didn't happen. The Laver-Rosewall match took place the following day, and even though these two warriors had played each other countless times, *World Tennis* described this as one of their most exciting displays, "sprinkled with all their finest shots"[299]. Throughout the conclusion to the 1970 season, Wilma and the boys travelled with Rosewall through Europe and Japan.

> The family were with me at the end of 1970, when I was playing in the Grand Prix events in London and then the Grand Prix Masters in Japan. We had to look after the schooling for the boys while they were travelling. We started off at Barcelona, and then London, Stockholm and Paris. There were four weeks and four tournaments, and then to Japan for the finals. We then went from there to America, so we had Christmas 1970 with our friends in Scottsdale, Arizona, at the John Gardiner Tennis Ranch. The Arizona facility was just opening and created a lot of interest with its focus on tennis and good accommodation. The ranch became the main base for me in America. Mr Gardiner set up the first junior live-in camp in Carmel Valley, California, and later developed the ranch in Arizona. The first camp in Carmel started in 1957, and it gradually got bigger and bigger. The family returned home at the start of the Australian school year (February 1971) and I then started out on the 1971 WCT circuit.

◇◇◇◇◇◇◇

Reports at the end of the year confirmed that a settlement of sorts had been reached between the ILTF and the WCT. This followed the meetings and intercontinental telephone hookups. There was a great

299 *World Tennis*, March 1971

deal of secrecy between the parties. Neil Amdur of *The New York Times* wrote that the way everyone was acting so "close mouthed" you would have thought they were about "to sign the Treaty of Versailles". The proposed agreement allowed contract pros to play at Wimbledon, the French Open and the US Opens during 1971, and provided that the two parties would "work together towards the development and spectator appeal of the game throughout the world"[300]. It was expected, nonetheless, that the Italian and French Championships would suffer due to scheduling problems with WCT events. More and more Australian players were signing up with WCT at this stage, with Ruffels, Stone and Crealy all deciding to sign as pros. Commentators saw it as a sad state of affairs for Australian tennis. Graham O'Neill of *The Australian* wrote that tennis had "had it" in Australia:

> *Australian tennis is in its death throes. The seemingly bottomless barrel of talent which provided us with two decades of superstars has been plumbed and scraped dry. The money which would be needed to attract the stars away from lucrative European and American circuits during the year could not be offered by any Australian sponsor.*[301]

There were no such concerns in the United States where tennis was the new 'boom' sport. A sign of the boom was Rosewall's association with the John Gardiner Tennis Ranch in Arizona.

---

300 *The New York Times*, 9 December 1970

301 Quoted in *World Tennis*, February 1971

CHAPTER 7

◇◇◇◇◇◇◇

POLITICS... AND MORE POLITICS

At the end of 1970, members of the tennis elite and its governing bodies were still debating just who had been the best player of the year (notwithstanding any ranking system). In an era of professional tennis, should it be the person who won the most money (Laver), or the person who won the major tournaments (Newcombe and Rosewall)?

Perhaps the $210,000 Tennis Champions Pro Classic, starting at Madison Square Garden in January 1971, would help answer the question. This was the same series of winner-take-all matches played in 1970, where players qualified through to a final four, and then a final match—all qualifying matches were played for a weekly prize of $10,000 on a new acrylic fibre surface called Sportsface. The event kicked off at Madison Square Garden, before moving to Rochester, Boston, Philadelphia, Detroit, Cleveland and Los Angeles.

In one early match Laver convincingly beat Rosewall at Madison Square Garden by 6-3, 6-2, 7-5, almost three years after Rosewall beat Laver at the French Open in 1968. One interested spectator was US player Julie Heldman, who wrote: "Ken's head began to droop, he played games with his racquet and his sighs were accompanied by typical Rosewall gestures of despair."[302] Laver seemed to enjoy this winner-take-all format and he romped through 11 qualifying matches, pocketing cash prizes. He had set himself the task of winning 13 straight matches in this event, seemingly because he felt aggrieved at only being ranked number four in the world for 1970.

In contrast, Rosewall's start to the new year was disappointing, marked by a first-round loss, 6-3, 6-4, to Owen Davidson in the Philadelphia Indoor Open event. "I was off before I was on," said a subdued Rosewall after the match. He had not dropped a set to Davidson in two previous encounters, and Davidson himself commented that his win felt "like beating the teacher"[303]. It was embarrassing for Rosewall as the following day he was due to receive the Golden Racquet Award for player of the year in 1970. The Philadelphia event was the first of the WCT circuit events for 1971 and, in spite of his heroics on the winner-take-all circuit, Newcombe scored a victory over Laver in the final by 7-6, 7-6, 6-4.

With major professional players participating in these money-making events in the US throughout December 1970 and January 1971, none of the big stars took part in the state tournaments on the Australian circuit—all of which were won by the Russian, Alex Metreveli. A cheeky poem, *Ode to the Vanishing Tournaments* by John Sheridan, appeared in the June 1971 edition of *World Tennis* magazine:

Australia, Australia, of what have you done?
Such paltry prize money that players won't come.
Remember the tourneys a few years ago
With Rocket and Muscles and Ashe and Emmo?
But now your position is just too damn silly
With all the State titles won by Metreveli.

In order to accommodate some of the 'big stars', the 1971 Australian Open was played in Sydney in March and sponsored by Dunlop, an organisation

302 *World Tennis*, April 1971

303 *The New York Times*, 11 February 1971

prepared to enter into a collaborative arrangement with WCT. It was fortunate for Australia, as without this arrangement the country was in danger of being dumped from the world calendar, it also meant that, this year, the Australian Open had a full entry of the world's best pros, although some fell by the wayside at an early stage. The much-vaunted Laver, who had already earned $124,000 during 1971, lost early to Mark Cox (6-3, 4-6, 6-3, 7-6). Newcombe looked equally uncomfortable when he lost to Reissen (7-6, 1-6, 7-6, 7-6). On one afternoon *The Sydney Morning Herald* reports of the difficulties tournament referee Cliff Sproule had in getting matches played at all, as players were glued to television sets watching a title bout between Muhammad Ali and Joe Frazier.

Before leaving Sydney, Laver predicted that Rosewall would win the event. Laver's own $885 prize money cheque was described as 'pin money' compared with his average weekly earnings of $12,400 for the first 10 weeks of 1971.

It was another occasion when Rosewall gradually wove his way through the field beating Okker in the semi-final (6-2, 7-6, 6-4) and Ashe in the final (6-1, 7-5, 6-3). He won a grand slam event, with all the best players, without losing a set. In fact, the 36-year-old Rosewall had won the last two grand slam tennis tournaments, and he held aloft the Norman Brookes Challenge Cup for the first time since 1955. Regrettably, however, the event was not a major success, with organisers suffering a $110,000 loss, and only 45,000 spectators attending the 10 sessions of play (over seven days and three nights).

The early losses of Laver, Newcombe and Roche robbed the event of spectator interest. Laver showed a distinct lack of interest in playing doubles after his singles loss, having booked a seat on a flight back to the United States on the day of his early round doubles match. The major sponsor, Dunlop, announced that it was not prepared to negotiate with WCT the following year. It would only deal with the WCT contract pros as individuals. The lackluster effort of some of the big names in the event, where seeded players "fell like raindrops", was seen to be a weakness in the "guarantee" system.[304]

304 *World Tennis*, February 1972

> It was a good field—the contract pros did a deal with Tennis Australia (or the then LTAA). I wasn't under a specific contract by this stage but the ILTF still prevented us from playing Davis Cup. It was the last Australian Championships held anywhere but Melbourne and it was a satisfying event for me because Sydney, and White City, was my home. I have good memories of being at White City, at least except for the 1954 Davis Cup! My father got to see some good tennis, as he was there. I played well that week.
>
> I can remember that match between Mark Cox and Rod. It was an evening match, with damp, heavy conditions. That suited Mark because he was such a clean hitter. He beat Rod without taking his sweater off. It's always remembered that Mark Cox is one of the few players (or maybe the only player) to beat the Rocket without taking his sweater off.

The final match in the Tennis Champions Classic was played back in New York on 19 March 1971, and Laver won with almost embarrassing ease over Okker (7-5, 6-2, 6-1). The match lasted just one hour 15 minutes. The prize money at stake was $50,000, with $35,000 going to the winner—it seemed Laver was always at this best when the big bucks were at stake.

The year continued on an interesting trajectory for Rosewall. He played and won the South African Open in April, a victory achieved without losing a set. He was then unable to play in Rome due to a shoulder injury, and decided to absent himself from the French Open. *The New York Times* wrote that both he and Laver decided not to play an event on slow, red clay so soon before Wimbledon. It meant being faced with tough five-set matches without tie-breakers, and the top stars might have wondered whether the slog was worthwhile if they could earn just as much playing a few nights on the WCT tour. Somewhat caustically the newspaper also suggested the players didn't like the 20 per cent tax on prize money imposed by the French government. This year only 16 of the 32 WCT contract pros entered the French Open, after all, it was a non-WCT event. As a result, the ILTF accused the WCT of not keeping its side of the bargain made earlier that year and instead concentrating its efforts on building a circuit in the United States while neglecting Europe. For the second year in a row Jan Kodes won the French Open, on this occasion defeating Nastase by 8-6, 6-2, 2-6, 7-5.

> My reason for not playing on that occasion? I wanted to spend time with my family. It wasn't as though I was playing in any opposition event. Whenever I was home I used to practise with some of the younger players—the junior players that were in and around Sydney. At bit before this—in the late 1960s—I used to play with John Alexander. And before that I also used to play and practise with Newk [Newcombe]—before he started to get better.

◇◇◇◇◇◇◇

Rosewall played in two tournaments in the lead-up to Wimbledon. At Bristol he lost in the quarter-final to Ashe 7-6, 7-5, and then in the South of England tournament his Wimbledon preparations looked in disarray when he lost to unheralded Frenchman, Georges Goven. Part of the problem might have been a lack of match practice, as he had played only four matches over the previous six weeks. The Wimbledon seedings placed Rosewall third after Laver and Newcombe.

The Bristol tournament had been brought up by WCT as part of the settlement it reached with the British LTA, however, bad weather plagued the event and *World Tennis* called it a fiasco.

There was a little play on Wednesday, a ludicrous 13 minutes on a lethal court on Thursday, and nothing at all on the Friday. The press was reduced to recording the number of buckets of water removed from the courts. The event was eventually cancelled with prize money shared between the four semi-finalists.

It was beginning to look like it wasn't Rosewall's year for a Wimbledon title. In the second round he flirted with defeat in his match with Bob Carmichael, who at one stage led 2-0 in the fifth set. From that point Rosewall was said to reach "into his memory book for the shots that made him famous"[305] and eventually won six games in a row to win that final set 6-2. Then Rosewall passed a difficult test against his occasional doubles partner, Stolle, winning 6-4, 7-5, 7-9, 6-4. Here commentators wrote he was "throwing his racquet at his own mistakes"[306]. Meanwhile, some of the other top WCT players were having their own problems. Laver and Ashe both tumbled in fourth round matches, with Laver losing to Tom Gorman, by 9-7, 8-6, 6-3. It was actually Laver's second loss to Gorman in just 10 days, as the American also beat him on an indoor board surface in the Queen's Club event.

No one was sure what the outcome would be in the quarter-final match between Rosewall and Richey, the determined Texan, who had now earned his place among the world's best players. In spite of Rosewall's mediocre tennis in the tournament to this point, *The New York Times* wrote that this was a match that "will live long in the memory, a classic fought without quarter over 64 games and four hours with the centre court in bedlam"[307]. In retrospect, Richey should have probably won the battle between these two pocket-sized stroke-makers. He won the first two sets, and then led 4-2, 0-30 on Rosewall's service. Later he led 7-6 with his serve to come in the fourth set. As the crowd roared Rosewall on, the Australian fought back to win that fourth set. In the fifth set, Rosewall was exhausted, and in three successive service games trailed 15-40. But he held on, and then held four match points in the tenth game. He couldn't put the doughty Texan away on any of those, and had to wait a further two games. It was a marvellous match on the part of both players, with the occasionally volatile Richey controlling his temper and almost defeating the little master. Mike Gibson, writing in Australian newspapers, said he had never seen a crowd of 14,000 so hushed and silent as they were during Rosewall's fifth match point. Eventually, Rosewall saw his opening, and with the last volley thrust beyond Richey's reach, he lifted his tired arms above his head to acknowledge the crowd.

305 *The New York Times*, 22 June 1971

306 *The New York Times*, 28 June 1971

307 *The New York Times*, 30 June 1971

After all the drama, the score sheet showed Rosewall to be the victor by 6-8, 5-7, 6-4, 9-7, 7-5. Richey commented on the crowd's partisan support for Rosewall: "I guess it could have been worse. It could have been South America where they carry guns," he said. "Bitter … no I don't feel bitter. It's funny … in a weird ironic sort of way, I feel happy for the little guy." *The Times* newspaper went on to report that if the matter had been written in fiction, no one would have believed it:

> *Here were the boxer and the fighter, the artist and the craftsman, the old matador and the young bull. The one was hotly combative, the other coolly surgical. Yet in the sharpness of contrasts they were as one: quick little men with good groundstrokes, a taste for lobs, and an unyielding competitive spirit.*[308]

> Richey was a real fighter. A fierce competitor. He had a good stretch there for a couple of years. He learnt his tennis on clay courts. The worst thing about Cliff was that he was very hot-headed. He would lose his cool from time to time, and he wasn't as popular as some of the other players because of his actions both on and off the court. Most players thought grass wasn't his best surface but in one or two years he did well at the US Open. I had beaten him before on different surfaces and I guess I thought that if I played decently I'd be ok.
>
> We had two fairly long sets to begin with, which I lost, and then after that it was a matter of staying close with him. And things happen in the end. I would have preferred to have won a bit more easily, and then I might have had a better chance against Newk in the next round. Cliff was a tough competitor. He was tough to beat. So far as the crowd was concerned, I am not sure we would have taken too much notice as to whether they were for you or against you. I always had my supporters—because of my size or the way I played or whatever.

308 *The Times*, 30 June 1971

After that wonderful and spine-chillingly close encounter Rosewall was matched up against Newcombe in a semi-final. Rather than managing any miracles he achieved on that day, Rosewall was crushed by his tall, fit compatriot (6-1, 6-1, 6-3). The little man was tired and lacking fire, and the loss was possibly a predictable one. After the Richey match, *The Daily Telegraph* had written that the match and Rosewall's efforts had transformed sporting values into something transcendental, and it was hard "to see how a man of 36 will have either mental or physical energies left to carry him further"[309]. In simple terms, Newcombe played his best tennis and Rosewall suffered one of his worst losses in a major event. Famed tennis writer Richard Evans claimed that Rosewall was suffering from what he called a disease called 'Newcombe'. An ailment that took the form of: "A nightmare in which you believe a power-crazed machine is driving tennis balls into your guts. The ones that miss you whine past your ears and explode into the stop netting."[310]

Maybe Rosewall's legs gave out after the enormous efforts of the match against Richey, but Newcombe was playing methodically, and at the peak of his powers. In fact Rosewall thought it was the best that Newcombe had ever played against him.

> Newk probably would have beaten me anyway, but I was worn out. Newk was much better than I was that day.

Newcombe agreed, saying he played as well as he could play. He went on to win the 1971 Wimbledon Championship in a five-set battle against the American Stan Smith (6-3, 5-7, 2-6, 6-4, 6-4). A final described as "a dour, uncompromising battle of battering serves and fierce volleys"[311]. The result placed Newcombe in that elite group of players who have managed to win the Wimbledon title more than twice. And what of Rosewall? In an unusual gesture the Wimbledon Committee granted him membership of the All England Club, an honour traditionally reserved for players who win the title.

309 As quoted in *The Sydney Morning Herald*, 1 July 1971

310 *World Tennis*, September 1971

311 *The New York Times*, 4 July 1971

> It was a very nice honour. It was my third time in the final, and they must have thought I had worked hard enough to become a member. I was told to get dressed and come up to the members' area when I was ready. Herman David, the then chairman of the All England Club, presented with me with a membership that gave me rights to a members' badge and privileges to enter the members' area. I also have rights to buy tickets for the championships, and I have done that from time to time. I get a members' book, with contact details and a list of officials. Wimbledon will always be something special, and 1971 was a good tournament, although Fred and I lost in the doubles.

On Wimbledon men's singles finals day in 1971, the ILTF's management committee announced that it proposed to ban WCT contract pros from its tournament circuit commencing 1 January 1972. The warring parties had met throughout Wimbledon, but now it seemed that unless their quarrel could be patched up, all of the 32 WCT pros would be shut out of the French Open, Wimbledon and the US Open in 1972. The ban prevented WCT players from competing in tournaments run by associations linked to the ILTF, and using the courts of any clubs affiliated with national associations. Referring to Lamar Hunt of the WCT, Herman David steamed: "This man will not tell us how to run tennis."[312]

On its face, it looked like a return to the days before Open tennis. The ILTF's position was that only players accepting the authority of their *national associations* were entitled to compete in ILTF tournaments (most importantly, the grand slam events). The bad blood had been festering for a year or so. In 1970 WCT pulled its players out of the Italian and French Championships, and the professional organisation believed it was entitled to a greater share of the profits, a larger share of sponsorship rights, and a say in tournament circuit rules—including matters as mundane as what ball should be used. The British LTA was incensed at WCT's demands for appearance money and a share of the television rights. A tentative peace

312 *Sports Illustrated*, 22 May 1972

agreement was reached at the end of 1970, but organisers of the French Open were upset when top WCT players chose not to turn up in Paris.

Initially, the tennis press took the ILTF's side and challenged the WCT's right to make such demands. But observers became increasingly concerned that the stalemate might signal the end of open tennis. The ILTF realised that there was a serious challenge to its authority. Writing a guest editorial in *World Tennis* magazine, Rex Bellamy of *The Times* remarked that the world game was run by and for amateurs, and the ILTF's prime concern was "the general health and development of a part-time recreation, not the promotion of big-money spectator tennis". Having said this, it was the ILTF who controlled the famous tournaments that were "the vital shop windows and sources of income for the international game". Bellamy went on to compare the position of WCT—an organisation run by and for professionals:

> *As tennis developed into a big-money sport (a trend accelerated by open tournaments) it was inevitable that the successors of the old professional circus would reorganize, expand and grab a large share of the prestige and profit available in the game's new markets. Born in 1967, WCT became, within four years, the largest and most powerful organization in the history of the game—with 33 players (there were originally eight), offices in Dallas and London, and a staff of eight, plus the owners, Lamar Hunt and his nephew, Al Hill. At first the flight to professionalism lent impetus to Britain's advocacy of open tournaments. Later the ILTF realized that there had never before been such a threat to its authority.*
>
> *WCT expanded the game's horizons, set new standards in tournament promotion, and made existing and new publics more tennis conscious.*[313]

◇◇◇◇◇◇◇

The week after Wimbledon, Rosewall defeated Roger Taylor in the final of the Welsh Tennis Championships, an event he had won the year before. The players then moved on to the Washington Star event in

313 *World Tennis*, January 1972

Washington DC, a tournament full of upsets with Ashe, Graebner and Richey all losing in the second round. It was a WCT event, and 29 of the contract pros turned up to play, but the seedings for the tournament seemed unusual to say the least, as Rosewall ended up meeting Laver in the fourth round.[314] Securing his first victory over Laver since May 1968, the 36-year-old tamed his great rival 5-7, 6-3, 6-1. The result seemed to confirm that Laver was now better at one-off matches, like the professional series at the start of the year, rather than playing through a tournament. In a subsequent semi-final match Rosewall beat Wimbledon finalist Smith, 6-3, 6-2, and then trounced Reissen in the final, 6-2, 7-5, 6-1.

The following week, during a WCT event in Louisville, Kentucky (where Rosewall was beaten by the fast-improving Australian John Alexander and Laver lost to Bowrey), the ILTF general assembly made the unanimous decision to bar WCT contract pros from competing in ILTF tournaments or playing on ILTF courts in 1972. Member nations were told that anyone helping WCT would be expelled from the organisation, meaning the 32 WCT contract pros would play their own circuit in 1972 and leave Wimbledon, Forest Hills, the French Championships and every other LTA event "bereft of the great stars"[315].

The players then moved on to the US Professional Championships at Longwood Cricket Club, where the first day's matches disrupted by members of the National Association for the Advancement of Coloured People (an African-American civil rights organisation) protesting against the participation of South African players.

The players took time adjusting to the slow Uni-Turf embossed vinyl sheet surface, which might help explain why Laver lost to Reissen in a quarter-final by 1-6, 6-4, 7-6. It was the first time since 1963 that Laver had not reached the final of this tournament, an event he had won five times. It also meant that Reissen had beaten Laver on three out of four occasions during the course of the year. Columnists rightly noted that Laver had not won a tournament since May, but had been awarded much more prize money than any other player. In an evening quarter-final Rosewall, seeded sixth,

314 Here Rosewall had survived a match point in his first round match against American, Jim Osborne.

315 *World Tennis*, November 1971

swept aside the second seeded Ashe, 6-3, 6-4. For the time being it seemed that Ashe and Laver's great skills had departed them.

In the semi-final matches Drysdale ousted the favourite Newcombe 6-3, 1-6, 5-7, 6-4, 6-4, and Rosewall wore down Reissen 3-6, 6-1, 6-4, 6-3, mercilessly sending the American scampering back and forth across the court on a unpleasantly hot day. Rosewall was back in the final US Professional Championships for the fourth time and he used the opportunity to demonstrate all his best shot-making skills while completely overwhelming Drysdale 6-4, 6-3, 6-0. It was a hot day and the slow surface suited the Australian's game perfectly, as he stepped forward and clouted his groundstrokes from one side of the court to the other with pinpoint accuracy. Both Reissen and Drysdale faded in the heat. The good-looking and dapper Drysdale chose not to wear a hat, which was probably a mistake, while Rosewall was well prepared wearing a floppy hat and a handkerchief tied around his neck.

The following week the WCT players attended an event in Toronto. Here, Rosewall lost in a semi-final match to Newcombe 7-6, 6-2[316] and Laver lost to another of his tormentors, Taylor, the left-handed British player, in the third round.

In mid-August WCT advised the tournament director of the US Open, Bill Talbert, that five of its top touring professionals (Rosewall, Emerson, Stolle, Roche and Gimeno) would not compete in the major US event, and later announced that Laver wouldn't attend either. Their reason was presumably related to the proposed ban on contract pros from ILTF's major events the following year, although Rosewall always said he planned to return home to Australia for a rest. The statement set in motion a number of unrelated events: one of the major US Open sponsors Philip Morris threatened to terminate its contract; and Joe Cullman, chairman of Philip Morris, indicated the company planned to reconsider its commitment to future telecasts of the Open, and wished to renegotiate the price for the 1971 telecast. In his view the tournament no longer reflected the anticipated level of competition at the time the contract was signed. Cullman's move

316 Newcombe defeated Okker in the final of the event, 7-6, 3-6, 6-2, 7-6.

was regarded as an attempt to persuade the USLTA to go against the ILTF ruling (effective January 1972), and act to preserve the prestige of its own major event.

The WCT players (including Rosewall) claimed they wanted to save themselves for professional events later in the year, leading up to the year-end play-offs in Dallas. Their decision reverberated around the world. These top contract pros gave the tournament three weeks' notice of their intention to withdraw from one of the world's two major open events. From the spectators' point of view, the 1971 US Open was an odd event—with the missing eight WCT players, and the overshadowing consideration that all WCT players were to be excluded the following year. One observer noted: "Something's gone wrong with this tournament. There's a sort of spooky feeling about it—like everybody's waiting for the axe to fall next year."[317] Of course, it should be remembered that the event actually came alive due to the remarkable progress of 16-year-old Chris Evert through to the semi-finals of the 1971 women's singles event. She alone ensured that television watchers remained glued to their sets for the duration of the tournament.

> Of all the decisions I made during my career, I regret deciding to miss a major event. I really did just travel home for a rest, but on reflection it is a regret. I was the holder of the title. And there was no real reason for not being there to defend it. However, my body did need a rest from tennis, and there was the WCT circuit coming up in October and November.

In the absence of the top pros, the 1971 US Open was won by Smith, who defeated the Czech player Kodes in a four-set final, 3-6, 6-3, 6-2, 7-6. Kodes was a master of clay, and was said to have described the grass surface at Forest Hills as a 'joke'. This reluctant grasscourt enthusiast played with enormous flair to beat Newcombe in the first round (2-6, 7-6, 7-6, 6-3) and then work his way through the draw to reach the final.

317 *World Tennis*, December 1971

Between the 1971 US Open and the end of the year the professional players took part in a series of WCT tournaments earning points for the year-ending WCT Championships, staged in Dallas. Between September and the finals, events were played in Fort Worth (where Laver beat Rosewall 7-5, 5-7, 6-2 in a semi-final); Berkeley, California (where Laver again showed his superiority over Rosewall, winning 6-4, 6-4, 7-6); Vancouver (where Rosewall won a lop-sided final against Okker); Cologne; and Barcelona. The WCT tour continued through various European destinations before the players met for the Wembley tournament in London—a significant occasion as it pitted WCT players against some of the 'independent' professionals.

It was a disappointing tournament for Rosewall, played at the scene of many of his great title victories. He was stunned in the first round by the double-handed South African player, Frew McMillan, and lost 6-4, 6-2. Rosewall complained that the carpeted surface was fast—"if you got off to a slow start, it is impossible to get back into the match"[318]. In spite of this, it is hard to imagine the surface was any faster than the indoor boards or canvas laid out over ice, used when he previously played some of his great tennis at Wembley. It was an unusual tournament that saw the first major title victory of one of the independents pros, Ilie Nastase. He beat Newcombe in the quarter-finals, and then won an exhilarating final over Laver, 3-6, 6-3, 3-6, 6-4, 6-4. It was a wonderful display by the young Romanian, and there was no finer praise than when Laver said that he had played well himself.

It was during those WCT travels through Europe in 1971 that Jeff Borowiak, the American, attempted to explain to Emerson and Stolle that Rosewall reminded him of Bach. After explaining just who Bach was, Borowiak waxed lyrical: "Seeing Rosewall play the first time is like hearing Bach for the first time. It is impossible to appreciate what Ken is doing. He rarely goes for the spectacular shot. He will lob, get himself back into position and keep the ball going. There is a continuous flow and balance."[319]

318 *The New York Times*, 26 October 1971

319 *World Tennis*, March 1972

After the players' sojourn through Europe the final eight placings for the WCT $100,000 year-end championships were settled—Laver, Rosewall, Newcombe, Ashe, Okker, Drysdale, Reissen and Lutz. It was the culmination of a 20-city tour that began the previous February in Philadelphia.

The quarter-final matches were played at the Hofheinz Pavilion in Houston, with the final to be played at the Moody Coliseum in Dallas. This event was big-time pro tennis—$3500 for first round losers, $8000 for the two players who lost in the semi-finals, $20,000 for the runner up and $50,000 for the winner (the richest single prize in the history of professional tennis). In a quarter-final match Rosewall beat Newcombe (who missed more than 50 per cent of his first serves) 7-5, 6-2, 5-7, 6-3. Once again the accuracy of Rosewall's groundstrokes meant Newcombe was unable to storm the net. In the semi-finals matches Laver defeated Ashe 6-3, 1-6, 6-3, 6-3, while Rosewall easily beat Okker by 6-3, 6-3, 6-1. Poor Arthur Ashe had now suffered 12 straight career losses to the Rocket, including a loss in Bologna just a week before. Those semi-final matches were played on a Saturday evening, with the final due to be held the following Friday in Dallas.

Lamar Hunt went out of his way to inject glamour and excitement into this final match. He believed tennis had not been properly marketed in the past and planned for a big event. Charlton Heston, Neil Armstrong and Miss Texas were all present and played an active part in the opening ceremonies. Hunt flew in tennis writers from all over the world and "treated it as his own personal Super Bowl"[320]. It was the biggest event in tennis outside of the four grand slams.

> It was an interesting five days between the semi-finals and the final, which were filled with presentations and parties. We also had to arrange our own practice partners, as the other WCT players had left during that five-day period, and I remember hitting a lot with John Barrett—a good friend, and British writer and commentator.

---

320 D Sweet, *Lamar Hunt*, page 149

In fact, Barrett recalls that he and Rosewall noticed a tiny flaw in the court surface during those sessions, and during the match he was sure Rosewall occasionally aimed for, and succeeded in hitting this little bubble.[321]

When they met on court Laver was decked out in gold, from the collar of his shirt to his socks, while Rosewall opted for pale blue. All statistics pointed to a Laver victory. The great man seemed to grow an extra pair of legs when there was big money at stake, and he had beaten Rosewall in eight of their last nine meetings over a two-year period. Consequently it came as something of a shock to the afternoon crowd of 8200 when they saw Rosewall dance about the court and score a 6-4, 1-6, 7-6 (7-3), 7-6 (7-4) triumph.

Laver refers to it as a "stratospheric day" for Rosewall:

> *As you can tell by the score, I had a good shot at winning it, losing two tie-breakers. But Kenny was way up emotionally, and he played those tense tie-breakers particularly well. I think I lost it in the third set as he served at 3-3. It was a five-deuce game with five break points for me. I played it a little too safe. Maybe $50,000 on a match put a few more twitches in there and restrained me a little. When he escaped from that game he seemed to get looser, and his backhand and half volleys got sharper.*[322]

Forget about the ragged match play record against Laver over the last two years, this Dallas WCT was Rosewall's stage. The crowd, united in its support for Rosewall as the supposed underdog, cheered loudly and Muscles obliged with the most superb backhand volleys and the neatest, cleanest, backhand passing shots. Richard Evans wrote in his article, *Rosewall Becomes WCT Champion,* published in World Tennis:

> *The backhand volleys were in a class with those of Tony Roche. The backhand passing shots were all his own—sharp, deft crosscourts so well angled that they hit a point on the line eight or 10 feet from the net. He caught Laver repeatedly by volleying back to the same spot where Rod had been rather than to the open court. Poor Rod!*

---

321 Interview with author, 11 June 2012

322 R Laver with B Collins, *The Education of a Tennis Player,* page 228

And went on to recognise that Rosewall demonstrated his greatness when playing tie-breakers:

> *Six-all and another tie-breaker [in the fourth set] ... Rod serves the first point and loses it. There is not a nerve in Rosewall's blue-clad body. He makes three backhand volley winners, guessing Rod right every time. He wins the last point, he throws his racquet high in the air and he clasps his old friend and foe around the shoulders. The smile across that poker-Aussie-face is the biggest I have ever seen.*
>
> *When Muscles wins a match, his innate shyness disappears. After he was presented with his trophy, his car and his cheque, he burst into a witty, loose oration that was totally un-Rosewall and totally delightful.*[323]

Commenting on the match, Neil Amdur of *The New York Times* wrote that on this occasion Rosewall "volleyed impeccably", changing speeds off his groundstrokes, and serving "efficiently and deep enough with his new aluminium racquet". Amdur also spoke of Laver hammering three top spin bullets at Rosewall, "and the little man with the plodding gait and dark hair answering each shot with crisply punched returns". At one point Rosewall was struck by a ball in the eye in the third set. "It's the first time that ever happened to me," said Rosewall. In response Laver said: "I guess I hit him in the wrong eye. I should have hit him in the other one."[324]

Rosewall was presented with a gold trophy by Neil Armstrong, a red Triumph Spitfire sports car thrown in by a television sponsor, a one carat diamond ring, and a diamond studded bracelet for Wilma. "He's [Laver] had a pretty good run," said Rosewall after the match, "and I think it's about time he lost."[325]

After his minor slump during 1969 and 1970, Rosewall was back at the peak of his game. Were they friends—this pair of aging gladiators? John Sharnik calls it a "cordial vendetta", as they travelled the world often colliding in the finals of major events:

---

323 *World Tennis*, February 1972

324 *The New York Times*, 27 November 1971

325 *Sports Illustrated*, 6 December 1971

Between matches they were mates—in their fashion. They would practise together, discuss their games. But basically both were solitary types. Laver, withdrawn and fidgety, would fuss to himself over details like the crease in his tennis shorts, or the texture on the grip of his racquet handle. Rosewall, withdrawn and brooding would lie on a bench with a towel over his eyes while the locker room noise swirled around him. Then they would go and punch each other out for a couple of hours on a tennis court.[326]

We had been wearing coloured shirts during all of the tournaments. It was the players' choice, but WCT requested colours for the final. I am not sure if I wore blue for the quarter-final and semi-final, but certainly for the final. The following year was different. I just had on an orangey shirt and white shorts.

I started using a Seamco racket midway through 1971, which was quite good. I was the only player that ever used it. It was a different type of construction, with gromits for strings inside the aluminium. It wasn't that popular with stringers, as when the string broke, it required a full restring. I used it from 1971 though to 1975. After that I started to play with Wilson rackets.

As I said I ended up with the WCT trophy, and that was the original Kramer Cup. That was the trophy—made of gold—that the players themselves paid for 10 years before, and that ended up at my house in Sydney. In a weak moment I let myself be persuaded to hand it over to Mike Davies of WCT and it ended up in the International Tennis Hall of Fame at Newport, Rhode Island.

Neil Armstrong was at the match, spun the racket, and presented the trophy. It was nice gesture that he was there. The match was topsy-turvy, a flip of a coin as to who won. However, I think I played better than Rod throughout the match. Even though the third and fourth set were tie-breakers, I played well enough to have won. That's my opinion.

326 J Sharnik, *Remembrance of Games Past—On Tour with the Grand Masters*, page 5

> Apart from the compensation, there were good trophies. They presented me with a nice diamond ring—those typical big rings the basketballers and baseballers always get. And there was another diamond for Wilma.

◇◇◇◇◇◇◇

Later in December 1971 the independent pros played off the finals of the Pepsi Grand Prix in Europe, where Nastase scored a 5-7, 7-6, 6-3 victory over Smith. Neil Amdur commented that this event was a big prize money bonanza "drummed up by the ILTF to placate its stable of independent players"[327]. These were players like Richey, Smith, Kodes and Nastase, who decided they were better off not joining WCT. Big events like the World Championship of Tennis and the Grand Prix might have confused tennis fans, but the players themselves probably didn't care. It all meant more money in their pockets. There was some irony in that it was Kramer who was the main developer of the Grand Prix concept as it might have seemed like he was working against some members of the old Kramer brigade of pro players.

Towards the end of the year, Wayne Reid, the president of the LTAA, paid a visit to Dallas seeking assurances about further co-operation between the organisation and WCT. He negotiated a 'stay of execution' of the ILTF's rules concerning open tennis in the hope that this could save the Dunlop Australian Open event that ended in Melbourne on 2 January 1972. These negotiations were successful and ensured the tournament was exempt from the ban on WCT players.

The opening rounds of the Australian event were interesting when two members of the older brigade, Frank Sedgman and Neale Fraser, posted notable victories. The 44-year-old Sedgman won over fifth seeded Owen Davidson, and 37-year-old Fraser beat one of the Australian Davis Cup team Geoff Masters (7-5, 7-5, 6-2). This score was a little embarrassing as Sedgman and Fraser were joint coaches of the Davis Cup squad. There was even talk whether Sedgman himself might be included in the cup team.

---

327 *The New York Times*, 19 December 1971

The final of the tournament was also a showcase for the older players when 37-year-old Rosewall played a 36-year-old Anderson. This was probably stands as a record for the oldest pairing in a grand slam final encounter, but some observers wondered what this said about the current standard of Australian tennis.

In the semi-finals Anderson, described as a 'Queensland cowboy', made a wonderful comeback to tournament tennis by beating the Russian Metreveli 6-2, 7-6, 7-6 (having earlier beaten Newcombe). Rosewall endured a tougher than expected fight against fellow Australian Allan Stone, and was described as "slow getting to the ball" and "unimpressive"[328], but he eventually managed to wear down his opponent 7-6, 6-1, 3-6, 6-2. It was an extremely hot week in Melbourne, and this might have explained Rosewall's slowness about the court. The final was held on another sweltering day, but that did not deter the fans and there was a record turn-out of 12, 500.

Making a return to tournament tennis at this level, Anderson might have been somewhat nervous. Rosewall was able to beat his opponent quite easily (7-6, 6-3, 7-5) winning prize money of $2440. It probably seemed a mere pittance after the enormous purse he received in Dallas a few weeks previously. Before the tournament, Newcombe had called the prize money an insult and the least he had played for since open tennis came in.[329]

> We had record crowds—it just shows what a big sports town Melbourne is! The field wasn't all that strong in 1972 and a lot of the overseas players didn't really like coming to Australia and playing on grass. The year before a lot of the professionals who played at White City were not happy playing on grass. But grass courts were the dominant surface in those days. It wasn't really until 1978 when the US Open adopted a hard court surface that grass took a downward step. And then in 1988 when the Australian Open moved to Melbourne Park, it adopted a hardcourt surface.

328 *The New York Times*, 4 January 1972
329 *World Tennis*, March 1972

The big crowds on that Australian Open finals day in 1972 almost prevented Rosewall making an appearance, when the car carrying him, Wilma and sons Glenn and Brett broke down a mile or so from the courts. They were able to flag down a taxi, but there were so many cars on the road headed towards Kooyong they soon found themselves stuck in traffic jams. In the end Rosewall hailed a motorcycle policeman, who didn't recognise him and told the tennis star: "There's no point going to the tennis mate, you can't get in."[330] Fortunately, Rosewall persuaded the officer that he was required at the courts, and was given a police escort to the gate.

> It cost me money to play that tournament—you pay for airfares, hotels and meals during the week. And I got $2440! Although Owen Davidson and I won the doubles we probably only got another couple of hundred dollars. It was exciting to compete because there was so much interest, but there was no money!

The first major professional event on the 1972 WCT tour was the US Professional Indoor event at the Spectrum Stadium in Philadelphia. Here Rosewall won matches against Reissen, and then Ashe, to earn himself a place in the final against Laver. It had been a smooth-stroking Rosewall who worked his way back into the match from a first set deficit against Ashe, versus a machine-like Laver who ripped through Okker. In the final Laver defeated Rosewall 4-6, 6-2, 6-2, 6-2. The great 'Rocket' had returned to form, winning back-to-back tournaments after taking two-and-a-half months away from the circuit. The match was probably closer than it seems. Laver got the benefit of a bad call early in the second set, and it was evident that Rosewall's concentration was affected. "You have to take the calls as they come," Laver said later. "They go against me sometimes." In the same interview he spoke about Rosewall:

> *Whenever I play him I reckon I need two breaks of service in each set because he returns the ball so well and puts so much pressure on me.*

---

330 *World Tennis*, April 1972

> *I never let up on his service because I know I will lose mine sooner or later. He is more consistent than any of the other players. I can never play safe against him. Getting the ball back isn't enough. I must maintain the element of surprise, keep barrelling in and putting the pressure on him. I have to serve well to beat him and this time I served well enough to be able to take a few chances.*[331]

It was more or less the same the following week—Laver and Rosewall played through to the final of an event in Toronto, with Laver then winning in less than an hour (6-1, 6-4). In mid-March, Rosewall won the WCT event in Hollywood, Florida, beating Drysdale in the final, 3-6, 6-2, 6-4. That week Charlie Pasarell did Rosewall a favour by beating Laver in the second round.

At this stage WCT also took the provocative step of announcing that it was holding its own tournament for the 32 WCT-touring pros on the same dates as Wimbledon. Even though the ongoing dispute between the parties meant the 32 WCT players had been banned by the ILTF from 1 January, it was still hoped that reason would prevail and WCT players could take part in the three major events. However, Mike Davies of WCT announced that negotiations with the ILTF had broken down, and it was holding a tournament with $50,000 prize money in St Louis between 26 June and 2 July 1972. The consequence was that the field for the 1972 Wimbledon event would be limited to the world's leading independent professionals (or those who continued to play under the umbrella of their national associations—like Smith, Richey, Nastase and Kodes). All the WCT players, like Rosewall and Laver, had to play where the organisation told then, and had effectively not played in ILTF-sanctioned events since July 1971.

> All we really knew throughout the time was that WCT wanted a fee for its 32 players to play at Wimbledon. Obviously it was disappointing knowing that we would miss Wimbledon. But we

331 *World Tennis*, May 1972

> were under contract to WCT, and we didn't have a choice. We thought that WCT was a better organised circuit. We still didn't really have too much idea what the prize money would be like 10 or 15 years later.

The same issues remained at stake: should it be the ILTF and national associations or the professional promoters that were in charge of scheduling and sanctioning of events? Should the professionals be entitled to appearance money at major events? The ILTF complained that WCT wanted a percentage of gate receipts, car parking and television rights. Basil Reay, secretary of the ILTF, acknowledged the stalemate but went on to insist that the popularity of Wimbledon meant any decision concerning the WCT players was unlikely to affect attendance figures.

Commenting on these events in *The New York Times*, Neil Amdur wrote that many American tennis enthusiasts who watched other professional sports flourish, found the conduct of the sport's international leaders "inconceivable". It had established a category of independent professionals in order to prevent the contract pro groups from "taking over the game", and now appeared to want a return to the days of "shamateurism" (and under-the-table payments). In his view, many of the European nations wanted the sport run the way it had been many years ago, "through numerous committees that meet infrequently, as volunteers, and with an unrealistic sense of tradition—[with a propensity] to distrust an American-based sports organisation set up entirely as a business"[332].

Who was right and wrong in all this? Amdur thought that one problem was a lack of communication—between WCT in Dallas and the ILTF in London, with neither side entirely trusting the other. The players themselves weren't all that happy with the way things had worked out. Many were disappointed about not being able to play at Wimbledon, and the possibility that WCT's decision meant that they were limited to playing for an entire year in North America.

332 *The New York Times*, 19 March 1972

The Chicago stop on the WCT held some surprises for its top stars. Rosewall was beaten 6-2, 6-3 by Okker, the first time the Dutchman had managed this feat since 1968. Laver suffered a loss to the American, Lutz, and there was eventually a final between Okker and Ashe. However, the Rosewall-versus-Laver show resumed when the WCT pros played in River Oaks, Houston, in April. On this occasion the Australians played off the final, with Laver winning 6-2, 6-4, in a crisp 62 minutes. It was another day when the Rocket could do little wrong.

◇◇◇◇◇◇◇

The WCT cause was assisted a little when Richey shifted across and joined the group, stating: "I think Lamar [Hunt] has done more for the game than anyone. He's proved that professional tennis can be put on in a big-league way."[333] It was also true that by now Richey bore something of a grudge against the USLTA, after he was dumped from the US Davis Cup team in a policy dispute with officials.

At the WCT tournament in Quebec in mid-April Rosewall lost to Reissen in a quarter-final (4-6, 6-3, 7-5) and the big American went on to defeat Laver in the final. Then the following week in the final of an event in Charlotte, North Carolina, Rosewall beat the 25-year-old Richey, in his first ever WCT event (2-6, 6-2, 6-2). Earlier, in the quarter-finals of the tournament, Rosewall had wiped Reissen off the court by 6-2, 6-0.

In mid-April 1972 it appeared as if an agreement between WCT and the ILTF was close at hand—but there was little chance of a quick resolution to some of the practical matters. Any agreement required an endorsement from the majority of ILTF members at a meeting to be held in Helsinki in July, and WCT had already embarked on its plan to set up a tournament during Wimbledon. "We are committed to play St Louis the first week of Wimbledon," said Hunt. "I held that date open until 15 March, but we could not then reach an agreement." Looking forward, at least, there was some sort of accord between the parties; all WCT events were to be sanctioned by the ILTF, and the organisation would pay standard sanction

333 *The New York Times*, 12 April 1972

fees. It was agreed that once WCT-player contracts expired, the distinction between contract pros and independent pros would gradually disappear. Professionals would be eligible to play in either WCT or ILTF events. Efforts would be made to avoid conflicting schedules, and an attempt made, in particular, to schedule WCT events in the first third of the year. WCT also planned to develop two separate schedules to enable the greatest number of players to participate in WCT events.

A related issue was that in future years Davis Cup nations would be able to decide whether the WCT (contract) pros could play. It was a complex package negotiated over many hours and days. Kramer and former US Davis Cup captain (and now player agent) Donald Dell played a significant role putting it all together.

On 11 May, Rosewall commenced the defence of his World Championship of Tennis title, and won a five set quarter-final over Lutz, by 6-1, 3-6, 6-3, 4-6, 6-1. The match was played before a crowd of 8000 at the Moody Coliseum in Dallas. To some extent it seemed odd that the 1972 event was played within six months of the 1971 WCT Championship, but this conformed with the understanding that future WCT events would be played in the first third of the year. In other quarter-finals Laver beat Newcombe; Reissen beat Drysdale; and Ashe defeated Okker.

In the semi-finals of the event Laver staged one of his remarkable two-set down recoveries, and then blasted Reissen into a pulp, 4-6, 4-6, 6-1, 6-2, 6-0. The result was interesting, particularly as Reissen had beaten the great Australian two out of three times in earlier matches during the year. But, as always, when the big money was at stake, Laver seemed to slip into a higher gear. In his semi-final Rosewall defeated Ashe 6-4, 6-3, 7-6, despite the loser being fast and powerful, and continuing to improve. Rosewall was just too steady and too accurate on this occasion.

Once again the show-down between Laver and Rosewall in the 1972 WCT Championships involved playing off for a $50,000 prize. It was a dramatic, fluctuating match that took three hours and 34 minutes, and saw a climactic fifth set before Rosewall recaptured the championship by 4-6, 6-0, 6-3, 6-7, 7-6. The final set tie-breaker was finally won by seven points to five. Laver didn't appear to be at his best throughout the match;

he didn't serve well and made numerous backhand errors, but this did not mean the match was not nail-bitingly close and thrilling to watch for the 8000 or so at Moody Coliseum, and the national television audience, which was in the order of 20 million—the greatest number to have viewed a tennis match to that date. For many viewers it was also their first taste of the sport. Bud Collins didn't hold back in his descriptions of the match. "It may have been the best match ever played ... It was incredibly incredible."[334]

The fourth set was an extraordinary rollercoaster. Laver was on the edge of defeat but somehow scrambled to a tie-breaker, only to win seven straight points. In the fifth set Laver faced a match point at 4-5, 30-40, but then aced Rosewall and won his service game. The players reached 6-6, with the match to be determined on another tie-breaker. Once more Laver fell behind, and even double faulted at one point. Then he managed to turn things his way, and led 5-4, with two serves to follow. At that point Rosewall chose to attack the Laver serve with sizzling, underspin backhand returns, and in the space of two points he was leading 6-5. At that time he had something like a 'Drobny moment'. He served into the middle of the court and jammed Laver's aggressive backhand return, which clipped the net and fell back on Laver's side. It was over. "I hardly noticed that he floated a serve over the net. I waved at it with a backhand and tapped it into the net," said Laver about the final point.[335]

It appeared Rosewall might lose when the score stood at 4-4 in the fifth set. Laver had just broken back from 2-4 down, and was acknowledged as the best fifth set player in the game. He had easily beaten Rosewall in Toronto and at River Oaks just weeks before, plus Rosewall looked exhausted. Laver refers to this match as the biggest disappointment of his career, and still wonders how he lost the match considering the score in the tie breaker:

> *Two points. I never came so close and lost. But I had my chances and that's all you can ask. I had the serve at five points to four in the decisive tie-breaker. The odds had switched dramatically to me. I had to win it.*

334 *World Tennis*, December 1975

335 R Laver with B Collins, *The Education of a Tennis Player*, page 234

> *I looked at him and he couldn't stand up. Nobody was going to beat me now, after I had been down 0-3 in the fifth, after I had saved four break points in the next game to avoid 0-4, and after I zinged an ace on match point against me at 4-5. I couldn't lose it now.*[336]

Rosewall says this was the closest match he had played against Laver since the 1964 Wembley final, when he was beaten after leading 5-3 in the final set. Once more Rosewall won a treasure chest of prizes: a $50,000 paycheck; a Lincoln Continental motor vehicle; a diamond ring; and the giant trophy. The match was played at the height of a tennis boom in the United States when the public began to play, and to watch and read about open tennis. When these two marvellous Australian players threw everything at one another in a gruelling three-and-a-half hour contest, the Americans considered their efforts as synonymous with *greatness* in the sport. Laver himself reflects in *The Education of a Tennis Player* that it was a match that made tennis in the United States. After four hours of enthralling championship-level tennis, television ratings columnists wrote that the match out-rated pro basketball and pro hockey playoffs.

In the dressing room after the match, Rosewall broke down and cried.

> I'm not sure if it is the best match I ever played. It was one of the most memorable. It stopped the nation—they stopped showing the national news, and that was the first time ever. So that's something to be proud of, I suppose. It was a bit similar to the 1971 match—I think my form was pretty steady, and I deserved to win more than Rod. But he fluctuated more than me, and at the end he seemed to lift. Plus he could see I was getting tired.
>
> It had been a tough few days of tennis, playing on almost consecutive days. There was not that five-day rest like in 1971. I was certainly tired at the end, but looks are deceiving! Newk always says that when I dropped my head, that was when I was dangerous. I had played with Rod enough to know how we were

336 ibid, page 231

feeling on the court, but I also knew that his game went up-and-down, and I had lost a lot of games to him when I had been ahead. He was able to sometimes hit you off the court when he was behind in the third or fifth set.

All through the match I think I had more advantages, and a little more edge. I had my lucky moments: he missed a couple of running forehands and served a double in the tie-breaker, and then on that last point he hit the return into the net.

The struggle between the ILTF and WCT meant that the 1972 Italian and French Opens, and Wimbledon Championships, were stripped of star players. In spite of this the Wimbledon final turned out to be one of the great finals in the tournament's history, with Smith outlasting Nastase, 4-6, 6-3, 6-3, 4-6, 7-5.[337] It was a thrilling contest through to the end, with the Romanian saving three match points. And then on the fourth match point, Nastase muffed the simplest shot, missing a straightforward smash when standing at the net.

The earlier peace agreement forged between the ILTF and WCT meant that the top pros were able to compete in the US Open. In his description of the agreement Rex Bellamy wrote:

Both sides eventually made concessions. WCT restricted the scope of their activities and agreed to recognise the authority of the ILTF. In return, the ILTF gave up their misconceived attempt to smash the WCT circuit of tournaments organised by and for professionals.[338]

It was a resolution of the dispute but Gladys Heldman of *World Tennis* also called it "a devious method of getting Lamar Hunt out of tennis within two years"[339]. For one she thought this was sad for the game considering the contribution Hunt had made to tournament tennis.

337 Rosewall took a three-month break from the professional circuit after the WCT Championships and did not play in the WCT Holton Classic in St Louis during Wimbledon. That event was won by Newcombe.

338 *World Tennis*, March 1973

339 *World Tennis*, January 1973

I was disappointed when the WCT circuit eventually fizzled out a few years later. Lamar Hunt and the organisation ran into a lot of trouble. It was costing a lot more money, and the players were more demanding. Eventually, WCT gave into the players and allowed them only to play one event before they could qualify for finals. I am not sure whether that was players, the players' management, or a nucleus of organisations wanting to get WCT out of the circuit. The organisations never liked the idea of WCT having so many tournaments.

◇◇◇◇◇◇◇

Rosewall's first tournament following the WCT Championships was the US Professional Championships at Longwood Cricket Club in August 1972. This was the tournament he won in 1963, 1965 and 1971, but on this occasion he suffered a rare first round loss to Reissen by 6-4, 6-7, 7-5. In fact, it was his only first round loss since joining the pro tour in 1957. It was a strange tournament, with both Laver and Rosewall being unseeded after the powers that be decided that the 12 seedings should be based on players' performances in just one previous event. This was especially harsh in Rosewall's case, as he had not lifted a racket since winning the WCT Championships in May. Laver played through to the quarter-finals, but lost to Lutz by 6-4, 6-4. The final was played between Lutz and Okker.

The US Open proved to be the major international event in 1972. It was the first competition in almost a year between WCT players and independent professionals. The leading independent, Smith, was seeded first in the tournament, followed by Rosewall, Laver, Nastase and Newcombe. For many the question was just how well Smith, the recently crowned Wimbledon champion, would perform against WCT players who previously beat him regularly. And what about Rosewall and Laver, who dominated the tennis world, but had both suffered slumps during the year and were unseeded in recent tournaments? This question was answered almost immediately in Rosewall's case when he lost to fellow WCT professional, the Cambridge graduate Cox (1-6, 6-3, 7-6, 7-6), who was serving "decidedly well"[340] on the new, green and slippery grass. It was a disappointing result for the little man, who generally played well at Forest Hills. Indeed, the last time he played the event back in 1970, he had won. The score also shows that the final set (nine-point) tie-breaker was won when the score stood at 4-4. It was a case that *World Tennis* referred to as one of "those ludicrous 'match point-set point' situations that might as well be decided by the toss of a coin"[341].

> I agree that this was probably my only bad loss at Forest Hills. I had gone back to Australia after the WCT circuit in May and probably wasn't as well prepared as I could have been. I didn't play very well in the match against Cox. Having said that, he was an underrated player. Back at the first open in Bournemouth he beat Emerson and Gonzales, and he had a difficult type of game.
>
> It was a disappointing loss and Forest Hills was often a difficult tournament. You were lucky getting to practise on grass.

Forest Hills 1972 was full of remarkable upsets, in addition to the Rosewall match. On the third day the delightful but occasionally inconsistent Evonne Goolagong lost to America's 18th ranked player Pam Teeguarden; Stolle beat Newcombe 7-6, 6-4, 5-7, 7-6; and the unseeded, but hard-hitting Roscoe Tanner ousted Okker by 6-4, 3-6, 7-5, 6-3. Then in the last 16 the tenacious and persistent Richey wore down Laver by 3-6, 7-6, 7-6, 6-3. By the conclusion of the fourth round, seven of the top 10 seeds had been knocked out of the event. It was a painful exit for Laver, who was suffering from back spasms and wearing a brace. It was now some time since the Rocket had won a grand slam singles title—three years in fact.

The final of the US Open in 1972 was played out between Ilie Nastase and Arthur Ashe, with the flamboyant Romanian winning his first grand slam title. Nastase trailed in the final, but then rallied for a 3-6, 6-3, 6-7, 6-4, 6-3 triumph. Observers predicted that this marvellous shot-maker had the world at his feet. Certainly in *The New York Times*' review of *The*

340 Rosewall quoted in *The New York Times*, 3 September 1972

341 *World Tennis*, December 1972. From 1975 the US Open would use a standard 12-point tie-break system.

Fireside Book of Tennis: A Complete History of the Game and its Great Players and Matches, Fred Tupper suggested that Nastase's victory, together with the "hint that the great Australians are on the wane"[342] meant that a new group of players from Europe was about to take control of the game.

This 1972 US Open saw the establishment of the Association of Tennis Professionals (ATP). To be fair, discussions had probably been ongoing concerning this matter during the WCT-ILTF dispute. The new association, with Kramer as executive director, comprised 60 players (28 independent and 32 WCT) from 16 countries, and was formed to promote and protect mutual interests. Arthur Ashe was an articulate spokesperson, who referred to the ILTF and WCT as good organisations that sometimes didn't consider the players. However, the media often took players' interests to mean more prize money. Kramer tried to pour cold water on this, saying that the formation of the ATP didn't mean players would be demanding big prize money everywhere: "We will be working with the ILTF and the USLTA for the benefit of all."[343] The ATP would push for professionals to be allowed to play in the Davis Cup.[344]

The final three months of 1972 were a little topsy-turvy and disappointing for Rosewall. He lost early to Drysdale in a tournament in Montreal, and in the Pacific South West Championship was beaten by Okker in the quarter-finals (5-7, 6-3, 6-2). However, one result to note in that event was his third round victory over the American youngster Jimmy Connors. This was followed by a tournament victory in Tokyo in October, where he defeated Richey in the semi-final and Stolle in the final. He did play in the low-status event, the Australian Hard-Court Championships, at the end of November. In that tournament he played a quarter-final match over five sets against Sedgman. The 45-year-old Victorian, who won Wimbledon 20 years before, had the ferocious support of the crowd, but Rosewall won the match (6-3, 6-2, 6-1). In the final of the event Rosewall lost to the 22-year-old Queenslander, Geoff Masters (7-6, 1-6, 7-5, 6-2).

342 *The New York Times*, 22 October 1972

343 *The New York Times*, 18 March 1973

344 The existing arrangement was that contract professionals were entitled to participate in Davis Cup play when their WCT contract expired.

The following week Rosewall had an opportunity to make amends when he played Masters in the final of the Queensland Championships at Milton. It was an extremely close encounter, with the older man finally using all his skills and experience to win 6-2, 5-7, 6-4, 3-6, 7-5.

The marketing of the 1973 Australian Open was placed in the hands of a private organisation, Tennis Camps of Australia Inc, under the control of Frank Sedgman, former player-official John Brown, and Jim and Doug Reid, brothers of LTAA president, Wayne Reid. Dunlop decided not to continue sponsoring the event. The challenge for the LTAA was to see whether its decision to allow an outside promoter to run the event would succeed in restoring the tournament's reputation and lure the game's big stars. Sadly, however, this did not happen. Nastase, Smith, Billie Jean King and Chris Evert all chose to stay away, even though Tennis Camps of Australia Inc increased the prize money from $15,870 to $53,300.

Muscles was the main hope left for the promoters, but their hopes were short-lived with Rosewall losing at an early stage to a little-known German, Karl Meiler (6-2, 6-3, 6-2).

> I'd never even heard of Meiler before that event, but I deserved to lose and I got worse as I went along. Meiler was a big hitter; a European player who went for broke. I had been on antibiotics and wasn't feeling all that great. Wilma and the two boys were with me in Melbourne. After I lost the organisers asked me about playing doubles with Sedgman. I have to say I told them I didn't feel like it, so we went home. It was bad enough being on antibiotics. I couldn't get myself up and going.
>
> But Meiler was a good player, and it was a bit like he thought he probably wouldn't win, and just opened his shoulders and went for it. He was kind of player who won against players he shouldn't have beaten, but then lost to other players when he should have won.

Later that week, Newcombe won his first Australian Championships, beating New Zealander, Ony Parun, in the final. In the New South Wales

Open just a week later Rosewall lost to Anderson in the final (6-3, 6-4, 6-4), continuing his disappointing form on the Australian summer circuit.

◇◇◇◇◇◇

In early January 1973 Rosewall and Newcombe were named as the leading members of Australian team to play in the Davis Cup competition. The others named at this stage were Mal Anderson, Colin Dibley, Ross Case, John Cooper, Geoff Masters and Bob Giltinan. Rosewall and Newcombe's contracts with WCT had expired, and Newcombe planned to play a more limited program through the year, but this included Davis Cup matches. The LTAA focused upon a 'bring back the Davis Cup' mission, securing the sponsorship of Esso Australia Ltd to the tune of at least $25,000.

The arrangements for the WCT tour in 1973 were now in place. The tour was divided into two circuits: Group A (led by Smith and Laver) commenced tournament play in the US and then shifted to Europe; Group B (led by Rosewall and Ashe) began with events in Europe and ended up playing seven tournaments in the US. Once more all players earned points to qualify for the WCT Championships final in May 1973. This 64-player circuit was the largest professional tour in tennis history.

It was not a wildly successful start to the year for Rosewall, who lost to Cox in an event played at the Royal Albert Hall in London (7-5, 0-6, 6-4). The following week he atoned for this loss in the quarter-finals of an event in Milan, but was then beaten by Reissen, 6-2, 3-6, 9-7. On the other side of the Atlantic the mercurial Laver won two successive WCT events on the Group A circuit in the US. In Copenhagen, Rosewall again lost to Reissen in the semi-finals of the event. Then in Cologne he lost to the New Zealander Brian Fairlie (with an odd score—1-6, 6-2, 6-1) in a quarter-final match.

There remained considerable confusion in the game at its upper levels as the USLTA had now established a separate circuit for non-WCT professionals—the Independent Players' Association (IPA), which included most notably Ilie Nastase and Jimmy Connors. There was a level of conflict of interest in all of this: Bill Riordan, who was Nastase and Connors' agent, was also coordinator of the IPA indoor circuit. In retrospect, what seems significant is that Connors won six out of eight of these indoor tournaments and his belligerent style of play hinted that a new star was in the making.

Another event in mid-March saw an international contest between the United States and Australia, called the Aetna Cup. This was a best-of-seven contest (with five singles matches and two doubles matches). Australia won the event 5-2, with Rosewall clinching the victory by defeating the top American, Smith, in three sets (6-7, 6-0, 6-4). Bud Collins describes the match well:

> *Rosewall's 38-year-old legs out-sprinted the heavy drives of Smith as the fourth day began. Their shot-making feat was preserved for Rosewall when he saved a break point early in the third on one of his incredible half-volleys off a ripping Smith backhand. Often he was master puppeteer, jerking Smith here and there, yet Smith responded with wondrous lunging gets of his own. Rosewall changed directions a little better, volleyed a little sharper, and finally divided them with a copyright passing backhand for a 5-4 break in the third. It was one of those Rosewallian shots that caused writer Walter Bingham to gasp at Wimbledon three years ago, 'That's the greatest backhand since ... since Rosewall.'* [345]

It was the end of March and Rosewall had still not registered a tournament victory all year, suffering another loss at the semi-final of an event in Merrifield, Virginia to Ashe (6-4, 5-7, 6-4). Things could only get better when he returned to his 'hunting ground' at River Oaks, Houston, in early April. He beat Ashe in a quarter-final (6-1, 3-6, 6-4) and Kodes in a semi-final (6-2, 6-2). This resulted in a final encounter against Stolle, who once acted as Rosewall's ballboy! Rosewall was victorious (3-6, 6-2, 7-5), but the match wasn't without drama. There were four service breaks in the closely fought third set, and the vital break allowed Rosewall to level at 4-4. In that game Rosewall was helped out by a tricky net-cord, when a shot hit the net and bounced over Stolle's racket. "I was sitting right on the bloody volley," Stolle recalled, "That's the way the mind flops,

345 *World Tennis*, June 1973

I guess."[346] Richard Evans observed that Rosewall was probably lucky to beat Ashe in the quarter-finals, and also fortunate against Stolle. "Not vintage Rosewall," he wrote, "... but it would be a rash man who suggests he will not win any more."[347]

Even though Rosewall's 1973 form to this point had been patchy at best, the River Oaks victory placed him at the top of Group B standings. After that confidence builder, he proceeded to record victories in WCT tournaments at Cleveland and then Charlotte, North Carolina. The Charlotte event was distinguished by wins in the semi-final against the stocky, big-serving Tanner, who hailed from Lookout Mountain, Tennessee, by 7-6, 3-6, 6-4, and then Ashe in the final by 6-3, 7-6. Again Evans marvelled that occasional "fits of exhaustion were not sufficient to impair [Rosewall's] accuracy"[348].

The tournament in Denver the following week was the last stop on the 1973 WCT circuit, and by this time Rosewall was already assured of a berth in the WCT Championships finals, despite being blown away by Tanner in the quarter-finals by 6-1, 6-2. (The top four players from Group B were Rosewall, Taylor, Reissen and Ashe.) Laver and Smith had proved the most successful players on the Group A circuit, and were now touring through Europe. (The qualifying players from Group A were Smith, Laver, Alexander and Emerson.)

The finals of the WCT circuit were again staged in Dallas. The pairings for the quarter-final matches played on a Supreme Court surface (with a PVC foam cushioned base) at the Moody Coliseum were: Laver v Emerson; Alexander v Smith; Ashe v Reissen; and Rosewall v Taylor. Rosewall normally had Taylor's number, but this was a much closer match, with the older player finally prevailing by 4-6, 6-2, 6-7, 6-1, 6-4. The semi-finals were then played out between Laver and Smith, and Ashe and Rosewall. It was here that the surprises would occur. Laver and Rosewall probably regarded the WCT Championships as a personal competition after the events of 1971 and 1972, but this was no longer the case. First, Smith beat

346 *The New York Times*, 9 April 1973

347 *World Tennis*, July 1973

348 ibid

Laver in four sets (4-6, 6-4, 7-6, 7-5) and then Ashe fought off a brave Rosewall comeback in their semi-final by winning, 6-4, 6-2, 5-7 1-6, 6-2. It didn't seem to matter that Rosewall had 'owned' Ashe over the last few weeks. On this occasion the lanky American raced to a two-set lead, and was then up a break in the third before Rosewall spun some of his magic. This time it wasn't enough. The faltering Ashe regrouped in the fifth set. It was something of a changing of the guard as Rosewall handed over the title he had won the previous two years. During the match, a mighty Texan storm raged outside: "Thunder and lightning beat down ... momentarily dimming the lights and shaking the building to a cacophony of sound as the heavens raged in salute to the passing of an era."[349]

Consequently it was an all-American final, with Smith winning (6-3, 6-3, 4-6, 6-4), consolidating his place at the top of the sport, and prompting soothsayers to repeat their predictions that Australian tennis was on the wane.

> My recollection here is that I played a quarter-final against Taylor, which finished after midnight, and then I had to back up the next night against Arthur. As titleholder maybe I deserved a little more consideration. I didn't say much at the time, but I felt a bit hard done by with the scheduling. Rod and I played off for third and fourth, and I beat him again. It was probably a social match!
>
> I can remember there being some controversy in the final with Stan doing something that was not quite right. Arthur didn't complain, and just got on with the game. It was a question about a double bounce, or something like that.

Rosewall won that play-off for third and fourth by 6-3, 6-3. It meant that he had a unbeaten record over Laver in WCT finals.

Laver and Rosewall chose not to play in the 1973 French Open. Laver was apparently injured, while Rosewall announced he needed a rest and travelled back to Sydney. Rosewall was definitely playing at Wimbledon, and he regarded the 1973 event as probably his last real chance of winning the title.

349 *World Tennis*, August 1973

Hidden in the detail at the commencement of the French Open was an announcement that the tournament committee had allowed the Yugoslavian Niki Pilic to play. Pilic was a WCT professional who failed to play for his country in a recent Davis Cup tie against New Zealand. Instead, he was in Dallas playing out the finals of the WCT Championships doubles with his partner Allan Stone. Pilic, it seems, committed himself to play in the cup tie.[350] As a result the Yugoslav Tennis Federation suspended Pilic, although this verdict was now under challenge (or at least review by the ILTF). A definite decision from the ILTF was due to be handed down on 1 June, but in the meantime Pilic was allowed to play in Paris.[351] Pilic has been described as a dark and brooding player, whose actions and notoriety during the course of this incident probably surpassed his sporting achievements. There were some extraordinary features associated with all the controversy—the president of the Yugoslav LTA who imposed the suspension was Pilic's uncle.

This scenario escalated out of control in the following weeks when the ILTF upheld the ban of one month on Pilic for not playing in the Davis Cup match. It did so without giving reasons for its decision. The ATP immediately announced that at least 70 of its 97 members would boycott Wimbledon if Pilic was banned. Rosewall was among the boycotters, together with Smith, Newcombe and Ashe. Among the players who indicated they still planned to play were Nastase, who said he was under pressure from the Romanian Tennis Association, Connors and a number of British players. Those who were members of the ATP, including Nastase, were asked to resign from the association.

Certainly a problem for the boycotters was that Wimbledon always seemed to be a sellout no matter who was playing. Even during the 1972 Championships, when 32 of the WCT players were unable to play, attendance was the second highest ever. The seeding list was eventually

350 According to the ATP, the Yugoslavian association had merely 'designated' Pilic to play, and he should have had the privilege of refusing.

351 John Barrett comments that there was self-interest in all this. At the time Phillipe Chatrier was president of the French Tennis Federation and the ILTF. He nevertheless managed to have any consideration of the Pilic affair deferred so it did not interfere with the French Open. Interview with author, 11 June 2012.

headed by Nastase, with Kodes, Roger Taylor, Alex Metreveli, Connors and Björn Borg, the Swedish youngster, following.

In the days immediately before the championships there were further legal proceedings when Pilic appealed to the British High Court—the ban on Pilic was upheld, although the court stated that the case was not necessarily within its jurisdiction.

In among the painstaking negotiations to resolve the matter Herman David, the chairman of the All England Club, insisted the club would not back down. It was "backing the body which [represented] the whole world of tennis ... ATP are working for ATP."[352] Consequently, Wimbledon, which had pushed for open tennis just five or six years before, sided with the ILTF, rather than the players. Certainly Chris Gorringe, former chief executive of the All England Club, later wrote that at first glance the reasons for the strike appeared like "a *cause* not very *célèbre*"[353].

Kramer had never been popular among some followers of the game, and now the British press was screaming invective towards him and the upstart players' body. The tennis players were "flannelled fools who left school too early" and their main concern appeared to be "making money rather than playing tennis", wrote the British newspapers.[354]

Throughout the controversy Rosewall still had some hope of playing at Wimbledon. He received a call from John Barrett, by now an ATP advisor, telling him it would be wise to get straight on a plane to London to prepare for the championships. He left Sydney on Saturday 16 June, as Brett and Glenn played their Saturday morning football games—Brett was playing rugby union, Glenn soccer on an adjoining field. Rosewall's father picked him up for the journey to the airport when Glenn's team stood at 3-3. All the family wanted Rosewall to play the 1973 event and Glenn urged his dad to appear at Wimbledon—the only major tournament Muscles had never won.

The final vote for a boycott was taken by ATP members on the Wednesday prior to Wimbledon. There were some players, such as

352 *The New York Times*, 20 June 1973

353 C Gorringe, *Holding Court*, page 43

354 These quotes were attributed to Frank Rostron in the *Daily Express* and Fred Perry in the *Daily Mail*.

Rosewall, who raised the possibility of a reconsideration, however many (Rosewall included) were without voting rights. In spite these discussions, there was eventually no change in the ATP position and the boycott remained in place. It needs to be remembered that this ATP vote was not so much about Pilic. It was more about whether the players were beholden to the national organisations. Again, it was a question about who should be in charge of the game, and now the squabble was between the ILTF and the ATP. The players' union claimed they should have at least 50 per cent control of the game. Kramer was at the front and centre of the dispute, and the arguments were consistent with his long-held views about the role and position of a touring pro. The ATP players made a stand for the individual professional—and his right to determine where he would play or not play—against the role of the ILTF and LTAs, who (the players argued) were only interested in maintaining control of the game.

As it turns out the ATP executive ballot was striking enough in itself: three voted against the boycott (Smith, the defending champion, and Britons John Barrett and Mark Cox); and three in favour: Ashe, Jim McManus and Kramer. That left Drysdale, the chairman with a casting vote, who dramatically chose to abstain. According to ATP rules, the 3-3 result meant that the vote was carried, and the boycott fixed in place.[355]

> It's a shame that the issue was over Niki Pilic, who wasn't such a popular character, but at least it put the ATP in a good position as far as strength goes. Some of the players called for a strike. I felt a bit uncomfortable. I was only attending meetings as a member, I wasn't on the committee. Someone like John Barrett was caught between a rock and a hard place, being close to the All England Club and part of the Davis Cup team in England. He had to withdraw from some of the discussions.
>
> In theory I agreed with the association's position. I think it was a good move. Of course the ATP has been spectacular in its growth and success, and today's players should be thankful.

355 A subsequent ATP council vote was more decisively in favour of the boycott decision. Barrett resigned from the ATP in view of what he termed "unfair pressure" being exerted on some British players during this period. Interview with author, 11 June 2012.

For members of the ATP who complied with the boycott, this process meant being in London twiddling their thumbs for the period of the tournament and attending meetings discussing the future of the game. Just how the Davis Cup competition should it be structured: should it be via an inter-zone competition as existed over the course of the year as was presently the case; or an event somehow condensed into a fortnight? Another matter of discussion was the subject of World Team Tennis (WTT), which involved a proposed indoor inter-city circuit in the US between May and July, with male and female players competing. There was a problem with this concept as it conflicted with the three major events in the time slot—the Italian and French Opens and Wimbledon—and raised the question of players being paid salaries, which was against the ATP constitution. It was reported that Rosewall was the only ATP player in favour of WTT—with Laver saying that Rosewall might have wanted the security of a salary at his age, but the WTT concept was not generally good for the ATP.

Finally the ATP, and Kramer in particular, talked of establishing a body called the International Tennis Council comprising major sponsors and tournament directors, with the ability to override the authority of the ILTF. This type of contest—between players and officialdom—was new to the game, and commentators wondered about the repercussions. The players' union was seeking more power, and the amateur officials were stuck in their ways and unwilling to capitulate to their demands. Some international organisations imposed separate bans on their own players for participating in the boycott.

In the absence of the ATP pros the 1973 Wimbledon Championship was won by Jan Kodes over the Russian, Metreveli. After which, Rosewall participated in a tournament in Toronto that provided some indication of the future of the game. In the second round he beat the young Argentinian, Guillermo Vilas (7-6, 6-0) before being gradually worn down by the back-of-court, ground-stroking phenomenon Borg (2-6, 6-1, 7-5), who avoided Rosewall's sliced backhand and instead he pounded the Rosewall forehand. In another early round, Laver, who was playing in his first tournament in three months, lost to Ivan Molina of Columbia by 4-6, 6-2, 6-3.

◇◇◇◇◇◇◇

The early days of the 1973 US Open were played in the stiflingly hot conditions of New York in the last days of August. The focus of the tennis world was once more on the game itself, following a year of off-court drama with the Pilic affair and the player boycott at Wimbledon. Not much of note happened for the first few days, at least in terms of major surprises, and the press had to resort to discussions about the colours players were wearing. In one match Rosewall was said to look like a rose in pink as he beat Bob McKinley (who was wearing canary yellow).

The first major surprise of the tournament was Laver's loss to the "ever-smiling Indian, Vijay Amritraj"[356]. The 19-year-old shocked the gallery by beating the great champion 7-6, 2-6, 6-4, 2-6, 6-4 in the third round. The youngster was described as incredibly poised and polite, and was proving to be an irritant to Laver as he also beat him in a tournament in New Hampshire the previous month. Apart from Laver and Adriano Panatta of Italy, 14 of the 16 seeds were safely through to the fourth round of the tournament.[357] Some interesting match-ups in the fourth round pitted Rosewall against Richey and the now notorious Pilic against teenage heart-throb Borg. Rosewall trounced Richey 6-3, 6-4, 6-3, displaying his grass-court mastery, even though the tricky Forest Hills court was described as "a surface fit only for cows"[358]. The year of Pilic surprising the tennis world continued as he beat Borg in their last-16 encounter, in a match punctuated by the screams of young girls.

Amritraj's good fortune ended in his quarter-final match against Rosewall, with the youngster being eliminated 6-4, 6-3, 6-3. He seemed a little overwhelmed by the occasion: "I looked forward to playing him for a number of years just to see how great his backhand was. And as soon as I got on, I wanted to get off."[359] Amritraj's height advantage of eight inches had clearly not helped on this occasion. The other quarter-final results saw Newcombe (now to play Rosewall) beat Connors, Smith beating Parun, and Kodes beating Pilic.

---

356 *The New York Times*, 2 September 1973

357 Panatta was beaten by the Australian Allan Stone (7-5, 6-7, 4-6, 6-3, 6-4)

358 *The New York Times*, 26 August 1973

359 *The New York Times*, 6 September 1973

> Vijay tells the story that he got Gonzales to help him at this time. Apparently Pancho said I'll help you, but only on the basis that you listen to what I say and go with that. Gonzales said, 'Don't serve to Rosewall's backhand!' Amritraj listened, but then served to the backhand: 0-15; again he served to the backhand, 0-30; then again, 0-40; and then again, game.
>
> Amritraj says at the change of ends he looked around, and thought, 'Where's Pancho?' But he wasn't there. Vijay played out the whole match and lost. Then he went to the clubhouse and said, 'Has anyone seen Pancho?' He was then told that Gonzales had left. Vijay then went back to the hotel and asked whether anyone had seen Mr Gonzales, and was told he had gone back to Los Angeles!

Newcombe's form was something of a mystery as he had played few tournaments during the course of 1973, but on this occasion he showed his mastery by beating Rosewall in the semi-finals (6-4, 7-6, 6-3). Commentators suggested that Rosewall hit few of his great backhands, and "age and his lack of a big service finally went against him"[360]. On the other hand, Rosewall was suffering from a mouth infection and might not have been playing at his best. The other semi-final produced a rousing contest between Smith and Kodes, with the Czech player winning 7-5, 6-7, 1-6, 6-1, 7-5. It was fêted as the best match of the tournament, and provided strong defence against the claim that Kodes was merely 'damaged goods' as Wimbledon champion, due to the player boycott. It was also almost humorous that Kodes had always been one of the harshest critics of Forest Hills grass surface.[361]

In the final Newcombe was back on the winner's podium when he gradually subdued Kodes to win the event in five sets, 6-4, 1-6, 4-6, 6-2, 6-3. The US Open was a hugely successful event, with a record crowd of 15,241 attending the final match.

360 *The New York Times*, 9 September 1973

361 The grass was replaced with a clay-like surface for the 1975 event.

> Kodes was a surprise as he wasn't known as a grass-court player. He got a lot of confidence from winning Wimbledon.

After the US Open, Laver announced he was available to play in the Davis Cup for Australia in a semi-final match in Melbourne, having earlier agreed to play if Australia made the final against the US.[362] The complex rules that now applied allowed WCT players to compete in the Davis Cup once their professional contracts expired. During the course of 1973 the WCT contracts for Newcombe, Laver and Rosewall had all run out.

During September and October 1973, Rosewall played in events in California and Japan. In the final of the Japan Open he beat top-seeded Newcombe 6-1, 6-4. Players then travelled to Sydney to compete in what was termed the Australian Indoor Championships. In the semi-finals Rosewall qualified to play Laver in their first meeting since the 1972 WCT final in Dallas, and Newcombe played an Australian rising star, Phil Dent. The match between Rosewall and Laver was once again a nail-biting encounter, with Laver winning 6-4, 3-6, 8-6. The third set of the contest lasted more than two hours, and there were seven service breaks, as each player sought to gain control. But it was not a classic match. Rod Humphries wrote that it varied "from the superstar level to that played by a couple of tired men in their thirties"[363].

It was regrettable that the result of such a tightly contested encounter held the key for the number-two singles player in Australia's upcoming Davis Cup semi-final against Czechoslovakia. Australia suffered from an "embarrassment of riches"—its team was being described as "the strongest team Australia, and quite likely any country, has fielded in the history of Dwight Davis' much-travelled bowl"[364]. Before this Rosewall was probably considered a certainty to play Davis Cup singles, but then Laver won a tournament in Hong Kong and beat Rosewall in the Sydney indoor event. It made the selectors' job a difficult one. In the final of the Australian Indoor Championships, Laver beat Newcombe over five sets, 3-6, 7-5, 6-3, 3-6, 6-4.

362 The concept of a Davis Cup Challenge Round disappeared after the event that was played in 1971.

363 *The Sydney Morning Herald*, 11 November 1973

364 *The New York Times*, 11 November 1973

> Rocket and I were drawn to play each other in the semi-final in Sydney—supposedly to determine who would play a week or so later in the Davis Cup match against Czechoslovakia. I lost the match. Frase put Newcombe and Laver in the singles, and Newcombe lost to Hrebec—and no one has heard of him since.

The Davis Cup semi-final against Czechoslovakia took place at Kooyong in mid-November. The grass-court surface was described as bumpy and uneven, and the two Australian singles players were Newcombe and Laver. Rosewall was disappointed, believing it to be one of his last chances to play Davis Cup, but recognising that the two players were particularly good on grass. At that stage he still thought there was a chance of playing singles against the US in the final—an indoor event to be held in Cleveland. On the first day of the semi-final Hrebec scored a stunning victory over Newcombe, while Laver defeated Kodes, 6-3, 7-5, 7-5. It was an electrifying performance by Laver, but for Newcombe it was a bad day at the office. He could neither "pronounce [Hrebec's] name, nor handle his blasting shots"[365] and lost in four sets. Rosewall was selected to play doubles with Laver the following day. The occasions these two great rivals had played doubles together were rare, and they were faced with a marathon encounter on a swelteringly hot day before finally subduing Kodes and Hrebec 6-4, 14-12, 7-9, 8-6. On the final day, Australia won the two remaining singles matches to chalk up a 4-1 victory.

The result of the Davis Cup semi-final meant Australia had the opportunity to include its best players in a Davis Cup final (or Challenge Round) for the first time in many years, arguably since 1956, prompting Arthur Daley to call the team: "the oldest, the richest, and the best ever assembled"[366]. It finally comprised Rosewall at 39, Anderson at 38, Laver at 35 and Newcombe, the baby of the group at 29. The American team was Smith, Gorman, Erik Van Dillen and Reissen.[367] It was also notable that this would be the first time the Davis Cup final match was played indoors,

365 *The New York Times*, 27 November 1973

366 ibid

367 Ashe and Richey remained under contracts with WCT

emphasising the shift of the game (and its most prestigious trophy) away from the environs of country clubs and grass courts.

By this time another controversial issue facing world tennis was the advent of WTT, with a number of big stars like Newcombe, Alexander and Graebner signing contracts with the organisation. Although plans remained somewhat tentative, the proposal was that competition between teams representing major American cities would be scheduled between May and July 1974, and in years thereafter. The initial message from Kramer and the ATP was that it might suspend players who played for WTT. Its logic was that ATP members were obligated to play in the major European tournaments, particularly the French and Italian Opens.[368] The fact that WTT players were being paid guarantees was also in direct contradiction with ATP policy. Observers nevertheless accepted that guarantee payments might be attractive to a player like Rosewall, who wanted to cut back on tournament play. Americans believed that tennis was ready for a team concept, which would bring the sport in line with other major American sports like football, baseball and ice hockey. An interesting personality in all of this background play was George McCall, who assumed the role of WTT commissioner. Just a few years before he had led the charge towards pro tennis, heading the NTL in 1968. He was confident that WTT would be a success, telling the press: "There is room for everyone in tennis."[369]

The Davis Cup final match in Cleveland did not come without its problems for the "Australian Armada"[370]. There were technical problems with the condition of the court, the auditorium was poorly lit, and the match was played in the middle of a freezing winter. Newcombe beat Smith in the first match (6-1, 3-6, 6-3, 3-6, 6-4), and told *The New York Times* that it was the toughest five-set match he had won in the last five years. Then Laver played a remarkable match against Gorman. He was

368 The WTT response was that it planned to allow players to enter these championships

369 *The New York Times*, 11 November 1973

370 The expression 'American Armada' had been used to describe the seemingly unbeatable US Davis Cup team comprising Bill Larned, Maurice McLoughlin and Beals Wright in 1911. That team nevertheless lost in the Challenge Round to the Australasians: Norman Brookes, Alf Dunlop and Rodney Heath. The strength of the Australian team in 1973 made it also appear unbeatable.

often outplayed in the first three sets, but then stepped on the accelerator to cruise through the final two sets. The score was 8-10, 8-6, 6-8, 6-3, 6-1.

> We played in the old Civic Arena, which is no longer there. The conditions were wintry—so it was pretty hard getting warmed up. Fraser decided to put Rod and Newk in together. I suppose in a way I would like to have played. But both the boys were playing well—even though the first day was a long day as both matches lasted five sets.

In the doubles Australia played a Laver-Newcombe combination, and they blitzed the Americans Smith and Van Dillen by 6-1, 6-2, 6-4 in a wonderful performance. The pair had played together in only two tournaments during 1973, and yet they dealt out the worst defeat for an American doubles team in the history of the Davis Cup.[371] That Neale Fraser, the Australian team captain, ultimately chose Laver and Newcombe rather than Laver and Rosewall might have surprised some.

On the final day the Australians preserved the perfect record with Newcombe beating Gorman 6-2, 6-1, 6-3, and then Laver beating Smith in four sets, 6-3, 6-4, 3-6, 6-2. The records showed that the result was the worst performance by an American team since the 5-0 blitz by Australia in 1956. In spite of this happy result for the Australian team, the event at the Public Hall in Cleveland was not regarded as a success, with abysmal crowds of no more than 4000 each day. Perhaps it was the freezing weather, and the fact that local Clevelanders were actually more concerned with the fortunes of their local gridiron team, the Bruins, than watching Davis Cup matches. None of the major US television networks carried coverage of the Davis Cup final, and it was shunted off to the Public Television Network, gathering a fraction of the ratings.

The Davis Cup final was played amid further threats from the ATP to ban players who signed contracts with WTT from any of its 19 events in 1974. Newcombe had now signed a contract with the Houston franchise,

371 It was also significant that Smith and Van Dillen were unbeaten in seven previous Davis Cup encounters.

and was told of this threat after beating Gorman. He was a former president of the player's association, but on this occasion he stated: "I'm sick and tired of being banned and all that goes on. It's given me a pain for five years, and it's going to be more of a pain for the next five years."[372]

Just a few days later Rosewall admitted that he was considering an offer with the Pittsburgh Triangles, and subsequently entered a contract with that franchise. For its part the ILTF announced that it planned to meet in January 1974 to decide whether to sanction WTT. The European nations all saw the concept as a direct threat to their tournaments.

Newspapers reported that Rosewall was ranked number seven in the world for the year ending 1973 and Nastase was placed at number one, after winning the Grand Prix Masters event for the third straight year.

372 *The New York Times*, 3 December 1973

CHAPTER 8

DREAMS DON'T ALWAYS COME TRUE

One of the major changes in the tennis world in 1974 was the introduction of World Team Tennis (WTT). It was the ultimate in professional team sport US-style, with franchises based in 16 American cities. The new concept, based on "the traditional American love affair with team sports"[373], served up a brand of one-set matches. There was noisy crowd involvement, and players took the roles of good guys and bad guys. It was all very different to the staid world of grass-court tennis played at the All England Club. One of the main advocates of WTT was Billie Jean King, who professed that she wanted to bring tennis to the masses.

The first match in the WTT brand was played at Philadelphia on 6 May, when Billie Jean King's team, the Philadelphia Freedoms, took on the Pittsburgh Triangles. Playing for the Triangles were the Australians, Rosewall and Goolagong. Billie Jean's husband, Larry King, was one of the promoters of WTT. The new concept broke all the rules. For years Russian players had avoided questions about their professional status but now, due to an agreement between WTT and the ILTF, top Soviet players

373 *The New York Times*, 23 June 1974

were farmed out to American franchises. Not only that, but some of the past greats like Wimbledon champions Maria Bueno, Karen Susman and one of Rosewall's pro rivals, Butch Buchholz, all announced their intention to step back into the WTT tennis format. Newspapers reported that Billie Jean King and Evonne Goolagaong both had multi-year contracts worth over $1 million.

In early March 1974 the American and Australian players competed in the annual Aetna Cup contest in Hartford, Connecticut. Laver, Rosewall, Newcombe and Roche played against Ashe, Smith, Gorman and Reissen. Rosewall played as the third singles player and lost his match against Gorman, while the Australian team scored an overall win by 4 rubbers to 2. It was not a particularly impressive start to the year, and neither were Rosewall's losses in the Tucson Open against Drysdale (6-4, 6-4) or the final of a tournament at Columbus in early May against American Jeff Borowiak (6-1, 7-5).

Would the new WTT concept would succeed? The scoring concept was bizarre. It was just like VASSS from back in the 1960s. The first player to win four points won the game (with no-add, and no deuce), and there was a tie-breaker at six-all in any set. The matches involved ladies' singles, followed by men's singles, ladies' doubles, men's doubles, and then mixed doubles. The new format drew a crowd of 10,611 (with 7322 paying customers) to the Spectrum Arena in Philadelphia for the match on 6 May. Neil Amdur, much more used to writing about conventional tennis, commented: "In an atmosphere of bedsheets and banners, lucky number scorecards, spectators shouting without being reprimanded, substitutes and play-by-pay statistics—WTT arrived on the professional sports scene."[374]

It was more like a football game than tennis. In among the banners were bold statements like: 'Our Queen is a King' and 'Be Gone, Evonne'. The Philadelphia team, wearing outfits fashioned by Ted Tinling, won the match 31-25. During Rosewall's match with Fairlie, the New Zealander, the crowd, or opposing players, were screaming out advice like: 'Kill him, Brian' and 'Rosewall, you're a bum'. Rosewall seemed a little mystified

374 *The New York Times*, 7 May 1974

by it all at the start, and told the press: "It's a completely new concept. The younger players may be able to adapt better than the older players."

At one stage during the opening match Rosewall got so angry about some persistent barracking against him by opponent Buster Mottram that he was almost forced to settle the matter with his fists. He said something about wanting to jam the ball down Buster's throat, recalled Billie Jean King. She had responded: "Go sit down you little punk", but patted Rosewall on the arm as if to say it was all part of the new experience.[375] "We're almost back to one night stands," lamented Rosewall. "The only difference now is that I don't have to help lay the court".

Crowds shouting out support for their teams during WTT matches was encouraged. In one match in New York the crowd shrieked advice to 36-year-old Manuel Santana that he shouldn't respect his elders when he was substituted on to play 39-year-old Rosewall.[376] The Australian won that set 6-1.

> I put up with these new arrangements, but can't say I really enjoyed it. From a traditional point of view it was difficult—but I could see how it was exciting. It was now 'sudden death' in every game. For me the timetable of the WTT season worked with our own family arrangements. We took the boys out in their middle term of school in Australia, and we all went to live in Pittsburgh as the designated player-coach for the Pittsburgh team. The year was never meant to be a major year on the circuit for me. I had quit the WCT tour and planned to meet my WTT obligations, and also play at Wimbledon—Wilma and the boys would travel to Wimbledon as spectators, too.

While this quirky new form of tennis was playing to cities round America, the WCT circuit progressed through to its final series in Dallas. In that event Newcombe played off the final against the Swedish youngster, Borg. There were some ironies here as the 17-year-old had come further and

375 *World Tennis*, August 1974

376 *The New York Times*, 10 May 1974

faster on the men's circuit than anyone since Rosewall and Hoad, back in the 1950s. At Dallas he beat Ashe and Kodes on successive nights in the play-offs, before losing a four-set final to Newcombe. *The New York Times* described the vast difference between the atmosphere at the WCT finals and the new WTT event:

> *No mood could be further removed from the informal [WTT] format than the tense proceedings at Moody Coliseum, site of the $100,000 WCT finals. Spectators sat in hushed silence, rewarded played with enthusiastic, but polite applause and booed members of the press for typing and trying to do their job while matches are in progress.*[377]

Again, at the same time in May 1974, the Australian wonder team of 1973 was unable to play in the 1974 Davis Cup preliminary rounds. Without Laver, Newcombe and Rosewall, Australia was represented by Alexander, Bob Giltinan and Colin Dibley, who were faced with the onerous task of playing the Amritraj brothers in India. Playing on courts reputedly made of cow dung was never going to be easy, and the Australians lost the tie by 4-1. One Sydney reporter wrote that while Rosewall's name had been included in a Davis Cup squad for 1974, he wasn't asked to play in the matches in Calcutta. This may have been because of his announced commitment to WTT.

The politics of the game also re-appeared when WTT players were banned from playing in the Italian and French Opens in 1974 because the WTT schedule conflicted with their events. This had a significant impact upon Connors, the current holder of the Australian Open. He could legitimately claim that he had some chance of winning the grand slam for the year, but his WTT obligations with the Baltimore Banners prevented him playing the French Open. Some months later the feisty Connors issued a law suit against the ILTF and the ATP (including individual officers Kramer, Dell and Ashe) because he was excluded from playing in that event. In the absence of Connors, Borg had little trouble winning both the

377 *The New York Times*, 10 May 1974

Italian and French Opens in 1974. He established new levels of excellence playing clay court tennis.

> In June there was a three-week break from WTT to allow players to participate at Wimbledon, but I missed out on the opportunity of playing in Paris again.

No one really expected Rosewall to win Wimbledon in 1974. He was into his 40th year, and commentators referred to him as a 'part-time player'. When the seedings for the event were released on 18 June, Rosewall was seeded ninth. Ahead of him (from one to eight) were Newcombe, Nastase, Connors, Smith, Borg, Kodes, Okker and Ashe.

In an early round Rosewall once more met Amritraj. This was Rosewall's first tournament play since March, and he was understandably rusty. Nevertheless, it was superb to watch the "copybook strokes" of both players and the sharp angles from "little Ken". At one stage the players were at set-all and Rosewall frittered away a lead in the third set. He was even two points away from being down two sets to one, but managed to narrowly win a close tie-breaker. Then it was all over very quickly, by 6-2, 5-7, 9-8, 6-1. "Today I thought I had a chance," said Amritraj. "I was up there every time, but I couldn't push him. He's as sharp as ever."[378]

The tournament finally came alive when there were a series of stunning upsets in the third round. Borg, the wonderboy, was defeated by El Shafei 6-2, 6-3, 6-1. The poor young man then had to squeeze his way through a crowd of crying "tennis teeny boppers" as he left the court. According to a newspaper report he was "tired, sick of it all, and wanted to go home"[379]. On the same day, Ashe lost to his hard-hitting compatriot Tanner, 7-5, 6-3, 8-9, 6-3, and in another major upset Nastase was beaten by the American, Stockton.

378 *The New York Times*, 26 June 1974

379 *The New York Times*, 2 July 1974

◇◇◇◇◇◇◇

That year, it was a nasty wet and waterlogged Wimbledon, with players facing lengthy rain delays, and coping with the testing dilemmas dealt out by grass courts. In the fourth round Rosewall faced Tanner and his booming left-handed serve, which seemed almost specially fashioned for the grass court surface. The match was played on centre court, and the crowd winced when Tanner took the first set at 6-2. But then the little master, with the best return in the game, gradually managed to tame the rocket-like delivery and snuck back into the match. He won the second set 9-7, the third 6-3, and recovered from 2-5 in the fourth to win five straight games and take the set, 7-5. For the 39-year-old, with little match practice, this meant an assignment in the quarter-finals with top-seeded Newcombe.

> Tanner was always a dangerous player with a dangerous serve. He had beaten a lot of good players. I have a feeling that he might not have served fast all the time in that match. Maybe other players told him I generally returned faster serves better than a slower serve. He was trying to spin serves in occasionally, and I played quite consistently, and got a lot of balls back.

Newcombe defeated Rosewall in the 1970 Wimbledon final, and again in the 1971 semi-finals. But on this occasion Rosewall won with almost embarrassing ease (6-1, 1-6, 6-0, 7-5). He gave 'Big John' a lesson in tactics, with the most telling weapon being the trademark Rosewall sliced backhand. In the third set, things seemed almost too easy—*World Tennis* wrote that after losing the second set: "Rosewall made a few sour faces, slapped his thigh a couple of times" and then went to work "with the clinical accuracy of a surgeon"[380]. There was a change in the fourth set when Newcombe appeared to be gradually getting on top. The score stood at 5-5, and 30-all, when Rosewall netted a backhand to give Newcombe his first break point. Newcombe had a number of further break points, but on each occasion he muffed service returns. Finally, Rosewall won his serve.

380 *World Tennis*, September 1974

In the next game Newcombe led 40-15 on serve, but erred under pressure. First, there was a smash hit out of court, then a Rosewall backhand hit the tape, and then a Newcombe volley was hit wide into the tramlines. Finally, it was all over. Unusually perhaps, the good little man beat the good big man. In *The Times*, Bellamy wrote that Newcombe appeared to be playing "half a dozen Rosewalls":

> *All were playing well; and wherever Newcombe put the ball, one of them was bound to turn up. At times the man's statuesque helplessness was pitiful. He looked the way Samson must have felt after that famous haircut. Rosewall seemed to regard Newcombe's fearsome service as an invitation to a party. The little man seldom looked happy on the court, because he is a perfectionist beset by reminders that perfection is out of reach—in his case, only just.*[381]

Rosewall felt he now had a chance of winning Wimbledon, and talked of his burning desire to win this championship: "From the time I first held a tennis racket I've thought of Wimbledon. Even in this day and age of big money tournaments, Wimbledon maintains this magnetism."

Newcombe said: "I think he can win it. And I hope he does. He's running out of time."[382]

> I don't think that Newk played all that well in this match. Maybe he already had his three championship wins. It was also unusual that we had three sets as one-sided as that. It was relaxing having the family with me during that Wimbledon. This was this first time we had all been there together, and the boys were 11 and nine. We were staying at the Royal Garden Hotel in Kensington. It was all a good education for them.

On the same day Smith defeated El Shafei, and he was Rosewall's next opponent in the semi-finals. Connors was pushed to five sets, and earned himself a semi-final berth against Stockton.

381 R Bellamy, *Game, Set and Deadline: A Passion for Tennis*, page 90

382 *The Sydney Morning Herald*, 4 July 1974

The semi-final against Smith was a remarkable story of Rosewall, the 39-year part-timer, scrambling back to victory from two sets down, and match point down. The final score was 6-8, 4-6, 9-8, 6-1, 6-3, in a match lasting three hours and eight minutes. Similar exploits might have taken place on Wimbledon's centre court. In 1927 Henri Cochet recovered from two sets and 1-5 down against Bill Tilden, but at no stage was he match point down. In contrast with Rosewall's travails, Connors' journey to the final was relatively straight-forward, winning over Stockton by 4-6, 6-2, 6-3, 6-4.

At the crucial stage of the match against Smith, Rosewall trailed 6-8, 4-6, and 4-5, with the 6' 4" American serving for the match. It was here that Rosewall changed his tactics. Rather then following a plan of attempting to pass down either side, he cleverly dinked his returns to Smith's feet. The American fluffed these shots as he stormed to the net. Then a more confident Rosewall stepped in and backhanded a ball to a far corner, and the score was 5-5. In the tie-break that followed soon after, Smith reached match point at 6-5, but fell into error due to Rosewall's precise backhand. In the final two sets Rosewall played as well as he had against Newcombe—his backhand passes were at their most penetrating and accurate, and there were also delicate lobs thrown in for good measure. It was a stunning victory.

> Wilma and the two boys had planted a note in my sweater before the Smith match reading: "You can do it"–and I did. Stan and I had played a few times. He was a big guy, and difficult to play against. He had a good, aggressive game. I think after losing his serve at that point in the third set he was demoralised. It was strange to win the last two sets so easily. He was a great player. Stan is now president of the International Tennis Hall of Fame.

All this meant there were some remarkable statistics to consider—Rosewall was the oldest finalist since 1912, and the only man to play Wimbledon finals 20 years apart.

One correspondent wondered if the successive victories over Tanner, Smith and Newcombe were an even greater achievement than the second WCT victory in May 1972.

Sadly, however, there was to be no repeat of the heroics against Newcombe and Smith on finals day in 1974. Rosewall was given no chance by the hard-hitting, athletic Connors.

It was Rosewall who was now the unambiguous crowd favourite just as Drobny had been 20 years before, but Connors probably didn't care less about a matter as sentimental matter as that. There was always going to be a remarkable contrast between these two players. Some weeks earlier Peter Ross Range commented on their different style of play: "Connors plays an unconventional, explosive game characterised by leaping, flying, lunging and crunching from the back court—the opposite of, say, Ken Rosewall's textbook strokes."[383]

Dave Anderson, a venerable journalist, observed: "He's [Connors] petulant. His small eyes peer out from a narrow face framed in a pageboy. With his shirt-tail flying he moves with the aggressive arrogance that has endeared Pete Rose to most baseball fans but he lacks that certain style that tennis devotees demand."[384]

In the final Rosewall was demolished by Connors' weight of stroke—crushed by 6-1, 6-1, 6-4 in just 93 minutes. He was out-run and out-hit, with columnists saying he left his A-game in the dressing room. On the other side of the net, Connors' performance was incredible. However, he did not necessarily win the support of the crowd who wanted Rosewall to finally win the Wimbledon title.

Richard Evans wrote that Rosewall "was engulfed by the unquenchable flame of youth"[385]. There may have been a couple of chances at the start of the second set when he had break points on Connors' serve, but the boisterous American played bravely, and was devastating. It was not the happiest way to walk away from the centre court, but Rosewall managed a smile at the end, and waved to Wilma, Brett and Glenn in the players' box.

383 *The New York Times*, 23 June 1974

384 *The New York Times*, 3 September 1974

385 *World Tennis*, September 1974

Glenn had spent most of the match looking through a camera lens, hoping to record his Dad's triumph on film.

> I have to say I was pretty much shot to pieces by those earlier matches. It was a tough few days, with matches backed up because of bad weather, so I had to play some difficult matches on successive days.
>
> Every time I played Connors we met in the finals of events, and I was probably exhausted by that stage. In those matches he knew he had me on toast. He was an impressive player, and beat a lot of good opponents. His record speaks for itself, but he probably wasn't very popular with other players. Both Panchos [Segura and Gonzales] were his mentors for a few years.
>
> When we got back to the hotel that day in turned out Glenn had actually left his camera under the seat in the car—we never got that back!
>
> Overall it was a good time that year. Wilma and the boys were there, and I played well. Then when Wimbledon finished we went back to Pittsburgh. We finished the WTT season, and then I played in the US Open.

The week after Wimbledon, Rosewall and Connors faced each other once again in a WTT match-up between the Baltimore Banners and the Pittsburgh Triangles. As if to rub salt in the wound, Connors rallied from 4-5 to win that encounter 7-5.

Connors was seeded first in the 1974 US Open, which was played the week after the WTT season finished. The remainder of the top eight seeds were Newcombe, Smith, Borg, Rosewall, Okker, Nastase and Ashe. The event was notable because it was the last US Open to be played on a grass court surface. The West Side Club decided that it could no longer maintain good turf, and decided to replace it with clay. The board of the ATP however voted against the choice of a clay surface, with its preference being for a cement-like surface, like Plexipave.

Rosewall's first match in the US Open was against countryman Dibley, who he beat 6-4, 7-6, 6-1. Parton Keese in *The New York Times* wrote that Rosewall wore a look as if to say: "What is a man my age doing here?"[386] Rosewall spoke of trying to make the difficult transition between the single sets played in the WTT format and the best-of-five set matches of a grand slam contest. It seemed that he did not expect to be a major contender towards the end of the second week. It also appeared that he had not completely enjoyed the WTT experience. A couple of months later he announced that he was retiring from the competition, and would not participate in the 1975 event.[387]

> Like I said, we had the boys with us for the US Open as we took them out of school for the middle term. They did a bit of special school work with us in Pittsburgh. On this occasion in New York we stayed at the old Westchester County Club, and checked in there the day after a professional golf tournament had finished. We actually had the same rooms that Sam Snead had used the week before. We used a rental car to get us to and from the courts each day and Vitas Gerulaitis, one of my teammates on the Pittsburgh Triangles, organised parking for us at one of his friend's places.

Once again playing in a major event brought out the best in Rosewall. He beat the young Mexican Raul Ramirez (6-1, 6-7, 7-5, 6-3) to earn a quarter-final sport against Amritraj. At the same time, the match alongside on courts inside the grandstand was between Ashe and a 22-year-old Argentinian, Guillermo Vilas. It was the start of a year in which Vilas would make tennis fans sit up and take notice, not just of him but of tennis players from all over South America. He eventually won the bonus first prize for the top points gathering in the Commercial Union grand prix, and also the Grand Prix Masters final.

386 *The New York Times*, 29 August 1974

387 The WTT concept lasted five years, but in 1978 most of the top female players indicated they wanted to play through the 1979 European circuit, which spelt the death-knell for the competition. There was a subsequent Team Tennis competition with four Californian teams from 1981-91, and WTT was re-established in 1992.

In the quarter-finals Rosewall beat Amritraj 2-6, 6-3, 6-3, 6-2. After the match Rosewall said he wondered if Vijay knew he was in a hurry—that afternoon he had to rush to the airport where Wilma and the boys were returning to Australia after their lengthy stay in America and Europe. Rosewall's next assignment was Newcombe in the semi-finals, who had beaten Ashe in his quarter-final match. On the other side of the draw Tanner upset Smith in four sets, and Connors defeated Metreveli.

The unpredictable New York weather dealt a blow to the US Open schedule the following day, when rain washed out most of the matches. The following day resulted in a repeat of the Rosewall-Newcombe match at Wimbledon, and Rosewall once more defeated Newcombe (the defending champion) by 6-7, 6-4, 7-6, 6-3.[388] In the other semi-final Connors scraped through in a series of tie-breaker sets against Tanner.

After dropping the first set against Newcombe, the ageless Rosewall simply teed off and hit for the lines. *The New York Times* explained that Newcombe's defeat was due to "a Rosewall arsenal that included a perfect lob for every emergency, an extra sense of anticipation at the net, a fantastic backhand and return of serve that have frustrated all his opponents, and a knack of returning Newcombe's mightiest overhead smashes"[389].

It was an odd sort of match. Newcombe led by 5-2 in the third set and appeared to be in command. From there he missed a number of volleys, and allowed Rosewall back into the set. The big man actually held two set points, but could not nail down his scrambling countryman. Newcombe committed another volleying error in the third set tie-breaker. While this was happening, Rosewall was not making any errors of his own, and his precise slicing style of tennis took the big man apart.

Regrettably, however, none of these wonderful assets were on show in the 1974 US Open final when Rosewall again took on Connors. "Age withered before the onslaught of youth," wrote *The New York Times*, as Connors once more crushed his opponent by 6-1, 6-0, 6-1.[390] It was the worst defeat

388 Rowley notes that Rosewall arranged for Smith to be his warm-up partner before the match, a wise choice as the American's game resembled Newcombe's, in *Twenty Years at the Top*, page 196.

389 *The New York Times*, 9 September 1974

390 *The New York Times*, 10 September 1974

ever suffered in a US national men's championships final. Everyone who witnessed the match came away wearing "the glazed expression of those caught too near an exploding bomb"[391]. Connors was once more able to tell the world he had never played as well: "I felt I was gliding. I was on a cloud. It was a terrific feeling," he said. "I did not miss a ball today. I thought that the Wimbledon final was the best I ever played but this was better. I've never served any better."[392]

The writer Peter Bodo considered Connors to be the first real professional in the game—a great athlete insulated during the transition to the pro game, who brought to it "a peculiar blend of qualities that distinguishes the ideal pro: pride, personality, talent, a devotion to his craft that borders on monomania, and a healthy mercenary instinct"[393]. Maybe he was just what players like Rosewall envisaged as the future of the sport as they travelled about on their uncertain calendar of one-night-stands back in the 1950s and 1960s, struggling to build a professional tennis circuit.

Obviously the match wasn't a happy experience for Rosewall, who was variously described as a dejected, beaten and tragic figure. However, he still had people rooting for him, wrote Dave Anderson, "for two reasons—his age and his manners"[394]. But it was a crushing defeat, and it seemed unfair that Rosewall had to face up to this again so soon after the match at Wimbledon.

Perhaps the circumstances were a little fortunate for Connors. Richard Evans made the point that Jimmy had won the world's two major grass-court events without once facing Newcombe, Smith, Nastase or Ashe. And earlier he claimed he was ill with gastroenteritis just days before the tournament.

> I lost quickly. All the matches I played against Jimmy were in finals. He is 18 years younger than I am, and when I played him

---

391 *World Tennis*, November 1974

392 *The Sydney Morning Herald*, 11 September 1974. Connors reached the semi-finals of the US Open as a 39-year-old in 1991. He was the oldest player since Rosewall to reach that stage of the event. Connors was beaten in the semi-final by Jim Courier, 6-3, 6-3, 6-2, who then lost the final match to Stefan Edberg.

393 Quoted in J Drucker, *Jimmy Connors Saved My Life*, page 57

394 *The New York Times*, 28 November 1974

> I was just about worn out. Once again that US Open was delayed with rain and I was pretty disappointed with the way I played when I did get on the court. Jimmy was too good. I left the US pretty much straight after the tournament, and arrived back in Australia five days after Wilma and the boys.
>
> It was the sort of thing that might have spurred a younger player on, but at 39 I was aware that my best tennis was behind me. I still had commitments in Japan and Australia, but was seriously considering moving into the comparatively leisurely life of coaching.

A few things had gone wrong for Rosewall on this occasion: there wasn't a left-hander available for him to practise with on the day of the match; not only was he meeting Connors in a final, but the match was played on a Monday after heavy rain delayed and backed up matches; he missed getting a massage the night before; and tournament officials gave him inaccurate information about precisely when the match was to be played. In spite of all this, it is hard to argue with the decisive nature of the result. Rosewall was affected by the loss, and started seriously talking about retiring from the game.

It was reported that Rosewall was finally listening to Wilma, and would cut down his schedule even further in 1975. As it happened he only played in about seven tournaments in 1974, plus WTT. By the end of October he signed a five-year contract with Cathay Pacific Airways as a sports promotion coordinator. He also signed a contract with a medical insurance company—Oak Insurance—to promote their product.

Politics had become a part of tennis ever since the advent of the open game—and another major political statement was made in 1974 when India refused to play South Africa in the Davis Cup final, because of its apartheid policy.

In October, Rosewall travelled to Japan, reaching the final of the Japan Open, beating Stockton, the Wimbledon semi-finalist, 6-3, 6-0. In the final, played the same day, he lost to Newcombe by 3-6, 6-2, 6-3. In the Australian Indoor Championships played in Sydney the following week

Rosewall lost to Richey in the semi-finals by 7-6, 5-7, 6-1. Getting from Tokyo to Sydney on that occasion was full of logistical difficulties. First, the Japanese event was delayed by rain, and Stockton and Rosewall were then off-loaded on the flight to Sydney and arrived two days late. It was probably too much to expect that Rosewall could be well prepared for the event in those circumstances.

Richey had only ever beaten Rosewall on one previous occasion, and that was four years before. Another feature of the Australian indoor event was the legendary 'tennis twins'. Hoad and Rosewall, resuming their doubles partnership, after a 10-year break. Regrettably they were beaten in the first round of the event.

> That doubles arrangement was a difficult one. Graham Lovett, the promoter, was keen for us to play together and Lew was back in Australia especially for the event. We weren't all that optimistic about how it would go, and ended up losing to a couple of guys who hit the ball as hard as they could.

The rain was so bad during a tournament in Hong Kong the following week that the event had to be abandoned and prize money shared between the four semi-finalists: Newcombe; Rosewall; Parun and Tanner.

In a fourth round match against Mike Estep, the American was foot-faulted by a linesman on his second serve, when serving to stay in the match at 5-6, 30-40 in the deciding third set (match point, no less). Estep flung his racket to the ground, and the crowd hooted in a show of annoyance. The umpire even became involved, telling the linesman to change his call. By this time Estep decided he had had enough in any event, and stalked off the court!

After Hong Kong, the players played in South Africa where Rosewall was a surprise loser in the quarter-finals to Ramirez.

◇◇◇◇◇◇◇

By the time Rosewall participated in the New South Wales Open in December 1974 he was 40 years old, and eventually lost to Tony Roche in a quarter-final of the event—a man who had been troubled by injuries for many years. The score was 6-2, 7-6. Not only did Rosewall lose, he was cranky about the tournament organisers, saying the event lacked atmosphere and there was a lack of umpires and ballboys. By this stage of the event, the top three drawcards—Newcombe, Rosewall and Björn Borg—had all been eliminated. For Rosewall, it meant the end of his playing commitments for 1974—a year when he did not win a tournament—and he chose not to play in the 1975 Australian Open the following week, which was sponsored for the first of four years by Marlboro, with significantly increased prize money.

After the lacklustre event in Sydney, the open was very atmospheric with people wondering if anyone could stop the Connors juggernaut. Newcombe believed that he was the man to stand toe-to-toe with the American. He even wrote a newspaper column claiming that Connors had been avoiding him for the last 12 months, which caused the match to be billed as a "meeting of the mouths"[395]. It was to be a prickly encounter to say the least.

Newcombe did manage to score a historic victory, winning the first major event of 1975, when he beat Connors in that final (7-5, 3-6, 6-4, 7-6). Newcombe was at his peak and had been in serious training mode for a month before the match, abstaining from KB Lager or any other brand of the "tasty brown stuff".

Connors was at the forefront of tennis news at this time. It was rumoured that his first words after beating Rosewall at Forest Hills, were "Get me Laver!" In reality, this was probably a comment made by Connors' agent Bill Riordan, rather than the man himself. Riordan never missed a money-making opportunity, and the result of his back-room manoeuvrings was to set up a winner-take-all match between Connors and Laver at Caesars Palace, Las Vegas, in February 1975. Laver had been out of regular tournament play for some time, but always managed to focus his attention on single matches, especially those offering $100,000 in prize money, even though each of the players was likely to reach close to this amount

395 *World Tennis*, March 1975

again from television rights. It was a sure sign of the tennis boom that gripped America and, after all the hype, Connors won in four sets 6-4, 6-2, 3-6, 7-5.

Meanwhile, down under, Australia sealed a victory in the Davis Cup eastern zone of the 1975 competition against New Zealand when Newcombe and Masters defeated Parun and Fairlie in a doubles match, 6-4, 6-4, 7-5. Earlier Rosewall beat Parun 6-2, 6-4, 2-6, 6-4, and Newcombe defeated Fairlie 7-5, 6-3, 7-5 in the first day's singles matches.[396] Shortly after, the top Australians—Newcombe, Laver, Rosewall, Alexander and Emerson—all joined together to play in the sixth Aetna Cup, against the US in Hartford. America was represented by Smith, Ashe, Reissen, Stockton and Lutz. The notable absentee was Connors, who refused to play on any team captained by Ralston. During the course of the match, Ashe observed: "The Aussies know how to play as a team, and the Americans don't. The Aussies put aside their differences, they don't bicker over who's number one or who's running things. The idea for them is to win and encourage each other."[397] Obviously it hadn't helped that Ashe was named as a party in the proceedings brought by Connors against the ILTF and ATP. Eventually, the Australians won the Aetna Cup by five matches to four, although Rosewall lost his singles encounter to Smith 6-2, 7-6.

The stand-off between Connors and Ralston had a long history. There were questions about whether the younger man should be selected in the US Davis Cup team in 1973, but Ralston considered this was unfair to those players who had been members of the team through inter-zone matches that year. Connors refused to play on the US team during 1974, and America lost to Columbia in a remarkable upset. Then, in some irony of timing, the weekend that Connors played Laver in the challenge match at Las Vegas, America was eliminated from the Davis Cup by Mexico.

Shortly after these events, Rosewall played and won an invitational event in Jackson, Mississippi, beating Buchholz in the final, 7-5, 4-6, 7-6. The next tournament on the calendar was the American Airlines event in Tucson, Arizona. On this occasion, Rosewall won through to the semi-

396 Rosewall beat Fairlie 6-1, 9-11, 7-5, 9-7 in a later singles match

397 *The New York Times*, 5 March 1975

finals after beating Amritraj 6-7, 6-0, 7-6. His opponent in the semi-final match was Nastase, who scored a significant victory over Laver. The match between Rosewall and Nastase became one of the most controversial encounters of the year due to Nastase's bad behaviour—especially as the ill-tempered histrionics were directed at the game's elder statesman.

On this occasion Rosewall won the first set, and was serving at 5-4 in the second. Throughout the match Nastase had engaged in petulant displays. At one time he mocked Rosewall, who had dropped his racket to the ground, by walking to the net and dropping his own racket. On that occasion Rosewall picked up Nastase's racket and tossed it away. He presumably was not used to this odd, ill-mannered behaviour.

When Rosewall was serving for the match at 5-4 he lost the first point, but then won the second point by serving an ace. The issue (at least in Nastase's mind) was that the same linesman who called Rosewall's serve 'good' had earlier called one of his own serves a fault—consequently, and with no warning, the Romanian simply walked off the court. Those watching on television heard Nastase say: "I play no more. No, I no play. It's no fun anymore."[398] What then happened was bizarre. Rather than accepting that Nastase had defaulted, tournament officials persuaded the Romanian to return to the court to continue. All these shenanigans threw Rosewall off his game. He lost his serve, lost the second set, and then lost the match 3-6, 7-5, 6-2.

The letter pages were full of comments about what should have happened in this scenario. Hadn't Nastase retired? What were the umpires doing by trying to persuade him to continue playing? It was game, set and match to Rosewall. While most of the criticism was against Nastase, some of the correspondents also suggested that Rosewall should not have caved in so easily. Another issue was whether this raised the question that tennis officialdom was something of a joke, even though the era of professionalism had well and truly taken off. The umpire was apparently a local official, and probably not up to the task of managing a badly behaved Nastase.

398 *The Sydney Morning Herald*, 7 April 975

> In that match I was playing well. But right from the beginning Nastase sat down on a chair and said he wasn't playing. I went over to him and said: 'Look, I've had some bad calls as well. Let's play on.' The central umpire should have suspended him straight away. Or else I should have walked up to the central umpire and told him to suspend him.
>
> He misbehaved a lot against me. Pancho Gonzales got upset with linesmen and umpires, but would never involve the other player. And the problem with Gonzales was that when he got upset, he usually played better!
>
> The central umpire made a big mistake, but I made a mistake as well because I should have picked up my rackets and walked off because he absolutely cheated. He was pretty good at that. I wasn't the only person he cheated.
>
> Nastase actually tried to be nice off the court, but he was so ugly on the court that it was difficult to be sociable with him. He did so many bad things and upset sponsors. Several places wouldn't have him he was so bad. He was his own worst enemy.

There might have ultimately been some justice in all of this as Nastase appeared subdued and below his best in the subsequent final match against Alexander, and the Australian player won by 7-5, 6-2. 'Nasty' was fined, but in retrospect it is hard to understand why he wasn't defaulted. The public was incensed by his behaviour and there was a flood of telegrams and telephone calls to PBS, the broadcasters of the match. When later writing about the match, Nastase said that he regretted the incident. He recalled Rosewall picking up his racket and tossing it to the side of the court: "Even I could tell I'd gone way too far, because for Rosewall that was about as strong a reaction as you ever saw from him."[399] Nastase's excuse was that he arrived late for the tournament and was suffering from jet lag.

Connors' challenge match series continued through 1975 when the American played Newcombe at Caesars Palace in April. Newcombe

399 I Nastase, *Mr Nastase*, page 147

spoke of tennis fans coming up to him and complaining of Jimmy's spoilt brat image: "People hope I beat the hell out of him. Even the US players on the circuit feel that way. I think him not playing Davis Cup has a helluva lot to do with that. They think his country should be bigger than his personality conflicts."[400]

Unfortunately this pre-match big talk did not help Newcombe's performance on the day as he submitted somewhat passively, by 6-3, 4-6, 6-2, 6-4. The match was said to have little of the spectacular play or crowd excitement that marked the Connors-Laver contest of a couple of months earlier. On the other hand, the sums at stake were enormous. Connors earned himself almost $500,000 in prize money and television rights; Newcombe was said to earn $250,000.

The same week Rosewall played the River Oaks tournament in Houston, always one of his happy hunting grounds. In that event he beat Richey in the quarter-finals (1-6, 6-4, 6-2) and then won over Harold Solomon, a qualifier for the WCT play-offs in Dallas (6-4, 6-7, 6-4). In the final he met Drysdale, who he swept aside by 6-3, 3-6, 6-1.

The WCT finals took place in Dallas the following week, with Laver qualifying for the fifth time (although he had never won the event). The other qualifiers were Ramirez, Borg, Solomon, Alexander, Tanner, Ashe and Cox. Perhaps the lustre of the WCT event was diminished, with six of the world's top 10 not playing the 1975 WCT tour (Connors, Newcombe, Rosewall, Nastase, Orantes and Vilas). Eventually, it was Ashe who stood alone as the WCT champion at the end of the week, having defeated Borg in the final (3-6, 6-4, 6-4, 6-0). Earlier the young prince of Sweden defeated Laver in a four-hour semi-final match that cemented his place at the pinnacle of the game. And this was confirmed when Borg won his second French Open title over Vilas by 6-2, 6-3, 6-4 in early June.

◇◇◇◇◇◇◇

Notwithstanding his limited match play, Rosewall was seeded second at the 1975 Wimbledon Championships. This was said to be because

400 *The New York Times*, 24 April 1975

of his consistency in selected events over the previous 12 months, but it was also a somewhat generous decision on the part of the Wimbledon seeding committee. Connors was seeded first, with Borg third, and then Vilas, Nastase, Ashe and Smith. Newcombe was absent due to injury.

It proved an upset-ridden championship once more. Smith, the former champion, was beaten in the first round by unknown Byron Bertram of South Africa (6-1, 6-2, 6-1) in a match described as "a carnage in 64 minutes"[401]. Nastase lost in an early round to Sherwood Stewart, who newspapers described as "the best player to come out of Goose Creek, Texas"[402]. Alexander and Kodes were also fancied players who lost in early rounds.

In the last 16, Rosewall faced Roche, the number-16 seed. It was the 40-year-old against the left-hander who had been through all manner of ordeals and injuries since 1970, which had led him to seek help from a faith healer from the Philippines. This unusual treatment might have been successful, as Roche delighted the centre-court crowd when he whipped Ross Case of Australia in the round before. There were more thrills to come. In their fourth round match Roche conquered Rosewall (6-3, 6-8, 8-6, 6-1).

It seemed the 1974 runner-up had run out of steam—there was a little drama in the match with Rosewall serving at 6-6 in the third set. At 15-30, a Rosewall backhand volley appeared to be out. The linesman signalled 'out', but then changed his call to 'good'. Roche questioned the call, and in the end it was agreed to play a let, but the umpire then became confused about the score and there was a sharp exchange between the players at the net. The confusion definitely distracted Rosewall, and he lost the next point and the game. Rosewall was dejected, believing the incident had changed the course of the match—he couldn't deliver his winning shots at the end and wore a hang-dog look, kicking at the turf and dropping his racket. There was one more chance to regroup when he had a break point at 1-3 in the fourth set. However, at that point the sturdily built left-hander served an ace and it was soon over.

401 *The New York Times*, 25 June 1975

402 *The New York Times*, 26 June 1975

In his press conference after the match Rosewall criticised the rule allowing players the right to appeal against a call: "I was playing it for in. This would have made it 30-all but when the umpire ordered a let to be played it upset my concentration."[403] Why have linesmen and umpires at all, Rosewall must have thought. He nevertheless gave Roche credit for his volleying and forehand, but it was a match that obviously upset the little master.

> I told the press: 'You better make it good fellas, because this is the last time you'll be interviewing me here.' This was probably more my fault than anyone else's—allowing myself to be upset by one call. Even so, Tony was a top player—and he had been through so much over the previous four or five years.

It was a great Wimbledon for Roche, although his success was unexpected. He had been struggling for so long, but in the quarter-finals he proceeded to take Okker apart over five sets (2-6, 9-8, 2-6, 6-4, 6-2). Roche had actually only travelled to Wimbledon to play in the doubles with Newcombe, who was forced to scratch from the event. Roche's semi-final would prove another flinty, five-set display before he was finally taken down by Ashe, by 5-7, 6-4, 7-5, 8-9, 6-4. The 31-year-old Ashe was more focussed than ever, and he proved a difficult obstacle for Roche on this occasion. In the other semi-final, Connors easily beat the big-serving Tanner (6-4, 6-1, 6-4).

The 1975 Wimbledon men's singles will always be remembered for Ashe's strategic play in the final as he cleverly took apart Connors' game. It was a wonderful victory by 6-1, 6-1, 5-7, 6-4. Connors' law suits were finally settled later in the year. He was quoted as saying he had "no more use for the 'bs'. I just want to have a good time and enjoy what I do."[404]

There were more tournaments to play. A week after Wimbledon Rosewall won the Swiss Open in Gstaad, with a victory over Meiler of West Germany by 6-4, 6-4, 6-3. Rosewall was better prepared for the match than he was for their Australian Open encounter back in 1973.

403 *The Sydney Morning Herald*, 30 June 1975

404 *World Tennis*, March 1976

In August, Rosewall played in the Volvo International, a clay court tournament in Bretton Woods, New Hampshire. After winning a quarter-final match over Alexander (6-0, 6-3) he joined Laver, Connors and Nastase in the semi-finals, where Connors beat Laver 6-4, 6-4. The other semi-final provided Rosewall with an opportunity to avenge his loss to Nastase at Tucson. The score, in Rosewall's favour, was 7-5, 1-6, 7-6. Presumably the crowd were well aware of the circumstances of the earlier match as they "cheered every shot, particularly his [Rosewall's] famous backhands that almost impossibly landed on the sidelines and caused Nastase sometimes to twist his head around in astonishment"[405].

The victory placed Rosewall in another final against Connors, where once again the heavy-hitting American was simply too good and won 6-2, 6-2. "Today was a day I didn't miss any shots," said Connors. Rosewall commented, "Jimmy is a great player on any surface."[406] At the same time he announced that he would not be playing the 1975 US Open for personal reasons.

> By now I had decided to spend more time at the John Gardiner Tennis Ranch. During that American summer season I actually wasn't playing many tournaments, except the event at Bretton Woods, and I was home in Australia during the US Open.

In September 1975 an Australian team of Tony Roche and John Alexander lost a Davis Cup tie to Czechoslovakia in Prague. Rosewall was back in Sydney, but announced that he had simply not played enough tennis to be ready to play on the slow-clay courts. "Maybe my presence there would have been a morale booster. But I don't know."[407] Australia had now suffered the indignity of two years of disappointing Davis Cup losses. These were some obvious explanations: Roche had played a full schedule of WTT matches in America which probably was not a great preparation; and Alexander was not a great player on European clay. Even so, Australian fans would soon

405 *The New York Times*, 10 August 1975

406 *The New York Times*, 11 August 1975

407 *The Sydney Morning Herald*, 30 September 1975

begin to realise that winning the Davis Cup on an annual basis was no longer a matter of entitlement as it had been back in the glory days.

Later in the year Rosewall played in a series of tournaments in Australia, Japan and the Philippines, suffering losses along the way to Masters, Lutz, Sandy Mayer, Barrazzutti and Ramirez. Just as people were questioning whether the Rosewall gloss had disappeared, he managed an extraordinary series of victories at the Gunze World Tennis tournament in November 1975. Here, Rosewall reached the semi-finals alongside Newcombe, Roche and Smith. He then beat Smith 6-4, 7-5 to advance to the final to meet Newcombe, who had defeated Roche 3-6, 6-4, 6-2. This meant that Rosewall would play Newcombe for the 20th time in their careers, lifting his advantage over his countryman to 12-8 when won by 7-5, 4-6, 6-1.

During the course of the year Rosewall also coached the Japanese Davis Cup team in a match against India, but was unable to prevent the Amritraj brothers scoring an Indian victory.

◇◇◇◇◇◇◇

The 1976 Australian Open was played through a period of unpleasant heat at Kooyong. Rosewall was the number-one seed for the event based on the ATP's computer ranking—notwithstanding Rosewall's limited schedule, he apparently deserved the status. Perhaps an unexpected series of victories in Japan assisted his ranking. It apparently did not seem to matter that he had been beaten in the New South Wales Championships the week before by long-time practice partner Ray Ruffels. Other leading players in the 1976 event were Newcombe, Roche and Stan Smith.

In his quarter-final, Rosewall struggled through four sets to beat a new Australian player described as a 'teen sensation', Brad Drewett (6-4, 3-6, 6-2, 6-2). The day before Drewett had beaten Rosewall's other 40-year-old compatriot, Mal Anderson.

It was not so easy two days later. On that occasion Rosewall was upset by the big, burly and unknown 21-year-old Mark Edmondson 6-1, 2-6, 6-2, 6-4. The young man from Gosford was "a big-serving youth who threw himself at every ball", wrote one commentator in *The Sydney Morning Herald*. It was a huge crowd that braved the heat to watch Edmondson "peppering Rosewall with a variety of passing shots". The conditions were incredibly unpleasant, with the temperature at courtside registering well over 40°C. It was probably easier for the younger man who wasn't even born when Rosewall won his first Australian Championship back in 1953. Edmondson was struggling to break through as a tour player. Over time he worked as a handyman, painter, nurseryman and cleaner to scrape together enough cash to help him travel overseas.

"That bloody heat," said Rosewall after the match. "Its good to see that Australia is at last getting some youngsters up near the top again, but I wish it wasn't me that was clobbered."[408]

There was very little similarity between the way Rosewall and Edmondson played the game. The young man had the build of a rugby league player, was possessed of a brutal serve, and had little of the finesse of the ground-stroking wonder.

> Mark came out of the blue. Newk had actually been practising against Mark because he thought he was going to win some matches, and might have to play him! I don't remember too much of my match against him. He was young, enthusiastic and strong. He had a pretty good serve and aggressive volley. He was a bit wild off the ground, but he played well. I was a little disappointed not getting to the final again. The tournament established Mark Edmondson.

Edmondson went on to beat Newcombe the following day in a four-set final (6-7, 6-3, 7-6, 6-1) without dropping his serve the entire match. The unknown Edmondson had "gunned down the grizzled veterans"[409] and was the first unseeded player to win the Australian Championships. Writing in 2012, Edmondson has proved to be the last Australian player to win our national championship.

408 *The New York Times*, 4 January 1976

409 *The New York Times*, 7 January 1976. Peter Stone wrote in *Tennis Magazine* (March-April 1976) that Edmondson was probably the first player to win one of the world's major grand slam events as "an unknown".

POSTSCRIPT

It was ultimately not long before Lamar Hunt and WCT were squeezed out of their role in the men's game—the Men's International Pro Tennis Council (MIPTC) stepped in and took over management of the men's game in 1975. This was a tripartite structure comprised of the players (the ATP); the ILTF (later ITF); and worldwide tournament directors. For a time through the late-1970s, there was a marriage of sorts between WCT and the ILTF-Grand Prix Circuit, but this gradually fell apart in 1981. The MIPTC, which considered itself to be the ruling body in the game, strongly supported the Grand Prix Circuit and harboured an ongoing antipathy towards Lamar Hunt. WCT removed itself from its Grand Prix connection during the 1980s.

What became the Men's Tennis Council decided to eliminate WCT events in 1990, and later still the ATP chose to break away and form its own tour—and it was this decision that resulted in WCT's final disappearance from the game. Bud Collins writes that Hunt and WCT were unfortunately and ungratefully frozen out of the men's tour in 1990, "after 23 years of raising standards within the professional game"[410].

410 B Collins, *Total Tennis — The Ultimate Tennis Encyclopedia*, page 912

EPILOGUE BY KEN ROSEWALL

◇◇◇◇◇◇◇

DEFINING MY LEGACY

I kept playing for a year or so after that Australian Open in 1976. The last two events of any note I won were the Hong Kong Open in 1976 and 1977, beating Ilie Nastase in one final and Tom Gorman in the other. These were part of the Asian circuit that had been put together over the previous three or four years. Through this period I was pretty much semi-retired and limited myself to playing in the Australian and Asian tournaments only. My friend, Japanese photographer Eiichi Kawatei, got me involved in some coaching in Japan.

I played in most of the Australian tournaments through this period. I lost in the semi-finals of the Australian Open to Roscoe Tanner in 1977, and the quarter-finals in 1978 to John Alexander (although that event was actually played in December 1977). Then the following year I was seeded seventh, but lost to Austrian Peter Feigel in the last 16.

◇◇◇◇◇◇◇

At around this time the International Management Group (IMG) was keen to keep Rod Laver involved in the game—he was their first client and they began managing me in about 1976. They established something called a Legends circuit, which included me, Stolle, Emerson, Owen Davidson and a couple of others. Most of us had phased out of the tournament circuit, but we played in these smaller budget events. Everyone was well over 35 by that time.

In around 1984 Al Bunis from Cincinnati started the Grand Masters circuit for players aged 45 and over, and he had players like Frank Sedgman, Torben Ulrich, Rex Hartwig, Sven Davidson involved—and even Pancho Gonzales played some of those events.

Eventually, IMG took over the Grand Masters circuit, and by then some the original Grand Masters were starting to retire while members of the Legends shifted into the new category. It meant that none of us ever completely retired and we continued to play in these events in clubs and hotels around the US—they were always quite successful events as the public got to see the top stars from a previous era. It wasn't for huge amounts of money, but it was still quite good, and I was able to travel with Wilma as the boys were getting to the end of their schooling.

The Grand Masters was pretty successful until we all started to crack up physically! And by then the circuit was finished. There is still this kind of circuit for older players in Europe and America—now called the Champions Tour.

With tennis doing well in the US we also set up our own organisation that arranged corporate days, mainly through the work of Fred Stolle, called Grand Slam Sports. Most of the guys involved lived in the US and the group included Sherwood Stewart, Ross Case, Owen Davidson, Cliff Drysdale and Marty Reissen—about 10 of us in all and we all put money in to support office expenses and other costs. I was only involved in this corporate day activity during the US Open, but Wilma and I enjoyed that kind of involvement and managed to have a bit of a holiday while the tennis was on. Unfortunately a lot of activity for this group dried up during the global financial crisis.

◇◇◇◇◇◇◇

Through some of this time I remained involved with the Gardiner Tennis Ranch in Scottsdale, Arizona. My contact with the ranch had always been through a personal understanding I had with John Gardiner, rather than as part of a specific financial arrangement, although I did have a half split in what was the Rosewall House at Scottsdale (the house with a court on the roof).

Initially the tennis ranch did well—but over time there was competition from a lot of different facilities in the area. And over time Scottsdale itself became mainly a retirement-type place. Eventually Gardiner sold his interest, and later died. His second wife ended up going back to the original Gardiner property in Carmel Valley, California, and unfortunately today the Scottsdale property is no long a tennis ranch but a spa. There's no longer a court on the roof back in Scottsdale. We had some good times there. Elton John played tennis on that court.

◇◇◇◇◇◇◇

I had various business interests in Sydney with Rex Mossop, one of our great rugby players some years ago. I also started buying into land syndicates with friends in Brisbane, including Ashley Cooper. At one stage we had an interest in a farming property just outside Toowoomba. Another property in Brisbane was developed into a hotel called The Homestead. My partners managed that, and they included a few of the retired tennis players. We eventually sold the place to a brewery.

◇◇◇◇◇◇◇

I was very lucky throughout my career to avoid having any serious injuries, but then I ended up having rotator cuff surgery in 1987. I think I actually damaged the muscle when I was at home doing some work or lifting things in between overseas tennis trips.

By that stage I was a semi-retired tennis player, and wasn't playing all that much. I was spending a bit of time at the Gardiner ranch as I had gone to the US to play some Grand Masters events in March 1987, and went to Gardiner's before competing in other tournaments. It was while I was there I played a high shot and felt things go in my shoulder. Like I said, I am sure that I weakened the muscle when I was home lifting things and the tendon tore when I went back to play.

I had some orthopedics look at it, and was told there was a risk of causing more damage if I played in more events. I said I wanted to play out the year, which I did. But it was under difficult circumstances as I had lost all the natural motion to play certain shots. I was ok on the serve and forehand, but not high shots. I could get away with it most of the time in the Grand Masters. We were back in the states later that year, in about September, and that was when I organised to have the surgery done in Tucson.

We got home to Sydney in about the middle of November. Like most of these things it was about 50 per cent surgery and 50 per cent rehabilitation. The surgery went well, but probably over all I haven't done as much off-the-court rehabilitation as I should. In saying that I have been lucky to have all the flexibility, and still been able to do most things, but I lost a bit of muscle. From a tennis point of view I lost the throwing motion. Whatever throwing ability I ever had with my right arm compared with left arm is no longer much good. The modern players are much more knowledgeable about looking after their bodies, dealing with injuries, and proper nutrition than we ever were. None of us knew much about that stuff in the old days.

I had my arm in a sling, and finally I got some movement back. Then I was able to start playing again about three months later at an event at Melbourne Park in March or April 1988. Whoever was the main sponsor brought out Smith, Gorman and Olmedo, and we had a friendly match-up between the Australian and the American players.

◇◇◇◇◇◇

In 2011 we were invited to Rome for the Italian Championships. I actually only played in the tournament once. It was always played in early May and the LTAA never sent an amateur men's team away that early, except in 1953 when I lost to Drobny in the semi-final and Lew lost to him in the final. Now they have created an award called the Golden Racquet award, and it was through the courtesy of Nicola Pietrangeli, who was one top Italian players for many years and is now one of the chief organisers of the Italian Open, that I was invited to the event to receive the award.

We had the long trip over, and then went to the tennis on the Wednesday, Thursday and Friday. On the Saturday morning Wilma and I were having breakfast at the tournament hotel, and when I stood up to go to the buffet I started to wobble and had to lean against the wall. I went back to the table and told Wilma I felt a bit dizzy, so I sat there for a few minutes. When I tried to stand up again I was still wobbly, so I thought I better go back to the room.

Wilma helped me up but as I was walking out of the breakfast area I started to fall over. It turned out that there actually was a medical conference taking place at the same hotel, so there were doctors all over the place. Two or three doctors came across, and they were all talking Italian to themselves as they gave me an examination. Then they said through an interpreter that I might have had a small stroke and it was best to go to the local hospital.

That's what happened. I was sent to a hospital in Rome and over the next couple of days I had all these tests. It turned out that I had a little clot at the back of my neck, and that's what had put me off balance.

The Italian tournament hosts were very good. They drove Wilma to the hospital and looked after her. We ended up being there longer than expected, but finally got a flight and were able to come home. When I got back I had a lot of the treatment with a neurologist at Macquarie Hospital in Sydney. They seemed to think everything was ok. I must admit I haven't been as active. I haven't been playing any tennis and I haven't been walking as much because I haven't been playing any golf. At my age that is something I should really keep doing.

The function for the Golden Racquet award was on the Saturday night of the Italian Open, and I ended up being in hospital. They talked Wilma into going to the function to receive the award, and Monica Seles was the other person being honoured. It was a bit difficult when it was announced that I wasn't there because I was in hospital and everyone thought I was on my deathbed! People in Sydney were worried, especially my sons Brett and Glenn. One of the ATP guys, Vittorio Magnelli, kindly lent me his mobile phone to use in hospital so the boys could call me. I tried to tell them it wasn't as bad as what appeared in the newspapers here. I have been lucky.

◇◇◇◇◇◇◇

Wilma had a difficult time through my playing career. She came from a family that wasn't in the public eye. She had been a nice player in her junior days, but when we got married she probably wasn't sure what she was getting into. And then I turned pro soon after we were married. I always thought that was my best chance of making our future a bit more financially secure so long as I stayed healthy. But she had a difficult time, particularly in that first year. I think the amount of travel we did nearly killed both of us.

She never really thought that I would last as long as I did. I think we had some good results, and some things that weren't so good. Certainly when we were in the middle of those early pro years and she became pregnant with Brett (May 1959) things changed a little bit. I was outside Australia a lot and that meant being away from her and the baby.

I always thought that the most money I could make was the best result in the end, so I committed myself to play as much tennis as I could play in those years. Sometimes Wilma was able to come with me. So we did have some trips together, but with the sacrifice of leaving Brett at home as a baby.

A couple of years later Glenn was born (August 1961), and that made it even more difficult for her to get away. Fortunately we had great support from Wilma's mother because she was able to come down to Sydney and look after the boys, with a bit of extra help from time to time.

All in all I had great support from my family. Unfortunately my mother died at a very young age so she really never knew the boys. My father remarried, and he was always very pleased with my tennis career, and I probably did much better than he ever expected. My stepmother was an ex-tennis player, who played a decent game, so they tried to support us as much as they could.

◇◇◇◇◇◇◇

We had some trips overseas with the boys and then I think one of the most enjoyable things was in 1974 when they were both old enough to enjoy the world and where they visited. It was a learning experience not only with World Team Tennis in Pittsburgh that year, but also having the chance to go to Wimbledon. They went through the excitement of me getting through matches that I probably shouldn't have won and also the disappointment of the final. And then lo and behold the same thing happened in the US Open. I did better there than I thought I would at my age (39). It was probably fortunate they were not there for the final—as that was more of a disappointment.

The boys have worked hard. They were studious at school—not top of the class, but really good. They had a good education starting at Pymble Public near where we live in Sydney and then up to Barker Boys College at Hornsby, which they enjoyed. They both participated in their regular sports, rugby and cricket, and the school cadet system. Brett enjoyed making things—like train sets and model airplanes. Glenn was more outdoorsy and into sports. At one time he managed to win the school tennis tournament at Barker College. I was home some of the time and managed to help him a bit. He plays a bit of cricket, and still plays in 40-and-over competitions.

Both were keen about what the future would bring. Brett went straight into learning to fly. He got his basic commercial licence after spending about eight months in Cessnock at the live-in flying school, then an instrument rating licence at Bankstown, and after that he looked for a job. This meant flying charter flights in Darwin for about a year and a half before he had enough hours to join Ansett.

He had a tough time because the pilots' dispute in 1989 took place just after he was married, so he and his wife had to travel overseas to work. He was overseas for 10 years at that time. He has persevered and is now just on 10 years with Virgin, and is a senior check captain living in Brisbane. We have friends who say: "We fly Virgin, but we haven't struck Captain Brett Rosewall yet!" He does a lot of simulator work and trains some of the other younger pilots. He has flown 737s, but he was flying 747s for Cathay Pacific for a few years. Brett has three children. William is 17, and the two twin girls, Ashleigh and Stephanie, are 14.

◇◇◇◇◇◇◇

Glenn studied accountancy at Macquarie University when he came out of school and worked with one of the big eight accounting firms for three years while studying at night, and then worked with a smaller firm and still studied. He got all his qualifications and travelled overseas, as he wanted to work in London. While he was there he was asked if he wanted to work with a financial firm either in London or New York. That was in about 1985. So he went off to work in New York with a company called Cresvale, and he was with them for about a year and a half before getting head hunted to go to Morgan Stanley. After about another 18 months he moved with them back to Melbourne. By that time he was married with his first child, Anson, who is now 22.

Shortly afterwards Morgan Stanley pulled the plug on their stockbroking business so Glenn got a job with Ord Minnett in Sydney, which also saw him spend another couple of years back in New York and, by this time he had a little girl, Olivia.

After this Glenn and his family returned to Sydney, and he had a chance to start up his own hedge fund company through getting involved with a company called BBY, of which he is now executive chairman. It is a private equity stockbroking firm, and he has been with them for 10 years.

Keeping it in the family, Anson also works at BBY as an adviser and trader, and is completing some courses at Sydney University. Olivia has started an arts degree, also at Sydney University, and hopes to make the move to law. All our grandchildren are pretty bright. Much more brains than me!

◇◇◇◇◇◇◇

Both boys have both worked hard, sacrificed a lot, and we are proud of them. I think they probably get questions like: "Are you Ken Rosewall's son?" It is not such a common name, and generally not spelt right either! Glenn was referred to in an article in the *Financial Review* the other day, but the name was spelt with an 'e' (Rosewell).

◇◇◇◇◇◇◇

On reflection the best thing that happened during my career was that I had the opportunity to be involved with so many changes in the game. I have been able to see tennis develop into a worldwide game, and the changes made in technology, rackets and strings, for better or worse. It is also amazing when you look around at the number of top players and where they are from.

The worst thing for me was the attitude of the amateur officials in those early days. That was very upsetting. 'Big Bill' Edwards was probably the worst of the lot and there was also LTAA president Don Ferguson—both held a negative view of the pro game.

Other things that were disappointing were the ban on WCT players worldwide (including Wimbledon) in 1972 and the ATP player boycott of Wimbledon in 1973. I acknowledge the boycott consolidated the players' association, but for me those things were especially disappointing because I was running out of time. I lost the chance to play two years there and, having won the WCT event in 1972, I would have been in with a decent shot for Wimbledon in either of those years.

◇◇◇◇◇◇◇

Could a 5' 7" (170cm) player with magnificent groundstrokes compete against today's players? I don't think so. With tennis being played mainly on hard courts, I think the technique and strategies of the game have almost put it out of reach for a smaller player and back in the hands of the baseliners. But I still think that if you are well over 6' (183cm) you have a distinct advantage over someone who is in the 5' 7-8" (170-2cm) bracket. There isn't the sort of variation that we might have seen a few years ago. A lot of people say how interesting it is when points are won with an overhead or a good volley!

You have to admire the expertise of today's players. When you see things like the excessive topspin that Rafael Nadal gets on his forehand—that is just exceptional. I don't know if that is how the game was supposed to be played, but it shows tremendous talent, with the help of the new equipment and strings.

People say they would like to see more serve and volley, but you just can't play that way. That was the problem for Pat Rafter, who played an aggressive serve-volley game. But the surface they put in at Melbourne Park took away from the game he played because the ball bounced too high, and immediately gave an advantage to a groundstroke player.

◇◇◇◇◇◇◇

If I had my time over and could change one thing, I would like to change the foot fault rule. When you think about the players becoming taller and bigger, the serve is now becoming such a winning part of the game. I would like to see the rule changed in some way so it doesn't give the server such an advantage. It might mean one foot remaining behind the line. Or even going to an idea that the server has to start from somewhere behind they line if they want to 'jump'.

◇◇◇◇◇◇◇

I am not sure what my legacy is. I am just one of many players who tried to do well and be a positive part of the game. I am proud of the efforts I made to spread the word of tennis during those early pro years, making the game acceptable, sociable and admired. That is certainly a good legacy. I'd like to thank all the people who supported me—whether it was because of the way I behaved, my size or the number of times I had good wins against top players. Although I had losses against top players as well. Thanks to those people.

It has been important for me to tell the story about the development of professional tennis over a period of 25 years. Obviously the world of open tennis is nothing like it was when I started playing in the early 1950s, but like I said, I feel privileged to have been playing when the sport was gradually evolving—to have been there, and been part of those decisions about playing tennis as a professional venture.

Ken Rosewall
September 2012

◇◇◇◇◇◇◇

ACKNOWLEDGMENTS

Writing *Muscles* ended up being a lot easier than I thought it might be. It started as an occasional distraction from the rigours of writing a PhD thesis on Australian labour law, but today the thesis remains unfinished and now I have run out of excuses not to complete it!

I am proud of leaving a little legacy to the tennis world, after writing *The Wizard—The Story of Norman Brookes, Australia's First Wimbledon Champion* and now this book, together with Ken Rosewall. Read in partnership the biographies tell the story of the first 75 years or so of Australian tennis—but they are nevertheless different. The book about Brookes offers a social history of Melbourne, while *Muscles* also tells the story of an extraordinary tennis player, but is also about the monumental changes to the game of tennis that took place in the 1960s and 70s. Ken Rosewall was a close observer of all those events, and was the right person to tell this story.

Obviously, a book like this would not make it out of the starting blocks without the full cooperation and involvement of Rosewall himself. Initially, he was a little guarded about the project, but over time it became clear that he wanted to tell the story of the early days of pro tennis and perhaps think a little about the contribution that he and the other greats—like Gonzales,

Hoad and Laver—had made to the game we play today. By the end of the storytelling process, Rosewall was fully engaged, checking and scrutinising all my draft chapters. I hope he is happy with the outcome.

I want to thank a group of people who helped me with the research and writing of the book. David Studham at Melbourne Cricket Ground's library is a marvellous sports librarian and looked after me like a genuine club member whenever I used the library. That was a great help. I have now become an occasional visitor at the Kenneth Ritchie Wimbledon Library, and was extremely well assisted by Audrey Snell in June 2012. I hope she manages to find a nice spot for *Muscles* in the library collection.

Many thanks to Ada Klinkhamer at the Australian Tennis Museum at Sydney's Olympic Park. She initially helped me establish contact with Ken Rosewall, and was our email conduit as we sent draft chapters back and forth. She is assisted by Dora Hutchinson and other volunteers. Maxine McKendrick and Liz Meloni at Tennis Australia in Melbourne helped me gain access to 30 years' worth of records from Lawn Tennis Association of Australia (LTAA) council meetings.

My great friend Julie Heldman is one of the few people I ever allow to read my raw, unpolished prose. This time around it was exciting to receive her comments as she played during the Rosewall era, plus one of my principal research tools was her mum's magazine *World Tennis*. What a wonderful magazine that was!

My friends at The Slattery Media Group—Geoff Slattery and Helen Alexander—have now helped bring both *The Wizard* and *Muscles* to life.

I am very lucky to have a circle of friends who adopt a non-critical and reasonably supportive approach to my current weakness for writing books about tennis. In particular, might I mention Ayesh Perera, Darren Harrop, Melanie Sloss, Kitta Good, the Tuesday night tennis gang, the various dinner party groups that Mark Engeman coordinates, Geoff Satchell, Richard Mitchell and Paul Caulfield (who kept sending me copies of movies and TV shows in an effort to get my mind on something else). Thanks also to Donald Ward, mainly because he was so helpful last year when *The Wizard* emerged from hiding.

Being in close contact with Ken Rosewall means one immediately has access to the aristocracy of the tennis world. It meant I was able to interview Butch Buchholz, one of the leading American pro players during the 1960s, and also Rosewall's good friend John Barrett, to get their special insights into this story. Thanks also to Rod Laver and John Newcombe, who were willing to endorse the book.

My family Rosemary and John Wheatley, and Wendy and Michael Hillman offered unstinting support in these ventures, and that is always greatly appreciated. I should also mention the help of my nephew Timothy Hillman, who frequently discussed new ways of looking at the Rosewall story with me, while we enjoyed a Saturday night pizza!

Finally thanks to Ken and Wilma Rosewall for their encouragement and assistance along the way. I feel very privileged to tell the story of one of tennis' great players. It has been a most enjoyable few months.

Richard Naughton
September 2012

◇◇◇◇◇◇◇

BIBLIOGRAPHY

BOOKS

R Bellamy, *Game, Set and Deadline: A Passion for Tennis*, George Allen and Unwin Ltd, London, 1986

R Bellamy, *The Tennis Set*, Cassell and Co, London, 1972

R Bellamy, *Three Decades of Champions*, Simon and Schuster, London, 1990

M Brady, *The Centre Court Story*, Fireside Press, London, 1954

B Collins, *My Life with the Pros*, Dutton, New York, 1990

B Collins, *Total Tennis—The Ultimate Tennis Encyclopedia*, Sport Classic Books, Toronto, 2003

P Cummings, *American Tennis—The Story of a Game*, Little Browne & Co, Boston, 1957

A Danzig and P Schwed (ed) *The Fireside Book of Tennis*, Simon and Schuster, New York, 1972

O Davidson with CM Jones, *Lawn Tennis—The Great Ones*, Pelham Books, London, 1970

J Drobny, *Champion in Exile*, Hodder & Stoughton, London, 1955

J Drucker, *Jimmy Connors Saved My Life*, Sport Classic Books, Toronto, 2004

R Evans, *Open Tennis—The First Twenty Years*, Bloomsbury, London, 1988

R Gonzales, *Man With a Racket*, Thomas Yoseloff, London and New York, 1959

G Greenwood (ed), *The Golden Years of Australian Tennis*, Murray Publishers, Melbourne, 2000

C Gorringe, *Holding Court*, Century, London, 2009

H Hopman, *Aces and Places*, Cassell and Co, London, 1957

J Johnson, *Grand Slam Australia—The Story of the Australian Open Tennis Championships*, Courtney Books, Victoria, 1985

J Kramer and F Deford, *The Game—My 40 Years in Tennis*, GP Putman and Sons, New York, 1979

R Laver with B Collins, *The Education of a Tennis Player*, New Chapter Press, New York and Washington, 1971 (updated 2009)

J McCauley, *The History of Professional Tennis*, The Short Run Book Co Ltd, Windsor, England, 2003

J Medlycott, *100 Years of the Wimbledon Tennis Championships*, Hamlyn, London, 1977

P Metzler, *Great Players of Australian Tennis*, Harper & Row, Sydney, 1979

I Nastase, *Mr Nastase*, Collins / Willow, London, 2004

R Naughton, *The Wizard*, The Slattery Media Group, Melbourne, 2011

J Newcombe, *Newk—Life On and Off the Court*, Pan Macmillan, Sydney 2002

J Pollard, *Advantage Receiver*, Frederick Muller Limited, London, 1960

M Robertson (ed) *The Encyclopaedia of Tennis*, George Allen and Unwin Ltd, London, 1974

M Robertson, *Wimbledon—Centre Court of the Game*, BBC, London, 1977

P Rowley, *Ken Rosewall—Twenty Years at the Top*, GP Putman and Sons, New York, 1976

J Sharnik, *Remembrance of Games Past*, Macmillan and Co, New York, 1986

D Sweet, *Lamar Hunt*, Triumph Books, Chicago, 2010

Tennis Australia, *Australia Open—Official Draw Sheets 1905-2004*

The Tennis Year—1979, Park Street Publishing Co, London, 1979

L Tingay, *Tennis—A Pictorial History*, GP Putman and Sons, New York, 1973

T Tinling, *Sixty Years in Tennis*, Sidgwick and Jackson, London, 1983

T Trabert, *Trabert on Tennis—The View from the Centre Court*, Contemporary Books, Chicago, 1990

A Trengove, *The Story of the Davis Cup*, Stanley Paul, London, 1985

R S Whitington, *An Illustrated History of Australian Tennis*, Macmillan Australia, Melbourne, 1975

NEWSPAPERS, MAGAZINES AND PERIODICALS

Australian Tennis

Australian Women's Weekly

International Herald Tribune

New York Herald Tribune

The New York Times

St Louis Post-Dispatch

The Sydney Morning Herald

Sydney Sun-Herald

The Herald (Melbourne)

The Observer

The Sun (Baltimore)

The Times

Washington Post

World Tennis

Interviews carried out by Richard Naughton with John Barrett, Butch Buchholz and Ken Rosewall

INDEX